Keep this book. You will need it and use it throug~~h~~ your career.

About the American Hotel & Lodging Association (AH&LA)

Founded in 1910, AH&LA is the trade association representing the lodging industry in the United States. AH&LA is a federation of state lodging associations throughout the United States with 11,000 lodging properties worldwide as members. The association offers its members assistance with governmental affairs representation, communications, marketing, hospitality operations, training and education, technology issues, and more. For information, call 202-289-3100.

LODGING, the management magazine of AH&LA, is a "living textbook" for hospitality students that provides timely features, industry news, and vital lodging information.

About the American Hotel & Lodging Educational Institute (EI)

An affiliate of AH&LA, the Educational Institute is the world's largest source of quality training and educational materials for the lodging industry. EI develops textbooks and courses that are used in more than 1,200 colleges and universities worldwide, and also offers courses to individuals through its Distance Learning program. Hotels worldwide rely on EI for training resources that focus on every aspect of lodging operations. Industry-tested videos, CD-ROMs, seminars, and skills guides prepare employees at every skill level. EI also offers professional certification for the industry's top performers. For information about EI's products and services, call 800-349-0299 or 407-999-8100.

About the American Hotel & Lodging Educational Foundation (AH&LEF)

An affiliate of AH&LA, the American Hotel & Lodging Educational Foundation provides financial support that enhances the stability, prosperity, and growth of the lodging industry through educational and research programs. AH&LEF has awarded millions of dollars in scholarship funds for students pursuing higher education in hospitality management. AH&LEF has also funded research projects on topics important to the industry, including occupational safety and health, turnover and diversity, and best practices in the U.S. lodging industry. For information, go to www.ahlef.org.

Professionals Agree on *Fundamentals of Destination Management and Marketing*

"I applaud DMAI, as the voice for the industry, for developing this essential resource. Now bureaus have a single source to obtain relevant advice for managing their destinations. CVB veterans, newcomers, and students of the hospitality industry will find the information in this textbook to be invaluable."

Reint Reinders, CHA
President & CEO
San Diego (California) Convention & Visitors Bureau

"Managing a destination is one of the most complex, political, and exciting careers anyone could hope for. It is the task of or chestrating all of the elements within a destination to create a positive image that will not only attract future visitors but also guarantee they will return and tell others about their positive experience. This book provides the essential tools, proven techniques, and critical resources that are required to be successful in this demanding profession. It will become a valued r esource on my book-shelf, and I will recommend it strongly to others in academia and beyond."

Dr. Joe Goldblatt, CSEP
Professor and Executive Director
School of Tourism and Hospitality Management
Temple University

"DMAI has taken the leadership role in creating a knowledge base about one of the most effective vehicles for stimulating vital economic development in cities, states, and nations around the world. Its new textbook, *Fundamentals of Destination Management and Marketing,* unravels the details as to what the role of convention and visitors bureaus should be and how those organizations can function effectively. This book will be a valuable source of information for colleges and universities to build courses that will produce knowledgeable people for careers in this dynamic dimension of tourism management. The team of authors assembled by DMAI represents the best minds in the business and they have created a wealth of information for both students and practicing professionals."

Howard E. Reichbart
Associate Professor
Hospitality and Tourism Management
Northern Virginia Community College

"As convention and visitor bur eaus continue to gr ow professionally and become mor e known through-out the travel and hospitality industry, the time has arrived for this much- anticipated book, *Fundamentals of Destination Management and Marketing.* This textbook is the first to detail all the many functions and roles of a CVB and its many contributions to the community—thr ough economic development, visita-tion by leisure travelers, and the impact of meetings and conventions. Any professional in the travel and hospitality industry will greatly benefit from this important research resource."

Spurgeon Richardson
President
Atlanta Convention & Visitors Bureau

"This book should not be on your bookshelf; it should be on the top of your desk. To paraphrase another title, this is the *Best Case Survival Handbook*, chock full of ideas and directions and a melding of the aca-demic with practical, on-the-street relevance. I ordered a dozen copies for our office."

Rick Antonson
President & CEO
Greater Vancouver (Canada) Convention & Visitors Bureau

Fundamentals of Destination Management and Marketing

Educational Institute Books

Fundamentals of Destination Management and Marketing

Edited by
Rich Harrill, Ph.D.

**American
Hotel & Lodging
Educational Institute**

**Destination
Marketing**
Association International

Disclaimer

This publication is designed to provide accurate and authoritative information in regard to the subject matter covered. It is sold with the understanding that the publisher is not engaged in rendering legal, accounting, or other professional service. If legal advice or other expert assistance is required, the services of a competent professional person should be sought.
—*From the Declaration of Principles jointly adopted by the American Bar Association and a Committee of Publishers and Associations*

Rich Harrill and the authors are solely responsible for the contents of this publication. All views expressed herein are solely those of the authors and do not necessarily reflect the views of the American Hotel & Lodging Educational Institute (the Institute) or the American Hotel & Lodging Association (AH&LA).

Nothing contained in this publication shall constitute a standard, an endorsement, or a recommendation of AH&LA or the Institute. AH&LA and the Institute disclaim any liability with respect to the use of any information, procedure, or product, or reliance thereon by any member of the hospitality industry.

Contents

10 Financial Management 173
Ed McMillan, CPA

11 Board Governance 191
Joe Lathrop, President, OCG International

12 Alliances 219
Fran Bolson, President and CEO, Lisle (Illinois)
Convention & Visitors Bureau

Jan van Harssel, Professor, Niagara University College
of Hospitality and Tourism Management

Acknowledgments

The Destination Marketing Association International appreciates the significant contributions (both direct and indirect) of the DMAI Education Committee to this first edition of *Fundamentals of Destination Management and Marketing*.

Destination Marketing Association International Education Committee

Maura Allen Gast, FCDME
Executive Director
Irving Convention & Visitors Bureau

Keith Arnold
President & CEO
Peoria Area Convention & Visitors Bureau

Barry Biggar, CDME
President & CEO
Bryan–College Station Convention & Visitors Bureau

Fran Bolson, CDME
President
Lisle Convention & Visitors Bureau

Gerald Cook
President
Overland Park Convention & Visitors Bureau

Carrie Fenn Moses
Director of Conventions, Eastern Region
Salt Lake Convention & Visitors Bureau

Sallye Grant-DiVenuti, FCDME
Director
Hampton Convention & Visitors Bureau

Paul Griffin
Director of Meetings and Events
Destination Marketing Association International

Rosalind Kincaid
Vice President Administration/ Human Resources
Atlantic City Convention & Visitors Authority

Diana McAdam
Marketing Services Manager
Las Vegas Convention & Visitors Authority

Mike Mooney
Vice President Finance & Operations
Greater Phoenix Convention & Visitors Bureau

Elise Rogers
Vice President Membership
Albuquerque Convention & Visitors Bureau Inc.

Jack Wert, FCDME
Executive Director
Greater Naples, Marco Island, & Everglades Convention & Visitors Bureau

Brian Whiting
President
Providence Warwick Convention & Visitors Bureau

About This Book's Sponsor

T HE DESTINATION MARKETING ASSOCIATION INTERNATIONAL (DMAI) serves more than 1,200 members of approximately 500 destination management organizations (DMOs) in thirty countries, making DMAI the world's largest such organization. Its mission is to enhance the professionalism, effectiveness, and image of destination management organizations worldwide. The DMAI's vision is to create an inclusive, accessible, and responsive organization for all destination management professionals in the world.

Context and History

The DMAI was founded in 1914 as the International Association of Convention Bureaus (IACB) to promote professional practices in the solicitation and servicing of meetings, conventions, and tourism. The original charter was formed that year in Detroit, Michigan, to share information on convention meetings and automobile shows. Recognizing the growing importance of tourism in convention and visitors bureau (CVB) operations, IACB officially added a "V" for *visitor* to its name in 1974.

As the organization continued to grow, its mission expanded to include professional development and certification. Today, the DMAI provides educational resources and networking opportunities to its members and acts as a resource and advocate for the CVB industry and the public.

Helping members become more successful in their jobs, these resources and opportunities include quality education and professional certification, industry research and information, public relations and branding, leadership and peer networking opportunities, and meetings and conferences with industry vendors and service providers. Many of these programs are designed exclusively for CVBs. Membership fees are based on a bureau's annual operating budget.

Membership benefits include:

- Regular meetings focused on areas of professional expertise called "shirtsleeves tracks"

- E-mail discussion lists based on the shirtsleeves tracks

- Alerts for Requests for Proposals (RFPs) from meeting professionals

- Access to MINT (Meetings Information Network), the world's largest convention industry database with profiles of more than 28,000 association and corporate meetings

- An invitation to Destinations Showcase, an exhibition that features face-to-face meetings with association and corporate professionals who come prepared with RFPs or bid proposals

- A membership directory

- *DMAI E-News*, a weekly e-mail newsletter that keeps members informed of industry news, programs, and activities

- Several membership programs for alliance and business partners

Organization

The DMAI, headquartered in Washington, D.C., has a governing five-member executive committee, comprising a chair, chair-elect, treasurer/secretary, immediate past chair, and president and chief executive officer. The board also has nineteen directors. The DMAI currently has fifteen staff positions, ranging from president and chief executive officer to project managers.

Professional Development

The DMAI's professional development programs began over eighty years ago, with the number of member services growing exponentially. For example, the DMAI Annual Convention is an educational conference offering programming and networking opportunities for all professional staff of CVB or tourist boards. General sessions include broad topics and in-depth breakout discussions. Interactive shirtsleeves tracks are offered each day to foster exchange of ideas and information among colleagues.

The DMAI conceived its overall educational programs in three steps, beginning with an introductory course on the CVB industry. This course, Fundamentals of Destination Management, provides information on CVBs, the practice of destination management, and DMAI membership benefit opportunities.

The second step, the Professional in Destination Management (PDM) program, is part of the DMAI's commitment to the continuing education of its members. This certificate program helps professional staff obtain the necessary knowledge and skills to become more effective and efficient destination leaders and CVB managers. The program's required courses cover the fundamentals of management as well as other skills important to each member's success. By taking courses from a variety of specialty areas—from marketing to finance—participants can broaden their knowledge and hone their skills as CVB professionals. DMAI members must complete four required classes and acquire thirty-six additional credits during a five-year period to receive a certificate.

The third step, the Certified Destination Management Executive (CDME), is recognized by the industry as its highest educational achievement. This designation is designed for veteran CVB executives seeking advanced education courses, and it is earned by completing three interrelated core courses, two elective courses, and a final examination. This intensive program was developed in conjunction with the University of Calgary (Canada) World Tourism Education and Research Center and Purdue University.

To date, the DMAI has graduated ninety-one CDMEs. In 2005, the organization will have about twenty new CDME graduates.

Other educational opportunities include the DMAI Sales Academy™, which emphasizes destination selling. The introductory two-day Destination Selling program addresses issues ranging from prospecting and initial contact to follow-up. It is designed for people with two years or less of experience in every area of destination sales: convention, tourism, membership, services, and communications. This course is also available online in conjunction with George Washington University and the DMAI Foundation. More experienced individuals can take Destination Selling Part II, which focuses on effectively working trade shows, partnering with hotels and convention centers, prospecting on the Internet, and advancing or closing the sale.

The Chief Executive Officer (CEO) Forum enables CVB CEOs and executive directors to meet and discuss relevant and innovative issues frankly and openly, and features in-depth discussions of management and leadership issues with direct application to a CEO's day-to-day responsibilities. Together, they learn about important issues facing the global tourism industry.

Finally, DMAI offers a series of stand-alone educational meetings, specific to the previously mentioned interactive learning shirtsleeves tracks, based on primary job responsibility or professional expertise. During these meetings, members convene with others in their professional area to share ideas, review programs that may or may not have worked, or discuss how to handle specific situations. The DMAI currently offers the following meetings: CEO Forum, COO/CFO Forum, Membership Shirtsleeves, Sales & Marketing Executive Forum, and Visitor Services Shirtsleeves.

Results

The DMAI cites many elements of success in its professional development programs. First, it strives to ensure that the content for certification matches bureau executives' needs and expectations for the benefit of their own CVBs. Second, the DMAI believes its formal certificate programs provide informal forums for open discussions regarding the state of the global CVB industry. Finally, the DMAI enjoys considerable involvement from its members, and in turn receives feedback that it uses to improve its professional development efforts. This feedback is critical to offering instruction to a multifaceted industry: the program must be broad, yet cover topic areas in sufficient depth. The DMAI has succeeded in this difficult balancing act.

Because it is based primarily on membership and participation, the DMAI closely monitors its registration at conferences, forums, and courses. Evaluation is a key to improving the quality of its professional development products, including both guest speakers and salient topics. The DMAI asserts that quality is paramount because registration fees support the professional development program itself.

The DMAI is expanding its delivery of professional development via online education. Internet-based education will assist in meeting the organization's goal of expanding members' choices regarding professional development training. The option of online education should increase registration in the bureau's programs and decrease time and travel costs for members without sacrificing the quality of the training. The DMAI is actively cultivating relationships with academic and research institutions that have hospitality and tourism programs to enhance its overall educational effort. This relationship will strengthen the bond between university departments that train CVB workers as well as keep CVBs up-to-date on current developments in destination management research.

Certification, Education, and Beyond

As demand for certification and professional development grows, the CVB industry offers diverse training to tourism professionals in related but specific skill areas. Goals for the DMAI's professional development programs include the expansion of certification to a more discipline-specific level—for example, marketing—in reference to the certification of a tourism or marketing professional.

Outside its professional development program, the DMAI already has accomplished many of the organizational objectives specified in its strategic plan. Concerning education, it continues to aspire to be the premier source for destination marketing education and training worldwide. In performance measures, it strives to be *the* global source for industry standardization and statistics. In branding, it desires to establish a recognizable brand for products and services offered by destination management organizations around the world.

Preface

LONG-TERM TRENDS in globalization, demographics, and technology are making many cities and regions new engines of economic growth centered on hospitality and tourism. Private developers, leisure providers, and entrepreneurs have long noted such trends and have positioned themselves advantageously. Prestigious business schools continue to add faculty with expertise in these fields to satisfy the growing demand for MBAs with tourism industry knowledge. Curiously, many governments have lagged behind in taking advantage of hospitality and tourism as a source of economic development, even as traditional industries such as textiles and manufacturing continue to move offshore in pursuit of cheaper labor and resources. In several locales, this lack of preparedness has resulted in a leadership vacuum in the hospitality and tourism industry that must be filled by the individuals and organizations using this textbook.

This book represents the first comprehensive attempt to describe the basic functions of the contemporary destination management organization—the convention and visitors bureau (CVB)—an organization whose leadership is indispensable to shaping this new global economic landscape. At the local level, these functions are interrelated to the extent that it would seem almost superficial to describe them as a landscape. The functions of destination management—from sales and marketing to research and performance measurement—are so interconnected that perhaps the best conceptual framework is an ecosystem.

The similarities between ecology and destination management begin with this textbook. Consider the word "ecology," today a common term in many environmentally conscious homes, businesses, and communities. In the 1940s, the late Eugene P. Odum was a young University of Georgia faculty member drawing up a curriculum for biology majors. He suggested that ecology be a required course, although few of his colleagues at that time knew what the word meant. He realized then that the emerging science he was advancing lacked a fundamental textbook describing its basic principles. In 1953, his *Fundamentals of Ecology* became the first textbook in the field and remained the only ecology textbook for about the next decade or so. Since then, Odum's book has been used by thousands of students and translated into a dozen languages. Several factors converged to catapult ecology into the spotlight on April 22, 1970—the first Earth Day. By this time, social, economic, and environmental conditions had intersected, capturing a generation's yearning for a cleaner, healthier environment and a search for alternative economic models. Similarly, advances in transportation and communications, increases in leisure time and spending, and the advent of the Internet have intersected to favor the emergence of destination management.

One notable aspect of *Fundamentals of Ecology* was that it examined the entire ecosystem, from the top down, rather than the ecology of parts of the natural world. Odum argued that ecology was not a subdivision of biology, and that it should be an integrated discipline that brings all of the sciences together instead of breaking them apart.

In many respects, Odum's holistic view of ecology mirrors destination management as a term that comprehensively describes the hospitality and tourism system. The destination management ecosystem includes the relationships between hosts and guests, suppliers and consumers, and complex networks of residents, government officials, and CVB leaders and employees. This textbook describes the relationships among products, members, sales and marketing strategies, research agendas, alliances, and services in the same way Odum described the relationships among individual species and broader ecological communities as well as the development and evolution of ecosystems. Much like a natural ecosystem, a change in one area of destination management often significantly affects other parts of the system. For example, a change in products developed and services marketed results in a change in sales and marketing, which results in a change in performance measurement, human resources, and so on. However, because many of these interactions among destination management functions are unseen, hospitality and tourism are often referred to collectively as an "invisible" industry, again resembling the frequently unseen interactions among ecological components. Although not readily detectable, both systems can be incredibly productive.

Some relationships in a natural ecosystem are described as symbiotic in that one or many species depend upon one another for mutual benefit or survival. In nature, these relationships are shaped and driven by environmental conditions, socialization, and instinct. Although the pursuit of territorial dominance may upset these delicate relationships, they remain consistent over time. Other factors are necessary to keep the destination management ecosystem functioning. Perhaps the most important factor here is *trust* among key stakeholders, including the general public, government entities, bureau members, meeting planners, tour operators, academia, business partners, and other convention and visitors bureaus. When relationships break down between these entities due to misunderstanding or negligence, the element of trust continues to keep the destination management system functioning. Trust means that the local CVB will always act in the best interest of the destination and community. However, before trust occurs at the destination and community level, it is first necessary for individuals to demonstrate trust in one another on a daily, interpersonal basis, meaning that deadlines will be met, phone calls and e-mails will be returned, and payments will be fulfilled.

To his credit, Odum did not remain a passive observer of the field he fathered, but instead became a passionate advocate of ecological protection. Later editions of his textbook included examples of the consequences of man's destruction of the environment. Odum's *advocacy* for social and policy change with respect to the environment undoubtedly helped keep his work at the forefront of the environmental movement and spurred other landmark works such as Rachel Carson's 1962 classic, *Silent Spring*. In the same way, users of this textbook should aspire to be more than proficient practitioners of destination management's functions. They should act as advocates of an industry that has demonstrated a capacity for increasing prosperity, elevating quality of life, and promoting understanding between countries and cultures.

Unlike Odum's work that was the product of a single author and perspective, this volume comprises many voices and viewpoints, sometimes in agreement, and other times slightly differing on the nature of destination management functions. Each author was carefully selected to contribute to the textbook based on such factors as years of experience, breadth and depth of knowledge, and ability to communicate this information to students, entry-level staff, and seasoned veterans alike. What may not be apparent to the reader, however, is that many of these authors know one another as colleagues and friends in the tourism ecosystem, and thus were able to share concepts and ideas in contributing to this book. As consultants and bureau professionals, they are united in their belief that factors favoring the continued growth and development of destination management are too compelling to ignore. Their very contributions represent acts of advocacy in support of destination management.

Trends Favoring Destination Management

Perhaps today's most influential force is globalization, driven by advances in technology, communications, and transportation. Due to the liberalization of economic policies, many traditional U.S. industrial sectors have relocated to pursue cheaper labor and resources elsewhere in the world, although industrial output many continue to increase in many areas. At the same time, the service sector, including hospitality and tourism, continues to grow at a steady state. Despite terrorism and epidemic, the underlying structural trends supporting the expansion of tourism have not changed significantly. The World Tourism Organization's *Tourism 2020 Vision* forecasts that tourism will grow at a 5.4 percent rate from 1995 to 2020. Of worldwide arrivals, 1.2 billion will be intraregional and 0.4 billion will extraregional travelers. Undoubtedly, CVBs will assume a greater role in economic development as tourism volumes and expenditures increase.

As the service sector continues to expand, so will employment related to hospitality and tourism. It is often said that these jobs tend to be low-wage with little opportunity for advancement. Yet, as tourism and hospitality become crucial to the economic development of many cities and regions, so will the entrepreneurship spawned by these industries and the development of a tourism- and hospitality-oriented government sector. High-value managerial and enterprise positions will develop over time in tourism-led economies, ranging from positions in local governments to the sale of high-tech equipment used by visitors for navigation and interpretation to the expensive, advanced materials now preferred by many sportsmen. Of all economic development organizations, perhaps the contemporary CVB is the only one that has sufficient experience with all these businesses to assess their strengths, weaknesses, opportunities, and challenges within the overall economy. Many of these upstart tourism and hospitality-related industries are already members of bureaus, and will look to CVBs for support and guidance.

After globalization, the factor most favoring the growth of destination management is the size of the U.S. "baby boomer" generation, which consists of the seventy-eight million persons in the United States born between 1946 and 1964. By the end of 2005, the first boomers will begin to turn sixty. They are projected to be a significant portion of the population until at least 2025, when they will constitute twenty-five percent of the population.

It is difficult to predict with certainty the impact of this cohort on the hospitality and tourism industry. Because recession plagued the front end of the twenty-first century's first decade, many boomers will delay retirement and continue working to realize their financial goals. However, few can deny that this group will take advantage of improved health care and retain their desire to travel, even forfeiting other luxury items to preserve the annual family vacation. The group will still have enough income and education to support the continued growth of the tourism industry, in turn ensuring the continuing ascendancy of convention and visitors bureaus as economic development organizations.

The Urban Institute has reported that boomers have a higher real mean income than their parents' generation, and about twenty-five to thirty percent of the boomers have four or more years of college. In addition, the Travel Industry Association of America (TIA) has reported that this group generated the highest travel volume in the United States in 2003, registering 268.9 million trips, more than any other age group. Boomers are also more likely to stay in a hotel, motel, or bed-and-breakfast on overnight trips and travel for business.

Getting in tune with today's technology, many boomers are turning to the Internet to book their trips and vacations. Although all CVBs recognize the importance of Web marketing, it remains to be seen whether the ability to use this technology will close the gap between the larger and smaller bureaus or whether escalating Web site budgets will create an elite class of virtual destinations. From the consumer's perspective, Web marketing is here to stay. TIA has reported that most travelers are computer literate, with two-thirds of some 95.8 million travelers making travel plans online in 2003. Use of the Internet to actually book travel continues to increase, with forty-four percent of all travelers who are online having made travel reservations on the Internet in the past year, translating to 42.2 million online bookings, up eight percent from 2002. The association reported that seventy-five percent of online travel bookers say they bought airline tickets for a trip taken in the past year, seventy-one percent booked overnight lodging accommodations, and forty-three percent made rental car reservations.

Moving Forward

The advances and innovations detailed in this book notwithstanding, there is still much work to be done in the destination management organization arena. Although Odum's *Fundamentals of Ecology* created a new a field, it did not immediately launch ecology as a profession or as a societal concern. Convention and visitors bureaus must work with universities, economic developers, and other organizations to publicize and communicate the fact that destination management is a rapidly developing field with many opportunities. Universities and colleges must also work with CVBs to offer internships to students interested in destination management. It is hoped that readers of this textbook will become advocates for career and professional development in destination management.

Today, thousands of people worldwide have had formal training in ecology through a course or an entire major. *Fundamentals of Ecology* remains a foundation of the field, regularly updated with new editions, and it continues to be widely used in college classrooms by instructors and in the field by practitioners.

Although certainly not intended by Odum, the textbook has become something of a rarity in the academic world in achieving "classic" status. Certain books are accorded this status by breaking new ground or breathing life into old discourses. Sometimes such works even result in a "paradigm shift"—a pronounced change in how the world is perceived. CVBs are now pivotally positioned to generate such a transformation in economic development, leading the way from twilight industries toward the growth of new industries and sectors, providing an organizational foundation for hospitality and tourism as a rapidly expanding source of economic growth. Although only time will tell if *Fundamentals of Destination Management and Marketing* will achieve classic status, the topics and issues it addresses are now among the most important of the new century, for tourism and, indeed, for economic development itself.

—Rich Harrill, Ph.D.

Rich Harrill, Ph.D., is director of the Institute for Tourism Research at the University of South Carolina. The institute is available to provide tourism and destination management research and editing services to local, national, and international agencies, organizations, and businesses. As part of his efforts, he has authored Best Practices in Tourism and Destination Management *(volumes I and II), which have generated interactions with national and international clients, in places from Rhode Island and Michigan to China and Vietnam. He holds a master's degree in city and regional planning and a doctorate in parks, recreation, and tourism management from Clemson University. Dr. Harrill is available to speak on the topic of destination management to organizations and agencies worldwide.*

Introduction

By *Michael Gehrisch*

Michael Gehrisch is President and CEO of the Destination Marketing Association International (DMAI), where he has fostered major initiatives in branding, performance measurement, and lifelong learning. He also serves on the U.S. Chamber of Commerce's Committee of 100 and is involved in numerous hospitality and convention/meetings-related organizations. Before joining DMAI, he was executive vice president of the American Hotel & Lodging Association and also held management positions with sales for WorldRes and with Marriott and Hilton hotels. He is a graduate of The Ohio State University and the Institute of Organizational Management Program at Notre Dame.

THE HISTORY OF convention and visitor bureaus (CVBs) dates back to 1896 when a prominent Detroit journalist, Milton Carmichael, suggested that local businessmen band together to promote the city as a convention destination and represent its many hotels to bid for business. At that time, spending money to bring conventions to a city was a questionable endeavor and, just like the recently invented automobile, the bureau experienced a bumpy start. Soon, however, the Detroit bureau proved successful, and virtually every major city worldwide began using a similar formula.

During the subsequent one hundred years, CVBs evolved a great deal. Bureaus today are full-service destination management organizations that lead the development of their community's hospitality and tourism sector and are often a driving force in the local economy.

What Is a CVB?

While their approaches and structures may vary depending on geography, bureaus have the overall mission of promoting long-term development and marketing of a destination. By creating a brand for the entire community, and all of its tourism-related entities, a CVB gets a destination into the public's consciousness, creating a continuous awareness of and demand for the "product." That demand comes in the form of business travelers, convention attendees, leisure visitors, and residents.

A CVB serves as a coordinating entity, bringing together diverse community stakeholders—from local government to trade and civic associations to individual businesses—to attract visitors to their area. Whether traveling for business or leisure, visitors benefit a city in terms of expenditures, tax dollars, and job creation, as well as in intangible ways such as community pride and quality of life.

CVBs serve as information clearinghouses, convention management consultants, and promotional bodies for the community at large. They lead familiarization trips for meeting planners and travel writers, allowing these decision makers and opinion leaders to experience the destination. Plus, CVB professionals travel themselves, attending industry trade shows to sell the destination to tour operators or convention and meeting planners. Once a sale is made, the CVB assists groups with meeting and tour preparations and introduces them to a range of local businesses that can help create the perfect stay and the potential of repeat business.

The Contemporary Bureau

Readers will note that the title of this book is *Fundamentals of Destination Management and Marketing*, reflecting a general shift in the industry away from a narrow focus on marketing toward a more comprehensive approach emphasizing planning and development, as well as marketing. Cole Carley's chapter on product development effectively demonstrates that the contemporary bureau must take a leadership role in facilitating the development of new destination attractions. However, bureaus must also manage the social, economic, and environmental consequences of these new activities. The contemporary bureau reinvests the return on investment from sales and marketing into tourism development and environmental protection, realizing that quality of life is the one issue that bonds visitors, residents, hosts, and guests. For example, the Lee Island Coast (Florida) Visitor and Convention Bureau, a progressive organization, takes an active role in preserving the "golden goose" through its shoreline management program.

However, sales and marketing will always remain at the heart of the industry. Although shaped by technology, research, and performance measurement, attracting visitors to destinations for economic purposes is a fundamental mission that will not change. Chapters here by Doug Price (sales) and Marshall Murdaugh (marketing) guide readers through the process by which bureaus facilitate the purchase of entertainment, food and beverage, and lodging by travelers and convention planners. The authors note the increasingly competitive nature of sales and marketing in a world where destinations compete against one another internationally, rather than merely within a state or between states. But again, this book maps new territory by making connections between sales and marketing and research and performance management.

Economic recessions and privatization over the last twenty years have caused CVBs to embrace accountability and evaluation research, as noted by Ruth Nadler Trojan in her chapter on performance measurement. Conversion and return-on-investment assessments, once considered luxuries, are now considered crucial to the survival of CVBs. Research departments are under increasing pressure to demonstrate that public and private investment in the bureau's marketing and advertising campaigns is money well spent. These departments also serve an internal function of making sure standards of performance in sales and marketing are not only met but exceeded. The DMAI can take credit for providing the leadership to bring such performance measures to the industry. The DMAI criteria and indicators for performance measurement tracking can be found in her chapter.

It should not be forgotten that bureaus are management organizations. It is evident in these pages that the contemporary bureau is adding new dimensions as it embraces a holistic, rather than strictly marketing, management ethic. From the top, management begins with the community leaders and officials responsible for monitoring the contemporary bureau and its policies. As Joe Lathrop notes in his chapter on board governance, these individuals have a responsibility to guide the bureau while leaving day-to-day operations to individuals trained in destination management. These individuals should act as advocates not only for the bureau, but for the destination management industry, as tourism still does not receive full credit as a form of economic development from some community leaders.

Top management must also take the lead in forming alliances, which are becoming increasingly important to a bureau's economic survival. As Fran Bolson illustrates in her chapter, corporate relationships have added a revenue stream through advertising and cobranding. As Internet costs escalate, partnerships with local Internet providers and Web designers are also becoming an important way of leveling the playing field.

With rotating board government and new alliances, the contemporary bureau director must be able to navigate internal and external political landscapes. The director must also be a high-profile advocate of the industry, exemplifying respect and trust. As destination management increasingly becomes an economic development force, many different urban factions and government officials will use the term for their own political purposes and attempt to use bureaus as political instruments. This trend is already evident in numerous U.S. cities where mayors seek "trophies" for downtown redevelopment, such as aquariums or professional sports stadiums, often enlisting CVBs to provide political support for these projects. Whether the bureau does or does not support these projects, the director must be adept at political maneuvering, balancing the interests of city hall with the interests of visitors and residents. However, the bureau is not without assistance in shaping its image through "spin, buzz, and hook." Danielle Courtenay's chapter provides detailed instructions for proactively devising a communications plan and handling media calls. Moreover, implementing good communications procedures has become crucial to an industry quickly realizing that it needs to change its image in the public's mind from visitor information to corporate economic development. In an appendix to this chapter, William Hanbury provides an inspiring first-person account of how a DMO responded to multiple crises resulting from 9/11. In an increasingly complex and challenging world, such accounts provide meaningful insight into what to do in a "worst case scenario."

Technology has become as important as communications in getting the word out, although often the two functions are inextricably intertwined. In her chapter on technology, Leah Woolford warns of "disintermediation," defined as removing the middleman. She explains that the term is a popular buzzword describing many Internet-based businesses that use the Web to sell products directly to customers rather than going through traditional retail channels. CVBs face a similar disintermediation threat from an online travel industry that is trying to displace them as the traditional and official tourism-related organization. CVBs still have strategic advantages, she explains, but they must assert their rightful place and position themselves firmly as the official representative for their destination to all market segments. Destinations can do this by taking a leadership role in technology adoption and online marketing through strategic planning and execution. While online travel companies are focused on profitable business models and gaining market share, it is critical that CVBs allocate realistic budgets in this increasingly competitive environment.

Although many CVBs still feature a hierarchical, top-down approach to management, others are moving toward a model with each department or function operating synchronously, but with greater autonomy. These changes, as described here by David Camner, are partly out of deference to talented and highly skilled employees, but also reflect a budgetary reality where a single employee might wear many hats. The move from destination marketing to destination management also means the addition of new staff with new skills and roles. The DMAI has proven to be a leader in providing innovative training for employees in these new positions, whether at the beginning or advanced levels.

As bureaus expand their repertoire of duties and functions, they also become more accountable to multiple publics. As the distinction between public, private, and nonprofit sectors becomes increasingly blurred, bureaus have begun to adopt a private-sector business model emphasizing efficiency, effectiveness, and accountability. Nowhere is this more evident than in finance. Ed McMillan's chapter shows that financial management for the contemporary bureau should be an integrated process, with bureau financial officers keeping abreast of federal financial reporting guidelines, but also setting policy for how funds are managed internally. His chapter features examples of policy guidelines from actual CVBs that can easily be adapted by other bureaus.

The new focus on accountability also extends to members. As explained by Jesse Walters in his chapter on member care, not only has the number of members grown exponentially over the years at most bureaus, but memberships have become increasingly varied. Where once the members were mostly hotels, most CVBs also now count restaurants and retail establishments as members, as well as most of their city's tourist attractions and museums. In short, any business that feels it might be attractive to individual leisure travelers or convention attendees might join a bureau.

As visitor numbers increase, so do visitor services, as described by Bill Geist in his chapter. According to Geist, once the sale has been made, it is the service a consumer receives that makes the experience memorable. An unforgettable experience causes the customer to tell family, friends, neighbors, and coworkers. Service, he notes, is a function that can give a bureau a competitive advantage.

The future of destination management is global, where formerly isolated regions—politically and geographically—are now open to tourism. Many of these areas are undeveloped, and thus they need expertise in planning and development in addition to marketing. Many destinations lack CVBs to develop products and attractions. New bureaus are necessary in these locales to replace bureaucratic state agencies that manage crumbling infrastructure and facilities, if they exist at all. These destinations have much to learn from the other international case studies as described by Paul Vallee (Canada), Tony Rogers (United Kingdom), and Elda Cerda (Mexico). Undoubtedly, future editions of this textbook will expand to include destination management around the world. Alliances such as BestCities.net are fulfilling the promise of hospitality and tourism through members in Boston, Copenhagen, Cape Town, Dubai, San Juan, Edinburgh, Melbourne, and Singapore, and Vancouver. The DMAI itself continues to add members across the globe.

Jan van Harssel's glossary helps clarify the language of CVBs, introducing new students and employees to important terms and serving as a useful guide to seasoned veterans who need a quick definition at their fingertips from time to time.

Using This Book

This textbook is the first comprehensive guide covering the basic functions of the contemporary bureau—an organization whose leadership is vital in guiding communities to take advantage of hospitality and tourism as a source of economic development. As such, this book will be indispensable for CVBs, chambers of commerce, tourism organizations, and university programs as they delve into such issues as product development, member care, finance management, technology, board governance, performance measurement, sales, marketing, communications, alliances, services, and human resources.

Reflecting many voices and viewpoints, the contributors to this textbook are internationally recognized experts, each offering insight from years of experience. Throughout these chapters, readers will find a continuing theme of intertwined relationships involving hosts, guests, suppliers, and consumers, as well as complex networks of residents, government officials, and CVB leaders and employees. The connections between products, members, sales and marketing strategies, research agendas, alliances, and services are also described.

Since 1914, DMAI has represented bureaus and tourist boards worldwide through outreach and education. DMAI is proud to be the sponsor of this book. Travel professionals will benefit greatly from the knowledge and resources shared by these seventeen outstanding industry experts and professionals.

Those within the travel business will find that *Fundamentals of Destination Management and Marketing* is an indispensable resource, helping hone the skills necessary for success.

Chapter 1 Outline

The Value of Service
The Leisure Visitor
      Recommend versus Refer
      Service upon Arrival
The Meeting/Convention Planner
      On-Site Assistance
      Around the Town
The Sports Event Planner
The Motor Coach Planner
Industry Partners
      In the Lead Position
The Competitive Edge

Competencies

1. Explain why it is important for CVBs to provide excellent service. (pp. 3–4)

2. Describe the ways in which CVBs can serve leisure visitors. (pp. 4–7)

3. Describe the ways in which CVBs can serve meeting and convention planners. (pp. 7–10)

4. Describe the ways in which CVBs can serve sports event planners, and identify how their needs are similar to and different from those of meeting planners. (pp. 10–11)

5. Describe the ways in which CVBs can serve motor coach planners, and identify how their needs differ from those of meeting planners. (p. 11)

6. Describe the ways in which CVBs can serve community businesses and industry partners. (pp. 11–14)

7. Describe lead generation and its costs and benefits. (pp. 12–13)

Service

By *Bill Geist*

Bill Geist is president of Zeitgeist Consulting in Madison, Wisconsin, a firm specializing in assisting destination marketing organizations across North America with strategic, marketing, and tactical planning and development. Former CEO of the Greater Madison (Wisconsin) Convention and Visitors Bureau, he is the author of Destination Leadership, *a primer for CVB boards. Also, he hosts the innovative CVB industry teleseminar series, "DMOU.com." He holds an Executive M.B.A. degree from the University of Wisconsin–Madison and a degree in political science from Kenyon College.*

REGARDLESS OF THE SIZE of a convention and visitors bureau (CVB), the services it provides often will define the organization and destination more effectively than any sales or marketing campaign ever devised. Once the sale has been made, the service a consumer receives makes the experience memorable. An unforgettable experience causes the customer to tell family, friends, neighbors, and coworkers. Service is a function that can give a CVB a competitive advantage.

This chapter will address the numerous services that CVBs provide to their very diverse set of customers (leisure travelers and meeting and event planners) and clients (CVB members, industry partners, and local businesses). Readers will encounter several different ways to describe a CVB's relationships with other organizations. The term used will depend on the context of the situation.

The Value of Service

CVBs can distinguish themselves through service in several ways. A CVB's services can level the playing field against its larger or more budget-rich competitors. If a major metropolitan CVB charges meeting planners for shuttle services or registration assistance, a suburban bureau might offer these services for free in an attempt to position itself as a cost-effective alternative. Meeting planners are a talkative bunch—one planner may tell other planners that they should consider this suburban CVB and its services, and soon the destination will gain a reputation as a place where planners are treated well. That is the service advantage.

CVB services can also direct first-time visitors or event attendees to attractions and facilities that will enhance their experience in the destination. Without the bureau, visitors would be on their own and might miss out on experiences that would cause them to tell their friends about the great community they just discovered and the wonderful time they had there.

The hospitality industry provides the experience remembered by leisure visitors and business travelers for years to come. People in the tourism business got into this field to make people smile. And when visitors' experiences are enhanced, the cash registers of destination businesses hum. At the end of the day, that is why CVBs exist.

The Leisure Visitor

CVBs serve many different types of customers, but virtually every bureau serves the leisure visitor. A destination may not have meeting facilities, sports complexes, or attractions that appeal to motor coach operators, but almost every bureau wants to attract individuals, couples, and families to its destination.

The first service opportunity for CVBs comes when leisure visitors bite on the promotional hook offered through the bureau's marketing efforts. They like what they have seen or heard and want to learn more. Chances are they will either call the CVB or search for additional information on the Internet. The service to the consumer starts right there.

If they call, they are expecting answers to a diverse set of questions, and they are expecting the person on the other end of the phone to have those answers. This is why it is crucial for the person answering CVB phones to have several attributes, starting with an innate love of helping people. If the person is not, by nature, someone who enjoys helping others, the caller will know that in seconds. In those moments, a first impression of the destination has been made, and it is not a positive one. In this case, customer service is *not* your secret weapon, and it has just cost your destination hundreds, if not thousands, of dollars of forfeited revenue.

The perfect person to answer a CVB's telephones is a true "director of first impressions"—someone with a cheery disposition who loves to help others and solve problems and, ideally, knows the destination like the back of his or her hand. But, when forced to choose, go for the attitude. The CVB should always create a list of frequently asked questions that includes all but the most unusual questions potential visitors may ask. Such a list will serve as an excellent backup document for those answering the phones and give them a sense of security in their first few weeks on the job.

When a prospective visitor comes to the CVB's Web site, the bureau has no idea what the person's interest or question may be. Consequently, it is crucial for the site to provide all available information about the destination. To the extent possible, every question must be answered, and every possible interest must be linked to its location in the destination.

Internet users are unforgiving. If a potential visitor cannot find what he or she is seeking on the Web site quickly and easily, the result is akin to that generated by the crabby receptionist. The consumer will look elsewhere. Experience with phones, as well as traditional mail and e-mail, gives CVBs a pretty good idea of the questions one would get in any medium. Thus, CVBs need to build Web sites that answer all these questions, and more.

The Durham (North Carolina) Convention & Visitors Bureau (DCVB) has led the movement to connect these two modes of providing visitor services. Knowing that its Internet site could not possibly answer every question on the mind of a potential visitor, it added a "live chat" feature to its Web site. With this option, Internet visitors can type a question to a DCVB staffer and, within seconds, get an answer.

Recommend versus Refer

As much as bureaus would like to direct potential visitors to their favorite places, there are both ethical and legal reasons why CVB services must stop short of recommending a destination business.

From a legal standpoint, a CVB's recommendation puts the organization in a precarious position. If the CVB actively recommends a restaurant and the customer gets food poisoning, the CVB can be sued. But if a bureau merely refers a visitor to its list of members or destination partners, its liability is significantly reduced.

From an ethical standpoint, CVB professionals must remember that they represent a wide range of hotels, restaurants, retailers, and attractions. Destination partners depend on bureaus to represent them fairly and evenly. If a bureau only recommends favorites or friends, it violates the trust between its partners and the CVB. Although it clearly wants visitors to dine at the finest restaurant in town (so they will tell their friends about it), the CVB must represent all its members/partners in a balanced way.

At the same time, the customer really wants to know the "best" places. To be as fair as possible to partners and as helpful as possible to customers, the smart CVB representative will ask a series of defining questions to reduce the options and thereby help direct the customer to a preferred choice. For example, a customer asking for the best hotel in town will not be pleased to get a list of twenty choices from the CVB. By asking their preferred price range, whether they desire room service, and whether they would be interested in spa services, the list—probably numbering three or less—will better mirror their interests.

Service upon Arrival

Assuming the CVB has succeeded in attracting the visitor to the destination, the next opportunity to serve this consumer may come at the visitors information center, sometimes referred to as the welcome center. Although most visitors to a community never find their way to the visitors information center, those who do provide the CVB with an additional opportunity to impress them with great customer service. They also afford the CVB the chance to sell them on additional attractions and experiences they may not have considered or known about.

The key components of a successful visitors information center include brochures, maps, courtesy telephones and, of course, an upbeat and knowledgeable representative behind the reception desk. Unless they are just stopping to use the restroom, visitors arrive at the welcome center with questions. A full complement of brochures and promotional flyers will provide visitors with a wide array of answers to their "Where do I...?" questions. When designing brochure racks, it is best to cluster similar brochures together—for example, hotels in the lodging section and restaurants in the dining section—to facilitate visitors' selections.

One of the most frequent questions a visitor will have at the information center involves location of a site or facility. Thus, the availability of an easy-to-read map of the destination is crucial. While providing the standard multi-fold city map is an option, most visitors will be better served with an eleven-by-seventeen-inch (or equivalent) map that identifies major thoroughfares and key attractions. Such a map can be inexpensive to produce and allows information specialists on duty to highlight directions or attractions with ease.

By means of a destination audit—an assessment of a destination and its management that should include an evaluation of product mix and marketing strategies—the Grant County/Marion (Indiana) CVB discovered that travelers to that destination found customer service at the visitors information center to be friendly and helpful. However, for those who asked destination questions at hotels, restaurants, and gas stations, the experience was frustrating, to say the least. The CVB changed this perception by producing its destination map in tear-off pads of one hundred and placing these pads at high-traffic businesses around the county. Although people behind the counter still did not have answers to questions about the area's James Dean sites, at least they could offer visitors a map, and that made a huge difference in their perception of the helpfulness of the destination's front line staff.

Courtesy telephones in the welcome center are an effective way to "close the sale" on behalf of your destination. Designed to allow only local calls, these phones encourage visitors to take the information they have acquired at the center and book a reservation or purchase a ticket on the spot. Some visitors centers actually place these phones in an enclosed entryway to provide twenty-four-hour access to hotels, even when the center is closed for the evening.

Taking this concept a step further, some visitors information centers have begun offering a concierge service in which a staffer will make the reservation for visitors. In an effort to stand out and provide a memorable experience to the visitor, this tactic certainly goes above and beyond travelers' expectations.

As one develops information center experience, one can think of other services to provide to visitors while they are at the destination. Many bureaus, like the Alabama Gulf Coast CVB, now offer Internet kiosks and wireless Internet access so that visitors can check their e-mail while on the road. Others offer a postal drop for those wishing to send postcards to loved ones saying, "Wish you were here!"

Hours of operation are also very important. Successful visitors information centers are not like traditional, Monday-through-Friday, 8-to-5 businesses. Many visitors do not arrive at their destinations between 8 A.M. and 5 P.M. on weekdays. Consideration should be given to staffing centers later in the evening, especially on Fridays. Centers should also be open on Saturdays, when those who arrived late on Friday are trying to get their bearings in their destination.

Depending on the destination, Sunday hours might not be out of the question. Fond du Lac, Wisconsin, is located between Milwaukee and Door County, a popular resort destination on Lake Michigan. The CVB there discovered that tourists, in a mad dash to get to Door County by nightfall on Friday evening, whizzed by its visitors information center on Friday afternoon. As those same tourists headed home on Sunday afternoon, many stopped at the center for information they could use on future trips to the area. The Fond du Lac CVB is now open Sunday afternoons.

The Meeting/Convention Planner

For CVBs that represent meeting, convention, and event facilities, bureau services can be the deciding factor in a customer's decision to bring its business to a destination. More important, CVB services can determine whether that customer returns to the area or looks elsewhere for the perfect destination.

The top priority for a meeting planner is to stage a mistake-free event that impresses peers and managers and comes in at or under budget. The CVB that can help the planner meet these goals is better positioned to win the business than a CVB that focuses on its destination strengths and price. In the site selection phase of the process, with all other considerations being equal, CVB services can often tip the scales.

Even when all things are not equal, services can keep a destination in the running. Say three destinations are being considered for a state convention. One convention center refuses to budge on price while the other two offer lower pricing. However, the services the first CVB brings to the table may counter the cost differential and keep it in the running. For instance, if the bureau can offer free on-site registration assistance, it could save the customer hundreds of dollars and hours of hassles. If the bureau offers free shuttle service for attendees, it could save the client thousands of dollars. Indeed, a well-developed services package could actually offer the planner the lowest overall event cost option despite providing the highest convention center bill.

Beyond the cost factor, a bureau offering a high level of service also provides the planner with other benefits that can reduce stress and save time. For example, once the event has been booked, the CVB changes from sales organization to service superstar. In this role, the CVB becomes a consultant and can assist the planner in several ways. Especially if the planner lives outside the area, a CVB can be his or her eyes and ears in identifying facilities, vendors, speakers, and more.

In many instances, the bureau can be an effective liaison between the planner and local government officials when special permits are required. For instance, if a pyrotechnics convention wishes to stage a fireworks display on its closing night, chances are pretty high that it will need the CVB to run interference at city hall to acquire approval from the police, public works, and the mayor's office. These officials can be a pretty intimidating roadblock for many out-of-town planners. The CVB, on the other hand, should have strong, ongoing relationships with each of these groups and a track record of successful events with which to advocate for the necessary permits.

Many meeting planners look for an official welcome to kick off their events. Because of its relationships with local government, the CVB is in the best position to handle the arrangements for top community officials to appear and address the crowd. This also plays well for the CVB as most public officials love the opportunity to "meet and greet," and secure a photo opportunity for the next campaign. A

CVB that gives politicians a stage is a CVB that cultivates friends in influential places.

Another opportunity for CVBs to "wow" meeting and event planners is to offer assistance in convention housing. When large events that require multiple hotel room blocks book a city, managing the hotel inventory is often a mind-boggling chore for meeting planners, and finding a hotel room can often be a frustrating experience for the prospective attendee. CVBs can resolve this stressful situation for both parties (and their partner hotels) by coordinating the reservations in the room blocks at participating hotels. By providing event housing services, the CVB agrees to serve as the reservation agent, attempting to fill rooms fairly throughout the destination. Orders can be processed by phone or mail, but the trend has shifted to fax and Internet processing since the late 1990s. In addition, many third-party housing services have emerged, and numerous CVB and meeting planners have engaged these experienced professionals to provide this often time-consuming service.

The CVB can also decrease planner stress by providing referrals to area florists, caterers, audiovisual companies, disc jockeys, bands, and professional speakers. These are all services that meeting planners utilize in staging a memorable event. The bureau not only assists planners when it makes such referrals, but successfully steers new business to its destination partners.

CVBs can play a significant role in serving a stressed-out meeting planner by offering to assist in pre-event communications with prospective attendees. Some bureaus offer to mail pre-event postcards and registration forms to encourage attendance. These communiqués also allow the CVB to promote its destination, often by including a visitors guide with the registration brochure. Thus, even if the recipient chooses not to attend the event, the bureau has succeeded in placing promotional literature in his or her hands.

With the advent of the Internet, some bureaus are taking advantage of this technology to reduce mailing costs and more effectively customize their message. The Fargo–Moorhead (North Dakota–Minnesota) CVB offers a password-protected section for meeting attendees to view and take advantage of special offers in the destination that have been created just for their meeting. The CVB's convention services team works with the planner to develop a customized Web page with conference agendas; answers to questions; driving directions and shuttle information; nightlife, theater, and conference information; and a set of special offers for attendees during their conference. Imagine being able to offer a service that saves the meeting planner and the bureau money, and makes all involved look like superstars in the eyes of the attendees.

Meetings and conventions can also be promoted locally. Often, the CVB can connect the meeting planner with local media contacts to develop stories and features about the event, something that works on two levels for the CVB. For the planner and the organization, it gains them exposure in the region and shows them that the community is excited they are in town. For the CVB, it reminds the community that it is indeed a desirable destination for meetings, conventions, and tourism. This is always important in communicating the value of the CVB to local opinion leaders.

On-Site Assistance

As much as the CVB can be a valuable assistant in the weeks and months leading up to a meeting or event, it can be an absolute lifesaver during the organization's days in the destination. If meeting planners are unfamiliar with the host community, their stress level is high. Even though they have done their homework, chances are good that they will need a quick assist with a last-minute crisis. For them, a crisis can be as big as a life-threatening situation or as small as forgetting to order flowers for the outgoing chairman of the board.

Aside from helping with the inevitable crisis, however, typical on-site CVB services run the gamut from providing registration assistance and complimentary name badges to concierge services and goody bags with coupons, pins, and pens. By providing registration assistance and name badge services, the bureau saves planners the cost of bringing their own staff to handle these relatively mundane tasks or outsourcing them to a temp agency. Many CVBs utilize volunteers in this role, keeping costs down for themselves, as well. Providing one of the bureau's visitors information specialists to staff a booth near registration as a destination concierge is another opportunity for the CVB to shine in the eyes of the planner, and help direct visitors to member or partner attractions.

Around the Town

CVBs can also help make attendees feel welcome in the host community, which can go a long way toward developing repeat business. Some service-oriented CVBs provide welcome banners over key thoroughfares, at the airport, and in the meeting facilities, as well as welcome cards for display in the windows of restaurants and retail stores. For large city-wide events or conventions, some CVBs will also encourage area businesses with reader boards on their exterior signage to post a welcome. It is one thing for attendees to see a couple of welcome banners around town, but imagine how impressed they (and the meeting planner) will be to see a welcome on fifty fast-food-restaurant reader boards throughout the community.

For large, multi-hotel conventions, transportation can be one of the biggest challenges that a meeting planner and attendees will face. In many cases, the CVB can play a major role in arranging for and, in some cases for key customers, subsidizing the cost of providing a shuttle service connecting the meeting facilities, participating hotels, and key destination attractions. This is especially crucial for destinations without an attached or adjacent headquarters hotel for their convention center and communities in which the hotel inventory is spread across town.

Finally, there is always the chance that the working relationship between the planner and the facility will deteriorate over a dispute. To whom can the out-of-town meeting planner turn when being hassled in some way by the meeting facility? The CVB is the planner's ombudsman in such situations, offering to mediate or otherwise resolve the problem.

Even when the event's stragglers have finally departed for home, the sponsor banners are removed, and the last exhibit booth is shipped out, the service role for a CVB continues. Follow-up communication showcases the bureau's pride in its destination and concern for the customer's success. "Did we meet (and, hopefully, exceed) your expectations? Is there anything we can do (or could have done) that would enhance your event? What can we do to bring you back next year?" All these questions exemplify the bureau's service-oriented attitude. Follow-up communication is not only a service attribute, it is also an effective sales tactic. After the event has been successfully staged, the follow-up communication is as much an initial sales contact for future bookings as it is a reiteration of service.

The Sports Event Planner

One of the fastest-growing segments of the travel industry is the sports tournament market. Prior to the mid-1990s, many CVBs treated this market as a part of their meetings and conventions effort. After all, most sports tournaments were viewed as big conventions with different clothes and staged in different venues.

Of course, the selection criteria of the sports event planner are quite different from those of the meeting planner, and that is why a significant number of CVBs today have a separate sports sales division and/or personnel. Although the way a CVB attracts, pitches, and lands sports events is different, the service side does mirror the meetings market pretty closely.

Like meeting planners, sports planners depend upon the CVB to run interference with local governments, park districts, universities, and sports facilities on use policies, rules and regulations, permits, and the like. In 2004, the Greater Madison (Wisconsin) Convention and Visitors Bureau (GMCVB) was instrumental in landing ESPN's Great Outdoor Games. Despite excitement in the community, residents near a park to be used for the target shooting competition voiced concerns and cited a city ordinance preventing firearms from being discharged within city limits. The bureau met with representatives from the neighborhood, understood their concerns, then worked with ESPN on a set of counterproposals for this event. The GMCVB then worked with the mayor's office, the city council, and the police department to secure a temporary waiver of the restriction on guns for the duration of the event in that park. Without those efforts, a major component of the ESPN Outdoor Games would have been canceled, and the chances of Madison having another opportunity to host that event or others like it would have been next to zero.

CVBs are also called upon to provide for or arrange event housing services. For sports groups, this is often more complex than working with meeting facilities because of the diversity of hotels utilized. Organizations that participate in and attend sports events run the gamut from wanting to stay at low-priced, limited-service properties to the finest hotels in town. As the choices become broader, the selection process becomes more complex. This is another reason why many CVBs are now outsourcing housing services to third-party vendors.

Indeed, most of the services discussed for meeting planners are appropriate for sports planners. Welcome signage, registration assistance, and an on-site information stand all can elevate the appeal of a bureau's destination over its competitors. Participant goody bags are especially appreciated if they contain coupons from area merchants. For many participants and their traveling families, sports tournaments can be a strain on their budgets. Coupons for restaurants and other necessities, even entertainment, can be a positive image-builder for the community to the cost-conscious tournament participant or fan. And offering a customized Web page for event participants and fans—like the Fargo–Moorhead CVB example—would be a real plus for families making their tournament plans.

The Motor Coach Planner

Although, like meeting planners, motor coach planners represent a group, their needs differ significantly from those of other CVB customers. Motor coach groups tend to be smaller than convention and sports groups, and generally get together for sightseeing. Consequently, registration personnel, welcome banners, and many of the services offered to meeting planners are often not crucial.

But CVBs can serve the motor coach planner in other ways. Most important (for both the planner and the bureau's destination partners), motor coach planners need assistance with developing itineraries for their tours. For example, they need to identify attractions, restaurants, and facilities that are "coach-friendly," with such features as special turnaround areas, covered loading platforms, special prices, and restaurants that can accommodate sixty people at one sitting. They also want to know the time it takes to travel between each experience on the schedule. The bureau can help in all these respects, providing services that save the motor coach planner time and embarrassment.

Although coordinating pricing and hotel availability is often part of the sales, bidding, and negotiating process in the meetings and conventions market, it is also a valuable service that a CVB can supply to a motor coach planner. When a motor coach planner contacts a bureau and expresses an interest in the destination, the CVB is well-positioned to serve as an intermediary to identify hotels that offer the perfect set of services and pricing for the customer.

For some motor coach planners that are either new to the destination or do not prepare running narratives for their excursions, CVBs can provide another valuable service. Many bureaus offer local guides who know the destination and its attractions inside and out. The good ones have wonderfully colorful stories about the region and can become stars of the show as the coach travels from point to point in the destination.

Probably more than any other group, motor coach parties love goody bags and welcome gifts. Whether it is a selection of local products or a pin, such gifts are often an inexpensive way to please customers and make them feel welcome. For some groups, CVBs will also sponsor a welcome reception upon arrival. These customers react favorably to the personal touch.

Industry Partners

As noted earlier, CVBs serve two main constituents: their customers (leisure travelers or group planners) and their clients (CVB members or partners and area businesses). The services bureaus provide to customers are vital to the destination. However, the services they provide to their members and business partners can be just as critical to success.

Bureau partners look to the CVB to assist them in attracting more business and increasing their profits. For bureaus that maintain a membership program, this relationship is somewhat defined. The business pays the bureau a fee each year in return for a set of services. Some CVBs offer a menu of services for different prices. For instance, a base membership (providing a listing in the visitors guide and on the bureau Web site) might cost $250. If the member wanted to be part of the convention lead distribution service, the fee might jump to $400, and so on.

For bureaus without a membership program, the precise expectations of area businesses are a little less clear, but they exist nonetheless. This is often powered by a belief that because tax dollars have been invested in the CVB, the bureau somehow owes them some services or benefits.

An enlightened few have expectations that are more "big-picture" in nature. For example, a funeral home director in Quincy, Illinois, was once chided for his membership in the local CVB. He was asked, somewhat tongue-in-cheek, whether he was looking for new business from the bureau. His response: "I support the bureau because they help bring business to the community, and that's a good thing for all of us."

Among the services a bureau can offer to the business community, communication is probably the most important. The bureau often knows when the town will be full of visitors and when it will not. Keeping attractions, restaurants, and hotels aware of impending heavy weekends allows business managers to effectively schedule their staff to meet the anticipated demand. Informing businesses of what kind of visitors are coming can be just as important. Some groups, like the Gold Wing Road Riders motorcycle club, can virtually consume a city and take great pride in doing so. Letting restaurateurs know that the Gold Wingers are on their way enables them to stock up on extra food. Other groups, by their very nature, do not eat out much, and area restaurateurs need to be alerted not to stock up unnecessarily even though every hotel room in town is full.

Other services are more tangible. Most CVBs list businesses in their visitors guide, specialty brochures, dining guide, and on their Web site. Most will provide a link to the companies' Web sites on the bureau's site, sometimes for a fee. This visibility in and on bureau promotional pieces helps businesses attract visitors and is a welcome service.

In the Lead Position

For those businesses that court convention, motor coach, and sports tournament business, bureau services are even more important. Offering a lead service works for both the bureau and the tourism industry partner. Many CVBs maintain a professional sales staff to identify potential clients for meetings, motor coach tours, and sports events. Ultimately, the pieces of business they identify are called leads if they qualify as being truly able to book their event or coach into the destination. The leads that will take some coordination and multiple hotels are usually handled by the CVB. Those that can easily fit into a single property are often relayed to the hotel or facilities community.

The ability to hand off prospective pieces of business to interested partners allows the bureau to move on to developing more leads. It also increases the bureau's reputation in the eyes of the partner, and partners get professional assistance in growing their business.

Due to extensive staff time required, generating leads is expensive; indeed, it is one of the largest costs of a bureau's operation. This is why lead services are often offered to members or partners for an additional fee. After all, if these businesses are getting a higher level of service than others in the community, it is only fair that they assist in the cost of the service. If the lead service is producing business for partners, they should be willing to invest in the program.

Many bureaus offer partners the opportunity to participate in co-op advertising. Such programs are built on the premise that many destination businesses could never afford the price of a half-page ad in a major metropolitan newspaper. Even if they could, few could run that ad with the frequency needed to make an impression in the minds of enough readers to increase business significantly. Enter the CVB, which can contract for a half-page ad and then sell sections of that ad back to partner businesses at a fraction of its cost. In this way, the bureau provides a service to the business while making its own budget go further and increasing the frequency of the destination's message in major publications.

This group-buying concept can also extend to other applications that can benefit industry partners. If its membership is large enough, CVBs can attempt to negotiate special pricing on products and services that businesses utilize. From long-distance and broadband services to special rates on overnight shipping, the buying power of a bureau's membership can qualify for substantial discounts on these and other staples of business. Discounts at office supply stores could be negotiated for CVB members. More important, group buying opportunities in health care and insurance should also be investigated and, if available, offered. Remember, a bureau is there to enhance the profitability of the businesses in the destination. Saving them money is just as important as bringing them new business.

The CVB also can provide an exceptional service to its partners by offering opportunities for professional and staff development and training. At its most basic level, the bureau can offer regular customer service and destination awareness training workshops for front desk and counter staff. Although it is a sad commentary on the hospitality industry as a whole, many CVB partners say they cannot afford customer service training for their employees. With the rapid turnover in many hospitality industries, this lack of customer service acumen is coupled with an alarming lack of knowledge about the destination. The CVB should address these issues whenever possible.

Smart bureaus can step in and offer group training using the same format as cooperative advertising. Industry partners can take advantage of the bureau's sponsorship of a professional service trainer at a rate significantly lower than what it would cost to hire such a speaker on their own. During the workshop, CVB personnel could also lead a session on the highlights of the destination to acquaint front-line staff with the answers to the questions visitors are sure to ask.

Many bureaus see this service as so crucial they will go so far as to offer these workshops for free. Others will work with partner motor coach companies and destination attractions to stage mini-familiarization tours for front-line personnel.

In this way, the people with whom a visitor initially interacts will have had first-hand experience in the destination attractions that they will be suggesting.

The Competitive Edge

The success of most destinations springs from the experience of the visitor. Although a notable handful of destinations can get by on their physical attributes, most consumers employ the level of service they encounter while traveling as a measuring stick to evaluate communities. The CVB is a crucial component of this experience.

From providing leisure visitors with the information they crave to making the life of a meeting planner less hectic, CVB services can be a competitive advantage over destinations that take a laissez-faire attitude toward their varied customers. And, as noted earlier, it can be a great leveler when competing against bigger, more impressively funded bureaus. Likewise, large CVBs would be wise to invest more resources into bureau services to stave off hungrier, more nimble competitors.

Service can be a great advantage in most destination competitions, given that most competitors can, in terms of infrastructure, meet the customer's requirements. The only other ace in the deck is price, but winning on price is a hollow victory because if a CVB wins on price, that means it could not distinguish itself from the competition in a more meaningful way. Anybody can win on price. Great service distinguishes destinations and CVBs.

Chapter 2 Outline

Competencies

1. Identify sources of sales prospects, and explain why current and past customers should be a primary focus of CVB sales prospecting. (pp. 17–19)

2. Describe the purpose of qualifying prospects and explain the role of asking questions in developing a sales plan based on customer needs. (pp. 19–20)

3. Describe the steps in the sales process, including determining strengths and benefits, overcoming objections, and following up with customers. (pp. 20–24)

4. Identify three key market segments for CVB sales and explain the role of the CVB satellite office in building customer relationships with these market segments. (pp. 24–25)

5. Explain the role of the convention service manager in the CVB sales process. (p. 26)

2

Sales

By *Doug Price*

Doug Price, CMP, is responsible for all professional development functions of DMAI, including life-long learning, professional certification, and academic affairs. He has more than eighteen years of experience with Marriott International and ten additional years of consulting experience. A recognized public speaker, Price is coauthor of License to Sell, *a book on personalized "high touch" selling in a high-tech environment. He also wrote a companion volume,* License to Serve, *which focuses on the importance of delivering outstanding customer service. He holds a B.S. in hospitality management from Florida International University.*

How do CVBs approach the challenge of selling a destination? They dedicate sales professionals to sell the particular strengths and benefits of that destination. In many ways, selling a destination is more challenging that selling a single hotel because of the enormous amount of knowledge one must learn about the place.

This chapter will examine the following topics: prospecting for customers, qualifying prospects, selling strengths and benefits, handling objections, following up, market segmentation and CVB satellite offices, and convention services.

Prospecting

A major tenet in the world of sales is: To keep your job, you have to beat your sales goals. Many people miss their sales goals because they do not know where to find prospects. Where do you begin to find prospects for your destination? Your research begins with past and current customers. An existing database will provide insight into the types of customers likely to book in the future.

There are many reasons why customers stop doing business with a CVB. A customer can move from the area, an organization can go out of business, or a company can be purchased by another firm. A meeting planner or tour operator might leave his or her position and the replacement might prefer other destinations. Another possibility is that a customer may have had only a one-time visit, or his or her needs have changed. Then again, a customer may not have been solicited a second time. Contact past customers to find out what made them book in the first place and who, if anyone, is getting their business now. These answers will identify the competition. This contact also gives you the chance to ask some probing questions, such as, "What could I do to get you to try us again?" If they liked the destination enough to buy in the past, why not rekindle their business?

17

Sources

You can employ a wide variety of sources to find prospects, and it's worthwhile to check them all. Among them:

- Referrals from past and current customers
- Business proposals from groups that previously had considered your destination
- Friends and family
- Trade shows you attend for lead generation
- Trade publications/magazines from various industry types
- Web sites of organizations that list meetings and events
- Database marketing lists that can be purchased for prospecting by phone, mail, or e-mail
- MINT—Meeting Information Network, for members of DMAI, which contains histories of more than 28,000 meetings
- Newspaper reports mentioning upcoming events
- Telephone directories that list associations, civic groups, and meeting/event companies
- Chamber of commerce members who share leads and refer you to other businesses
- CVB board members who have contacts that would consider your destination
- Road shows/sales missions that you make with your members and partners to solicit business in other cities
- Third-party planners who can bring business to you for a paid fee

Gaining Referrals

Customers currently doing business with you are the most important group to research. Not only might they buy from you again, they can be excellent sources for referrals. Who better to ask for referrals, testimonials, or more business than current and satisfied customers? They are already familiar with your destination, and you know about them. A careful analysis of current customers can yield a profile of the ideal prospect. Customers will respect your inquiry once they understand that you are trying to expand a market and could use their advice on potential customers to call. Learn as much information as you can about a new referral prospect. Be sure to ask for permission to use your customer's name when contacting a referral. Ask your customer if he or she could help with an introduction, or, if appropriate, arranging for a meeting over breakfast or lunch.

The Prospecting Process

It has been said that "the toughest door to open is your own car door!" This alludes to the fact that a destination salesperson must get out of the office and call on prospects. What does prospecting mean? It is networking, meeting with people in their environment. One of the main reasons enterprises fail is that people don't spend enough time and resources prospecting for new business. The minimum amount of time devoted to prospecting should be 20 percent, or one day per week. Some might say it's impossible to get out of the office. If you don't have time, pay someone to do some of the legwork for you. Hire an hourly telemarketer or a direct mail house. No matter what your destination, you must find customers. Once research has shown who would want to meet at your place, you have to get out there and actively solicit their business.

Qualifying Prospects

Qualifying the prospect means determining whether the prospect has an interest that you can and want to handle. The use of effective questioning techniques to qualify prospects has become a lost art. Preparation of the right questions and the use of active listening skills, coupled with patience, are the keys to proper qualifying. You will want to ask questions that will confirm some of your pre-call planning. This implies that you do your homework and respect your customer's time. Do not ask questions "live" that could have been answered if you had taken the time to review the wealth of information online or elsewhere about the customer, his organization, or product. You will also need to probe to learn what the prospect's needs and problems are. In qualifying, you are trying to answer three basic questions:

1. Does a need exist that your destination could satisfy?

2. Are you talking to the decision-maker or at least someone who has influence with the decision-maker?

3. Does the prospect have the resources (budget, good credit) to book with you?

Do not take the first glimmer of interest from a prospect and begin selling. It is very tempting to do that when you first hear someone describe a problem that you can fix. As stated above, you are selling while you are listening. The goal in qualifying is to discover and prioritize all of a prospect's needs and problems before you attempt to help solve them. Be patient. Listen carefully. Think on your feet.

At this stage, you are playing the role of a problem-solver. You should not present solutions until you have heard at least three primary needs surface or you have confirmed that no other primary needs exist. Ask an open question, such as: "What else would you like to improve from your last convention if given the chance?" Or pose a closed one: "Similar customers who have used all volunteer registration found service to be a problem—has it been a problem for you?" Phrases you might hear while qualifying a customer might be:

- The solution to my problem…
- What our organization needs is…
- I want a way to…
- I would like to have…

- I wish there was a way to…

- I'm looking for…

- What is important to me is…

Examples of qualifying questions are:

- What is the overall objective of your convention?

- Do your tour series include senior citizens?

- How important is air travel access for your attendees?

- What would persuade you to return to a destination a second time?

- What other destinations have you used?

Take notes while the prospect is answering your qualifying questions. Continue the process after each need is described by asking, "Are there additional needs you have?" Once you have a list of needs and have asked, "Would you say that covers all your needs?" then say, "Let me repeat all the needs I have heard so far." When the prospect agrees that covers them, ask, "How would you prioritize these needs from most important to least?" The answer to that question gives you the order in which to sell your particular strengths. That information also helps if you have to negotiate later.

Selling Strengths and Benefits

Consider the following four-step selling process:

STEP 1: Open the sales call.

STEP 2: Qualify the customer.

STEP 3: Sell to/meet the customer's objectives.

STEP 4: Gain and confirm commitment.

When you begin thinking about selling the special strengths and benefits of your destination, you are in Step 3 of the process. One starts with strengths because often this is where the customer starts to think. In other words, the customer will have a concept or image of your destination's strengths, and this enables you to relate your product to the customer's thinking. Your particular strengths are the distinguishable differences that you claim exist between your destination and the competition.

Begin by asking, "What does the customer really need?" Then ask, "How can I deliver it?" You are looking for a fit, and should keep in mind that your perceived strengths alone are not enough for customers to choose you. You have to be able to communicate information about your strengths that makes you stand out from the others. This is even more critical in a very competitive marketplace, particularly if the destinations do not have major distinguishable differences. In a highly competitive marketplace, unless you sell your strengths, the customers are forced to do the sorting, and nine times out of ten they will choose on the basis of price and availability alone. Selling special strengths minimizes the importance of price competition and enables you to undertake value-added selling for your destination.

Strengths run the gamut from location and price to climate and image. Among them are:

- *Access:* Convenient location with a good air, rail, and highway access in and out of your market

- *Dining:* Options of restaurants offered

- *Recreation:* Facilities to participate in or watch sporting events

- *Night Life:* Variety and proximity of nightly attractions

- *Attractions:* Options for sightseeing, spouse programs, themed events, pre- and post-meeting opportunities

- *Convention center:* The benefits and features of your center, including convention services and shuttle services

- *Hotel Package:* The variety of hotels, pricing availability, and their proximity to the convention center, airport, or attractions

- *History:* Significant landmarks, famous people, and historic stories

- *Affordability:* The overall affordability of your destination as compared to a competitor

- *Miscellaneous:* Miscellaneous strengths for your destination, for example, welcoming programs, international signage, shopping, language translation services

- *You:* The selling skills and passion you display over a competing salesperson. Customers buy you first!

In the end, your destination will not be superior in all these categories. A good exercise for a destination salesperson is to analyze the array of special strengths and write a sentence for each that demonstrates its value to the customer. The answers should be brief. You ought to be able to state concisely why you're the best one and in what ways you differ from the competition. Remember, you can prove your validity to prospects by giving references and testimonials from satisfied customers. Realize that these strengths and benefits will change for each individual customer because needs change for every person.

Handling Objections

It is often said that the sale begins when the customer says no. Until that point, you are merely a presenter or marketer of information. Moving the customer from "no" to "yes" is the skill in selling. Objections are a part of the selling process you must learn to enjoy overcoming. An objection occurs when a customer has serious doubts or questions about your destination prior to making a decision. But objections can be beneficial because they might represent buying signals.

A successful salesperson welcomes an objection and treats it with respect and care. If it is important enough for the customer to take time to ask questions or express concerns over a particular feature, it is important enough to ensure the customer gets the exact answer he or she is looking for—even if it means losing the group.

A proven method for responding, once you have clarified and confirmed, is to use the "Feel—Felt—Found" method. With this technique, you restate the customer's objection by acknowledging how he or she feels and noting that other customers have raised similar objections. Then you explain how you and they found a way to overcome the problem and reach a positive outcome. This demonstrates empathy and sounds like, "I know how you *feel* about the distance from your headquarters hotel to the convention center because other customers have *felt* the same way. But, once they *found* out how reliable the shuttle service is..."

If the objection is not based on a simple question, you should probe to uncover additional hidden objections. Do not fall into the trap of answering the objection only to have others arise. Handling objections this way is like trying to hold a slippery fish with your bare hands. You may be able to do it, but it is not pretty and the chances of dropping it are great.

After you have confirmed and understood the objection, acknowledge it and probe for more. You might say, "I can understand your concern with.... It sounds like that is an important issue and one that I would like to address. In the interest of your time, before I respond to it, are there any other issues I can address?" Wait for a response. If you get one, probe it. Understand it. Confirm it. Acknowledge it. Then ask for another. Continue to do this until the customer has no more objections. But after he says no, ask him one more time just to make sure. You will be surprised how many more arise because you ask twice.

This approach of asking for all objections allows you to reorder those objections to best suit your needs. It also allows you to make the strongest case for your destination. You decide whether to put the hardest one last or first. You may find that you can combine two into one and handle them together. Dealing with them at the outset allows you to plan and prepare, even if only for a minute or two. If the objection or concern is based on a feature that your destination cannot provide, say so. It is best to be frank with a customer. If your customer feels at any time you are being evasive, you will lose trust for this call and probably for the entire relationship. At the same time, if you answer honestly and state your reasons professionally, you build customer trust. When you feel that a customer's objection has been satisfied, verify by restating the solution: "Can you see how the shuttle service plan will have your attendees at the center in less than ten minutes?" If the customer agrees with your verification statement, consider it handled and move on. If not, an issue still exists. Keep probing and clarifying for all hidden objections.

Liabilities and Misunderstandings

Objections can be classified in one of two categories:

- *Liability.* Something you cannot provide. For example, if someone must have 3,000 rooms within a five-minute walk of the center and you don't have it, that is a liability.

- *Misunderstanding.* Perceptions that can be corrected. For example, if a customer is ready to choose a competitor because your destination's room rates are too high, he or she may not realize hotels will negotiate at certain times of the year.

List the most common objections you face with customers regarding your destination/convention center/attractions. Review the list and label each objection with an "L" for liability or an "M" for misunderstanding. Generally, 70 to 80 percent of all objections are misunderstandings, not liabilities, and that means you can correct them to your advantage. This is part of the selling job.

Following Up

The number-one way to differentiate yourself from your competitors, and be a superior salesperson, is to consistently follow up with your customers. It really is that simple because most salespeople are order takers. They do not have systems in place that enable them to follow up, and many don't understand the importance of it.

Sales and marketing research over the years has supported these two theories:

1. It takes nine impressions to make an initial sale.

2. It takes six impressions in a year to maintain awareness.

An impression takes many forms. It can be a letter, message, brochure, advertisement, article, or personal call. If your destination is number two in the customer's mind, it is even more important to stay in touch so that when number one stumbles, you come to the forefront of his or her mind. It costs less to do business with a satisfied customer than to constantly be prospecting for new ones. Once you have made a sale and built rapport, keep in touch. It is smart business and could lead to referrals. Here are some suggestions on follow-up approaches:

- Issue a personalized (hand-written) note after a meeting or when a sale is complete.

- Send cards on birthdays and holidays.

- Clip articles from magazines/newspapers about your customer's business and send them to the customer. To make a real impression, have the article laminated with your business card at the bottom.

- Issue releases about your business that could include new products, renovations, or key personnel changes.

- Send postcards to customers when you are on trips.

- Send out regular newsletters, either electronically or by mail.

- Make a personal phone call.

- Advertise, and send copies of the ads to your customers.

- Develop and maintain a dynamic Web site.

- Be creative. For example, start a "Cookie of the Month" club. Contract with a great bakery and have it ship a couple of dozen different cookies at the start of each month. Customers will be calling you with thanks. This idea also works with goodies such as popcorn, chocolates, and doughnuts.

All customers are important, but some are more important than others. For these, usually your top 20 percent, have a regular entertainment schedule that gets you and your top customers outside the office. This may include golf, fishing, theater, dinner, or a day at the ballpark or speedway. When possible, include spouses; it helps attendance and builds goodwill. At a minimum, you should be making six follow-up contacts a year with the top 20 percent of your customers. Whatever you do, do not take them for granted.

Market Segmentation and CVB Satellite Offices

Successful CVB salespeople find most of their business prospects from three primary market sources: associations (national, state, and regional), corporations, and tour operators.

Associations and Satellite Offices

Associations are generally non-profit trade groups based nationally in a city such as Washington, D.C., or they can be regionally based in a province or state. CVBs consider associations a prime market to solicit because planners regularly schedule their events and tend to work full time on that. Association planners recognize the importance of building working relationships with multiple suppliers, including CVB sales and service staffs. Association bylaws often mandate the types of meetings that are held and even when they are to occur and how they rotate booking patterns. This allows an association planner to book meetings and events at a destination several years in advance.

To get closer to association customers, the Los Angeles and San Diego convention and visitors bureaus opened the first remote sales offices in Washington, D.C., in the early 1960s. The focus was to serve as a public relations vehicle to the concentration of association meeting planners headquartered in the nation's capital, and to generate leads for potential business to their home offices for follow-up. More than forty years later, the number of cities with satellite offices, the locations of those offices throughout the country, and their responsibilities have expanded dramatically. Washington now is home to more than fifty CVB satellite offices, and there is a large concentration in Chicago, as well. Remote offices continue to open in other locations such as New York, Dallas, and northern California.

Remote-office staffs vary in size from one home-office sales representative to dedicated downtown offices with several salespeople and support personnel. Structures and responsibilities vary, too. Some regional sales offices produce single-property hotel meetings only, while others handle city-wide conventions, including facilities. While most remote salespeople function primarily as lead generators and liaisons between the home CVB office and the customer, a growing number of regional sales offices provide complete account management by working with the customer from the initial information exchange to generating the lead, booking the meeting, and following up after the meeting's conclusion. Much as a chain hotel company's national sales manager functions, the local CVB rep takes "ownership" of the account.

Regardless of office size, structure, or procedures, satellite offices exist to continually bring the CVB city's message to the customer on that customer's home territory. In an industry where business flourishes through relationships and trust, regional salespeople can build strong partnerships with their clients and provide constant product visibility by living, working, playing, and serving in industry organizations together. Being where the customer is located not only provides such conveniences for the customer as doing business in the same time zone or hashing out a problem face-to-face, it promotes thorough and intimate knowledge of the organization's structure, philosophy, and needs, enabling the salesperson to serve as an advocate for the client to the home city.

Corporate Business

Corporations are another important market segment. Companies often have meeting and event planners who devote only a portion of their overall duties to scheduling and planning meetings. Their companies have them performing an array of duties that can detract from building multiple supplier relationships. Companies also tend to operate with a short-term mindset toward meetings based on their economic forecast. If a company is publicly held, the annual stockholders meeting might be the only meeting the company must stage each year. Otherwise, a company's earnings statement or forecast will dictate whether funds will be spent on travel and meetings. Because companies tend to plan on shorter notice than do associations, they can benefit from CVB services. Often, however, the corporate planner is unaware of those advantages. Corporate planners tend to work directly with hotels and venues with which they are familiar or with whom they have an established corporate relationship. Companies will maximize their buying power by working with a limited number of hotel chains and travel partners so as to better leverage their resources. Be aware that corporate planners (or third-party planners who work for rep firms such as Maritz, American Express, and Confron) may be housed in an organization's financial department. Keep this in mind when prospecting for clients.

Tour Operators

Tour operators make up a large share of the group leisure market. They will book groups of all sizes and interests from senior citizens and ecology tours to incentive groups, sports teams, and student tours. Tour operators benefit greatly from working with CVBs because they need the local expertise that a bureau sales professional brings to the job. Often, they are booking one to two years in advance, and once they book a tour series, they will market the package to the public through catalogs, the Internet, and other media. Tour operators work both in their own country and internationally. Third-party rep firms are often used to book convention sales as well as leisure and international travel.

Convention Services

After a lead is contracted or confirmed for a destination, the group's needs must be serviced. Depending on the number of attendees in a group, the convention service department will work with a planner on all the details of the event, often up to two years before the group's arrival. The scope of responsibilities will range from site visits to group housing, registration, and providing brochures and other promotional materials.

It is easy to think of convention service managers as concierges for group meeting planners. They become the "go to" person, and their job is to never say no to a planner's request. Often, they have to find the answer to any question asked. This could range from "How do we get the mayor to welcome our group?" to "Can we hang welcome banners from the street lights downtown"? No question is too small for a convention service planner to answer.

An important way to measure the success of a convention service manager is the amount of repeat groups he or she handles. This means that if a convention service manager does the job effectively, groups will want to return in the future. This frequently is related to the outstanding service the group receives during its stay. The job of the CVB sales professional is easier when the convention service manager is able to provide the experience described to the customer during the sales process.

Acknowledgments

The author thanks Sandi Talley, CMP, Vice President of Membership and Business Development for DMAI, and Andi Araback, former Director of Convention Service for the Washington, D.C., Convention & Tourism Corporation, and current Executive Assistant to the President and CEO of DMAI, for their contributions to this chapter.

Chapter 3 Outline

Competencies

1. Explain the consolidated approach to tourism marketing and discuss its benefits to businesses in a destination. (pp. 30–31)

2. Explain the difference between market research and marketing research. (pp. 31–32)

3. Describe the process of branding and theme development. (pp. 32–35)

4. Explain the difference between branding and advertising. (pp. 32–33)

5. Explain why it is important for a CVB to have a marketing plan, and discuss the elements and tools included in a typical plan. (pp. 35–44)

6. Explain how the Internet can be used to integrate sales and marketing. (pp. 42–43)

7. Explain how to determine the effectiveness of a marketing campaign. (pp. 46–47)

3

Marketing

By *Marshall Murdaugh*

Marshall Murdaugh is a leading marketing consultant for destination management organizations. The recipient of the Lifetime Career Achievement Award from the Association of Travel Marketing Executives, as well as its former chairman, he served for thirty years as president and CEO of some of America's most successful tourism destination offices, including New York City, Atlantic City (New Jersey), Memphis (Tennessee), and the state of Virginia under four governors where he developed the award-winning "Virginia is for Lovers" marketing campaign. He received his B.F.A. degree from Virginia Commonwealth University where he also pursued graduate studies in marketing and business management and later served as a member of the university's adjunct faculty, teaching commercial recreation and tourism courses for seven years. Murdaugh has also been a frequent guest lecturer at George Washington University and New York's New School for Social Research.

MARKETING IS the principal function and mission of destination management organizations (DMOs). Indeed, marketing and convention and visitors bureaus (CVBs) are so intertwined that DMOs could be—and, in fact, once were—alternatively recognized as destination *marketing* organizations.

What is marketing and what does it include? Here are two often-quoted definitions. Peter Drucker, world-renowned management scholar and Clark Professor of Social Sciences at Claremont Graduate University, said in 1954, "Marketing is so basic that it cannot be considered a separate function. It is the whole business seen from the point of view of its final result; that is, from the customer's point of view."[1] According to Philip Kotler, noted professor of international marketing in the Kellogg School of Management at Northwestern University, "Marketing is a social and managerial process by which individuals and groups obtain what they need and want through creating, offering, and exchanging products of value with others."[2]

For our purposes, a practical definition for marketing's function is "the business of determining customer needs and producing planned efforts to satisfy those needs."

In its purest sense, traditional business marketing is characterized by these principal components: consumer research, price, product development, packaging, distribution, promotion, advertising, and point of sale.

This chapter will examine such topics as marketing functions in the contemporary CVB, market and marketing research, advertising and branding, marketing and strategic planning, and innovations in Web marketing.

Destination Marketing: The Consolidated Approach ———

CVBs are "umbrella" marketing or promotional agencies, under which the extensive collection of businesses that promote their own products and services related to travelers stand. Many in the trade refer to this as a "consolidated approach" to tourism marketing. Business partners under the CVB umbrella include transportation, accommodations, food service, retail outlets, attractions, outdoor recreation facilities, and cultural heritage agencies, to name a few.

Consolidated efforts provide greater strength, unity, and leveraged results for everyone. Segmented, fragmented individual program efforts yield less impact and success.

The marketing task of the bureau is to incrementally increase new visitation and its economic benefits to the community. This responsibility calls for strategic marketing initiatives that move the potential customer or visitor through the cycle of awareness, interest, desire, and ultimately action in planning and taking a trip. Exhibit 1 lists some guiding principles of tourism marketing.

Consolidated marketing also recognizes that a stronger marketing program for a destination results when all visitor interests, market segments, and regional interests are effectively combined to leverage an expanded program. Stand-alone marketing by individual market segments, such as cultural tourism and the arts, restaurants, nightlife, or special leisure markets is rarely effective in producing significant results. However, combining these various elements in united initiatives offers multiple opportunities and a far greater chance of achieving optimum efficiency. At the same time, this concerted effort provides greater funding resources to reach multiple and mutual objectives.

Expanding marketing efforts into a regional partnership may also be a successful method to enhance the visitor product, expand marketing funding, and achieve greater results. This is why many destination management organizations today seek to produce regional marketing partnerships that can deliver more motivational attractions and visitor attributes to entice the visitor. A related and important axiom of tourism marketing says that "as geographic distance increases between destination and potential consumer, so does the relative lack of awareness of the visitor amenities that exist there."

Motivating the Customer: The AIDA Principle

Influencing consumers to visit a destination requires that they go through each step of what is known as the AIDA cycle. This process varies by degree for everyone, but in its broadest sense it describes travel-buying decisions through marketing efforts related to:

- *Awareness*, delivered through such motivational initiatives as advertising and word of mouth;
- *Interest*, fostered through in-depth information, including collateral and media publicity;
- *Desire*, delivered through sales solicitation processes; and
- *Action*, the ultimate purchase decision.

Exhibit 1   Guiding Principles of Successful Tourism Marketing

- Target major efforts to your major markets. Allocate resources in direct proportion to the amount of return for the destination. For example, if sixty percent of the lucrative overnight market is within a three-hundred-mile radius, expend sixty percent of marketing effort on this audience. Go fishing where the fish are biting, so to speak, and place the major weight of your advertising, direct mail, and media publicity in areas that provide the greatest return. Limit your spending on emerging or secondary markets based on current percentages of return.

- Sell your strengths. Consistently focus your messages on your community's top attractions, appeals, or benefits as confirmed by consumer research. If satisfied, visitors will motivate more customers who will become aware of your other destination amenities after they have visited.

- Focus on amenities not found in competing destinations. These form the basis of the community's tourism personality. Use them to their full potential rather than relying on generic appeals.

- Do not be an island. Sometimes CVBs only market visitor amenities within their jurisdictional borders, but consumers do not care about political boundary lines. Enhance your destination by "market annexing" nearby attractions and services that will complement your product for the customer.

- Be convenient. You may not have the world's greatest theme park or museum, but if you offer nearby customer convenience, use that appeal to its fullest potential. For example, South Carolina once promoted itself as an alternative to Florida for northern snowbirds. Its message was "another day of sunshine."

- Be honest. Do not exaggerate or hype customer benefits. Build your message on fact-based reputation, not image.

- Use testimonials, whenever feasible, instead of stale promotional copy. For example, Natchitoches, Louisiana, touted itself as "naturally perfect" until Oprah Winfrey visited and called it "the best small town in the USA." Now the CVB shares her observation with everybody.

Market and Marketing Research

"You shouldn't spend the first marketing dollar until you've clarified your visitor markets and their potentials," says John Boatright, five-time chairman of the Association of Travel Marketing Executives.[3] Market and marketing research are the critical first steps in defining the size, scope, economic well-being, and customer profile of the destination. *Market research* seeks to quantify and value, among other things, the economic impacts of tourism to a community in terms of visitor impact: tax revenue produced and jobs generated or sustained by visitor spending. To learn more about return-on-investment models, visit www.destinationmarket ing.org and access performance measurements.

   Marketing research assesses consumers, identifying them based on demographic (age, income, educational level) and psychographic (interest, desire, attitudes) profiles.

A whole host of research tools are available to today's tourism marketer to gather certain information required for the market planning process, such as:

- The community visitor profile. This provides important guidance to many of the bureau's ongoing programs, including advertising, media publicity, and collateral development. It includes length of stay and trip interest or purpose, and it assesses community strengths and weakness via in-depth analysis of visitor and non-visitor attitudes, opinions, impressions, likes, dislikes, perceptions, and awareness (or lack thereof) regarding the destination.

- Marketing, brand, and advertising awareness studies. These yield an assessment of how a CVB's program is performing to increase customer interest and desire to visit.

- Motivational research. This is a more limited and focused approach for determining what community attributes can best be employed to produce new visitor interest, and how they should be described.

Although these tools track the leisure visitor, they also apply to the meetings market and convention delegates. Once the meeting planner is satisfied with the availability of hardware to fill his or her needs (meeting space and required dates, adequate room blocks and rates, transportation needs, etc.), the personality of the community becomes paramount. Meeting delegates, after all, are leisure visitors too.

There are also numerous marketing research opportunities specific to the convention and meetings market. For example, the meetings information network (MINT) system of DMAI evaluates opportunities for sales and marketing of new meetings business. Lost-business reports evaluate community impediments to booking, as well as major destination competitors and their marketing strategies. Another option entails industry benchmarking of convention cities' product, sales, and marketing advantages. Convention services evaluations enhance customer service for the bureau and the destination.

Analyses of customers and competitors also offer opportunities. The former determines interest in the destination and assesses challenges and complications, including perceptual issues that can negatively affect business decisions. The latter addresses the perceived and real strengths and weaknesses of a destination in relation to its primary competitors, enabling adjustments and improvements while supporting sharper, more precise and effective sales messages.

Other research addresses the perception of the bureau throughout the community by means of member needs assessment surveys that help the CVB focus on improvements to build support, partnerships, and alliances.

Branding, Positioning, and Theme Development

Branding is today's buzzword for a process that many people wish to employ, but few understand. Essentially, the brand is a collection of perceptions in the mind of the visitor. It is the psychological, emotional, and (one hopes) motivational link between the customer and the product.

Everyone in the tourism field, therefore, should be interested in brand development and enhancement. Although the CVB cannot be responsible for every customer's perception of the destination, it should craft a brand development program that supports the destination through a fully coordinated and effective marketing communications plan.

Branding steps include the following, guided by marketing research. First, define the unique selling points that separate your destination from the competition. Then produce and prioritize a series of crisp and clear motivational messages for consumers that address the positive visitor characteristics of the community. Next, craft a market "positioning statement" that describes the destination and separates it from other competitors in the eyes of the potential customer. Finally, consider creating a new theme line and graphic logo for the destination that supports the recently created positioning statement.

This branding program will guide development of the bureau's array of collateral communications programs, including direct mail, advertising, Web site positioning, media publicity programs, and exhibits. However, for this program to prove successful, it must also enjoy the proactive participation of the destination's constituents in their own marketing communications delivery systems. This often requires considerable effort, but the labor will prove worthwhile.[4]

Branding through Theme Development

Theme lines or slogans can galvanize community tourism interests and dramatically increase customer awareness and interest in the destination through stakeholder usage of the campaign. Award-winning examples include:

- "Virginia is for Lovers." This marketing campaign brought a multibillion-dollar tourism business to the state. The campaign was responsible for increasing new young adult traffic (ages 21–38) from 28 to 38.5 percent of the state's market in a three-year period, and won the top award for marketing excellence from the Discover America Travel Organization. Incidentally, a newly elected state administration tried to move away from this campaign, but backed off when research confirmed the campaign's continued strong effectiveness in producing new awareness and in heightening visitor interest.

- "Start Something Great in Memphis." This slogan introduced a new program of community team participation in tourism that became the centerpiece for the Memphis Convention and Visitors Bureau's multimillion-dollar marketing plan and won national award recognition from the Travel Industry Association of America.

- "New York. The World Capital of Excitement." This slogan provided a new focus for New York City's tourism program. The theme featured the "world capital" appeals of fashion, food, theater, culture, and more. Within a year of its introduction, CVB business participation dramatically increased from 1,400 to 2,700 members.

Successful tourism themes for major destinations, as outlined earlier, are supported by persuasive documentation of significant consumer benefits. Positive tourism destination themes have been shown to assist in generating public aware-ness, consumer interest, and, ultimately, intent to visit.

Initially, a clearly defined priority of messages that will best motivate visitors from all market segments should be addressed. This is best accomplished through a benefit analysis process that includes communications recommendations. Com-munications and marketing staff from the CVB and its constituents should pro-duce messages based on the destination's major motivational sites, community attributes, icons, and sensory experiences.

Following this analysis, the messages would be tested via customer focus groups both for the visitor and the nonvisitor segments. The nonvisitor segment includes people who have not yet visited the destination or whose social, eco-nomic, or psychographic profile does not match the destination's current visitors. Four focus groups are recommended, and locations for the meetings would be determined following a review of available research. During the focus group research program, a process of benefit testing (or tourism message testing) will define the order and content of the most effective messages for future use. E-mail-based consumer surveys are another acceptable validation testing method.

Next, messages should be crafted for consistent use in ongoing communica-tions vehicles, such as Web sites, publications, direct mail programs, trade show displays, media publicity, advertising, and sales solicitation programs.

Based on the resulting list of messages, creative strategies and platforms should be devised and tested. Because of its speed and affordability, CVBs are increasingly using online survey methodology to effectively test and confirm their creative campaigns and important sales messages.

Finally, the new theme line should be developed from these results to serve as the promotional banner for the destination. Graphic art treatments would then be designed for extensive applications.

The Meetings Market and Theme Considerations. Market research conducted over the past ten years throughout the North American meetings industry has con-sistently concluded that meeting planners rank the following destination attributes high on their list of requirements:

- Convenient location and ease of accessibility
- Favorable hotel pricing and availability
- Convenient proximity of hotels to meeting facilities
- Shuttle service and other convention services, such as welcoming programs, media attention, and pre- and post-meeting opportunities
- Spouse programs
- Nearby shopping, restaurants, attractions, tour options, and entertainment
- Language translation services, currency exchange, and international signage when required

However, when meeting planners are then asked what their top reason was for choosing a particular destination for a meeting, the answer is universally the destination itself.

Exhibit 2   Principal Building Blocks of a Marketing Plan

- Marketplace complications and major challenges—all the impediments or road-blocks to success, including perceived complications
- Marketplace opportunities—where the new doors to success can be opened
- Departmental reports and productivity goals—the core of the plan. Each department should produce a detailed business plan including a specific department mission, relevant national trends, current year productivity achievements, planned highlights for the new year, projected sales goals in firm numbers with comparisons to current figures, marketplace complications for each market segment, and a competitive analysis.
- Major strategies to be undertaken
- Primary target audiences to be reached
- Specific tactics or work programs to accomplish the strategies
- A comprehensive marketing calendar listing all major strategies by month, containing trade shows, sales forums, and sales missions to be undertaken; media relations, advertising, and direct mail placed; publications and collateral to be produced; and major membership development initiatives to be undertaken
- A detailed budget

This means that planners choose meeting destinations (after they are comfortable that adequate convention facilities are available) *based on the unique appeal of the particular destination*—the community's personality, culture, heritage, or qualities that distinguish it from other communities. Thus, when attempting to motivate meeting planners, CVBs should wrap their convention product and meeting "hardware" with their positioning statement and compelling leisure tourism benefits.

The Marketing Plan

A true marketing plan outlines the best business approach for fulfilling the CVB's mission. It also forecasts a quantifiable, goal-based economic impact on the community and builds leveraged partnerships among and goodwill from community stakeholders. In addition, the plan can provide the foundation for a long-range strategic plan. It also gives priority to market-driven programs and resources that will deliver results more effectively than disparate, committee-driven, activity-based initiatives. Exhibit 2 lists the elements of a typical marketing plan.

Plan Parameters

The marketing plan should provide strategic direction toward target markets, outline detailed plans for success, forecast specific results by departments, and deliver a step-by-step series of actions or work tactics.

Exhibit 3   Sample CVB Marketing Objectives

- Generate positive awareness of the community as a destination of choice for leisure travelers and meeting business.
- Stimulate interest and desire on the part of consumers to take action and visit.
- Maximize the length and frequency of stay to increase economic impact and enhance the value of the visitor's experience.
- Increase the business volume of the community's tourism business partners and constituents.
- Develop additional regional tourism products to enhance a visitor's experience.
- Maintain a research base for the community's tourism industry.
- Create positive awareness, understanding, and support of, and participation in, the bureau and its marketing programs.

Developing a marketing plan will also prioritize the work of the CVB by analyzing market opportunities based on anticipated returns and related costs. It should forge stronger community alliances over time, foster team spirit, and strengthen common purpose throughout the bureau.

The plan should be produced with full team input and support, with the conviction that the final product belongs to everyone on the staff and to the local community of tourism industry interests. Therefore, key community leaders and constituent groups should also provide initial input through the bureau's marketing committee.

Goal-Setting

Department heads should guide their staffs and supervise their department's plan input. For effective goal delivery, individual staff should be encouraged to initially develop measurable objectives from the bottom up, using benchmarked results from the past year and other market data as guides. This approach provides staff members an opportunity to envision their own targets and make a commitment to achieving them. They will then collaborate with management to adjust the goals in relation to current market support and conditions.

Plan Elements

The new plan should include several elements, ranging from an executive summary to highlights. The summary, of course, distills the plan down to a few pages and includes a review of the implementation process. Next might come an introduction that encompasses the marketing mission, bureau visioning process, and value statements that chart the course for success. The bureau's destination marketing process—how new visitor business will be attracted to the community through a consolidated approach and coordinated tourism industry action steps—is another important feature. The highlights would include major quantifiable goals to be achieved. Exhibit 3 lists the objectives that encompass the comprehensive response to the mission statement. All programming of the bureau should fit within the parameters of the listed objectives.

Following the plan's approval by the board, a high-impact, edited version could then be disseminated widely throughout the community to build support and stakeholder/partner participation. This could be accomplished via a Web site, open forum, press release, or other means.

Final Report Preparation

Two reports may be required. One is a strategic plan/long-range overview of bureau requirements based on input from the board and from management. New initiatives, funding opportunities, and strategic directions can then be reviewed and recommended to support the CVB's annual marketing efforts. The other is a community strategic tourism plan that focuses on tourism and tourists in a community and describes how the community will attract and manage visitors. It also considers the fundamental questions of the costs of tourism to the community and how the community will capture potential economic benefits.

Strategic Planning

Strategic planning means different things to different groups. There is no tried-and-true model for CVBs, and the actual process may vary greatly depending on the community and on the bureau's needs. The term "strategic" has recently replaced "long range" and refers to the act of producing a multi-year directional marketing approach—usually a five-year plan. The strategic planning process prepares a road map for a successful future designed to match the bureau's long-range marketing requirements to the needs of the destination.

Some bureaus use the annual marketing plan as a foundation for strategic planning. They then build upon it by providing a stepped financial plan and marketing program by each year. Pending available projected resources, the bureau can then address the major "big picture" issues of need, including program funding, major initiatives for marketing (including sales), advertising, and customer development. The strategic planning process may even be community-wide and take several days to a year, including intensive meetings with agencies that have an influential role and additional dialogue with principal stakeholders and key bureau management and senior staff.

The process should also include the bureau's strategic philosophy. This involves a review of the mission statement that puts forth the bureau's purpose and related objectives of the CVB board. The board should also discuss vision and value statements because they involve the long-term priorities and operational values of the organization.

Another element is strategic analysis. This activity involves representatives of broad-based constituent organizations, associations, and businesses. It includes a scan or overview of the current environment, including the political, social, economic, and technical environment. Next, a stakeholder analysis of community strengths, weaknesses, opportunities, and challenges (or SWOC analysis) is produced with participants from both government and business. The new opportunities—initiatives that can produce positive long-term results—are addressed for future planning.

Follow-up sessions with the staff and stakeholders can address action plans, budgets, and current program success—how each specific objective or recommendation from the SWOC analysis can be produced using tactics identified by the participants. The analysis includes the individuals and agencies that can individually or collectively bring about change and the elements required to produce that change.

A separate component may involve intense meetings with key senior management to analyze long-term opportunities that affect these plans.

Marketing Tools

Advertising

The purchase of advertising space (print, billboards, Internet) or time (television, radio) offers the principal mechanism for the CVB to generate awareness. In advertising—unlike in media publicity that is considered editorial coverage—the CVB controls the delivery system regarding audience size (referred to as "reach and frequency" of message placed), location and size of materials, and timetable for delivery.

Full-service advertising agencies provide ad campaign development, including research-based planning, creative concept development (copywriting, photography, graphic design), recommended media selection, and placement of the final product. In addition, such agencies can also provide public relations services, including media publicity, brochure development, event development, publications, and direct mail.

Traditionally, agencies were compensated by a professional discount (usually fifteen percent) from the media in which ads are placed, plus fees for work assignments. More often than not today, clients and agencies negotiate compensation based on standard percentage commissions, plus fees that could be billed monthly, based on individual assignments, or paid for work produced, such as creative development and media buying.

Many marketing experts believe that advertising has now increased throughout the world to the extent that ad messages have become little more than wallpaper, enveloping us from morning to night in literally thousands of messages. In fact, one New York–based market research firm reportedly now tracks ad expenditures for 900,000 different brands. Against this backdrop, advertising should be created that sets the client apart from its competitors.

Advertising's objectives should be clarified at the outset of a project. Should it stimulate immediate visitation, prompt customers to request additional tourism information, or both? Is the campaign designed to produce inquiries that will convert to visitation, build or support brand identity, or a combination thereof? More important, what real-dollar-volume visitor impact should the ad campaign produce? The final outcome will be revealed by postcampaign conversion studies that determine who actually came to the destination.

Measuring Return on Investment. Following the ad campaign's market reach and frequency of messages, bureaus should validate, through conversion analysis, how many ad respondents who saw the ads and then wrote, called, or visited the Web site for information were subsequently motivated to actually travel? Further, what was their party size, type of accommodations, and duration of stay? More important, what were their total expenditures, including tax receipts? And finally, how many local jobs were generated or sustained through this visitor spending?

Without this required evaluation of return on investment, the ad campaign—no matter how aesthetically pleasing—will be suspect. To learn more about marketing and communications return-on-investment, visit www.destinationmarketing.org and access performance measurements.

Several methods effectively keep the advertising on track. For example, marketing positioning studies address areas of relative positioning in the marketplace, including awareness, image, and message strength. Concepts, ads for print and broadcast, messages, tag lines, and logos are all tested. Care should be taken to not put consumers in the position of actually choosing theme lines and related artwork. Pre- and post-campaign analyses provide the classic benchmarking designed to effectively measure how the ad performs.

Measuring advertising effectiveness is efficient and modestly priced when the work is done by a firm using defensible methodologies and employing e-mail questionnaire techniques with large sample sizes.

Public Relations and Media Publicity

Today's great brands are built with public relations, according to the new bestseller, *The Fall of Advertising and the Rise of PR* by Al Ries and Laura Ries. Why? Because of public relations' high consumer acceptability as the most believable of all communications media. In other words, messages that appear on editorial pages or in stories—not in purchased advertising—get higher marks with consumers for credibility.

Several CVBs have long understood the positive benefits of this initiative, and rely on staff to market to and interface with writers and editors. In some cases, public relations firms support the effort by working on retainer or an individual project basis.

The first priority is producing customer awareness, and numerous approaches are available. Some include:

- Publicity releases and placement

- Travel writer familiarization tours

- Individual writer site inspections

- Community and government relations

- Crisis management (terrorism, natural disaster, disease)

- Press conferences and writer receptions

- Trade show participation

- Calls to travel writers

Evaluating Success. Clipping services can provide some measure of effectiveness by producing copies of articles that appear based on the CVB's work. They can also measure the dollar value of articles, based on what they would have cost in ad lineage rates. But more important, they can tell if the coverage is focused to the audience that can best be motivated to visit the destination.

CVBs should craft a media marketing plan component that applies new information gleaned from research, such as a SWOC analysis, identifying expectations for the successful annual delivery of positive media impressions expressed in terms of circulation.

In summary, what best builds destination brands today are publicity messages, not ads. The more favorable messages for the destination, the stronger the brand will become.

Collateral Development

All creative approaches for communicating—be they ads, booth displays, letterhead, newsletters, brochures, flyers, direct mail, photographs, posters, or other initiatives—should resemble one another as members of a communications "family."

Indeed, the brand identity should be managed by a CVB staffer, preferably someone with advertising or graphic design background, who has responsibility as the "keeper of the brand."

An effective approach for managing collateral work is the creative brief shown in Exhibit 4—a one-page form that helps guide development of all graphic materials and ensures that everyone involved is informed about and agrees on the direction. Before beginning any creative project, the project manager should fill out the brief and gain approval from all participants.

A few guidelines for collateral development are:

- Incorporate photos rather than line art because, generally, consumers find them more credible.

- Use photo captions whenever feasible.

- Convey sensory appeals such as smell and taste whenever practical to "romance" the brand.

- Put the customer (based on profile information) in the product through action photos, rather than static shots. And remember that baby boomers perceive themselves as being a generation younger than they actually are.

- Highlight the popular appeals of the destination up front.

Web Site Marketing and the Internet

Today, the World Wide Web has surpassed all other media conduits as the consumer's most popular source for travel news and information. Many people now use a Web site for travel planning rather than motor club magazines, newspaper travel sections, television travel shows, and general interest magazines, according to the Travel Industry Association of America. Therefore, as the world portal to the destination, the bureau's Web site is one of the destination's most critically important resources for motivating and facilitating travel decisions.

Exhibit 4   The Creative Brief

Project Name_____ Date_____

Originating Department_____ Project originator_____

Project description (size, shape, look and feel)

_____

Primary service/message_____

Secondary message_____

Competing activity?_____

Marketing objective_____

Where is the business coming from?_____

Target audience profile_____

What is the single most important point we can deliver to this audience?

_____

Mandatory inclusions/restrictions_____

Merchandise or distribution plan (please attach)_____

Timelines_____

pieces produced_____

Budget/budget code_____

Approvals (signatures required below from affected departments)

Methods of evaluating success_____

Courtesy of MMMarketing.

It is also true that destination Web sites compete with major players such as Expedia and similar online travel agents. Consumers are demanding more from travel sites and want immediate information rather than waiting for a brochure in the mail. Consequently, destination sites must provide as much information as possible to attract Web visitors.

Travelers are looking for a variety of travel products based on their changing needs. Some want just a hotel room. Others want a hotel package with extra value. Some want a destination vacation package with choice of hotel and choice of local attractions. Others need just attraction tickets or tours. Destination Web sites must accommodate all types of consumers.

The Destination Management Organization Advantage. A destination site has an advantage over the major national online travel agents because the CVB or tourism board is the official travel authority and ambassador of the city or destination. The CVB has the ability to work with local hotels and local attractions to provide extra value and fresh content to travelers. The CVB, more than anyone, knows what is special about its destination and how to leverage that. It is critical that the bureau capture this essence on its Web site and in online marketing.

However, in many cases, the CVB's destination Web site is relegated to the finance and administration department where information technology specialists manage the site. They know computers but not necessarily marketing or even the destination itself. To achieve optimum success, bureaus should have an Internet marketing strategy managed by someone who understands the tools and the targets.

A site analysis from a third-party provider—preferably the technology provider for the DMAI—may be a good first step in assessing future directions. Such an evaluation could also include a competitive analysis to track visitation to the site.

Special Internet Opportunities. Contests with exciting destination giveaways are great ways to create a buzz online. Web users will e-mail their friends and families about this type of program and create a word-of-mouth virtual marketing situation.

Destinations should also try targeted placements online, and develop a plan to reach all people who are searching for travel information and deals to or in the destination. Focus on the CVB's demographic market. For example, if it is a golf destination, consider targeting potential visitors through Internet advertising. This advertising might feature specific courses, upcoming tournaments, or even the destination's golf-related retail outlets. Other Web advertising options include sponsorship of editorial and "advertorial" programs, banner ads, integrated text links on travel sites, and targeted e-mail sponsorships.

One innovative new Internet ad medium now prequalifies visitor inquiries to ensure the questions are worth a salesperson's time and attention, and touts the guarantee of new destination travelers. When visitors to travel-related Web sites request an offer, the destination's message also appears. They then choose to receive destination information, but are screened to ensure tourism destinations that they are only receiving qualified inquiries. Then consumers are sent travel information, and the names are "owned" by the destination for potential repeat mailings. Also provided is an independent third-party conversion analysis to confirm visitors generated and their economic impact.

DMAI offers several valuable Internet marketing programs for members. For instance, the OfficialTravelGuide.com Web site serves as a travel portal for more than 1,250 destinations. The Web site attracts approximately one million visitors a year from more that forty million marketing impressions, and it hosts a state-of-the-art search engine that visitors can use to quickly access local-content Web pages. CVBs are invited to display and link their tourism Web sites on OfficialTravelGuide.com and participate in several marketing programs.

For leisure travel marketing, CVBs can participate in several co-op promotions throughout the year sponsored by OfficialTravelGuide.com that leverage bulk online media buys to provide CVBs much greater value, exposure, and traffic directly to their destination's Web site. For more information about specific programs available, go to www.OfficialTravelGuide.com/cvbpromotions.

DMAI has also developed a database of meeting planners (MINT) and spearheaded the creation of a separate, stand-alone Web site for meeting planners (www.CVBHotRates.com).

MINT, an exclusive convention and meetings database, has profiles of more than twenty-eight thousand meetings from fourteen-thousand-plus organizations, including associations, corporations, and government agencies. For information on the MINT database, go to www.iacvb.org.

The CVBHotRates.com project is a cooperative effort between major hotel brands and the CVBs in some of the top meetings destinations to provide meeting planners the best available rates on unsold hotel meeting dates, space, and sleeping rooms. CVBs can host their market's meeting inventory on the site and also utilize the software on their own Web sites.

Both OfficialTravelGuide.com and CVBHotRates.com are marketed by USDM.net, DMAI's official alliance partner for Web marketing and Internet technology. The group provides Internet marketing and technology services for more than one hundred destinations. Its services include a travel-industry-specific best practices approach to Web site, technology, and Internet program assessment; Internet marketing plan development; ongoing Internet marketing services to drive traffic and e-commerce; and economic impact conversion studies.

The Internet facilitates billions of dollars in travel commerce, and it is a powerful and highly accountable marketing force. It warrants CVBs' increased marketing focus and budgetary consideration.

Direct Marketing

Keeping in touch with clients, or potential clients, is a never-ending process, and most experts agree that personal contact is paramount for the best customer relations. Direct mail is yet another useful arrow in the quiver of destination marketing. It can foster opportunities by creating destination awareness with a brand new customer base that may currently be off the CVB's radar screen. Traditional direct mail yields low-percentage returns, usually in the low single digits. However, for product introductions, services, and enhancements, it can open new doors.

It is possible to purchase mailing lists by market segment from trade industry magazines or other third-party providers. An ad agency can help plan a campaign based on an agreed-upon creative brief, and an implementation outline that addresses required steps, as shown in Exhibit 5.

Merchandising and Direct Marketing. Communicating ongoing marketing campaign initiatives directly to principal targets through direct mail and personalizing it with individual, personally signed letters is one very successful concept for direct mail. One such approach has been the use of CVB display ads, along with major editorial articles from important publications in an ongoing merchandising effort. For example, when Memphis entered the meetings market several years ago with its aggressive ad campaign that compared itself to other destinations ("Help stamp out fat meeting costs."), the individual ads were sent to meeting planners with a personal cover note from the CVB sales managers. The campaign stimulated new interest, and the staff then initiated follow-ups.

Attention grabbers that provide a series of marketing messages delivered over the course of a season or year also have merit in retaining customer interest that

Exhibit 5   The Implementation Outline

Project name_____

Description_____

_____

Markets served_____

Program objective_____

Implementation steps/ timelines_____

Costs: manpower/ financial requirements_____

Methods for evaluating program success_____

(Those individuals who will contribute to the process, participate, or approve should sign off below).

Approvals_____   _____

Consider this implementation outline process for all other marketing projects. Courtesy of MMMarketing.

should be measured through the use of customer surveys by third-party providers to ensure independent analysis and helpful feedback.

Event Development

Public events hosted for travel consumers can provide substantial results in terms of visitor interest and resulting economic impacts. Most bureaus, however, market events rather than develop them.

Event development and economic evaluation require special skills. The International Festival and Event Association (www.ifea.com) has provided event development guidance to hundreds of community promotion agencies for the past forty-five years. Likewise, the International Event Group of Chicago provides extensive educational training in the valuing and securing of sponsorships for events. Both are excellent resources for CVB event programming.

Gala receptions or customer "road shows" replete with tabletop displays, great food, and a myriad of entertainment options are another method of grabbing attention. But if these events are not followed by on-site familiarization tours by the bureau for these customers, they will have minimal impact until the next client event comes to town.

The CVB's planning process should involve a thorough review of objectives to be achieved, including a postevent evaluation process, as well as the desired results. Supportive sales calls before the event can also boost attendance and share valued information with clients. Above all, these occasions should be imbued with the personality of the destination, reflected by local food and entertainment.

When New York opened its new convention sales office in Washington, D.C., in 1994, it invited the meeting planner fraternity to meet the new office staff at a gala and unveiling of the bureau's new trade show exhibit headlined by the world-famous Rockettes. Client lists were selected based on criteria provided by the convention development department. Invited media covered the special occasion, and additional photos were produced by the bureau for its future use. A photographer also captured the moment with shots of invited meeting planner guests used in follow-up direct mail delivered by each sales manager. Special gifts were provided to all guests as they departed, helping make it a truly memorable evening.

Sometimes it is important to include the intended guest participants in the actual planning process. When Virginia's tourism industry hosted the travel trade of New York City and Chicago to say "thank you" for putting the state on the map, rather than a hard-sell approach, it asked invitees what their event preferences were: Sit-down lunch or buffet and bar? A presentation from the governor? Special entertainment and music choices? The optimum site to meet their needs? After the survey results were implemented, attendance at the annual event grew by thirty percent.

Gifts. If a CVB decides to incorporate client gifts as remembrances, they should be selected with the objective of matching the quality of the destination; for example, an elegant champagne glass might not suit a place noted for NASCAR. Also, resist the urge to place a logo on the item (or at least pick a discreet, out-of-sight area for it). Remember, it is the gift—not the logo—that is intended to create a long-term positive memory for the destination through its use by the recipient.

Alliances

Alliances may consist of bureau members for destinations with membership programs, or business partners who work with CVBs to leverage their own individual business needs.

The Importance of Alliance-Building

Membership is one of the most compelling bureau functions, if for no other reason than dues generate revenue. But staff should continue to be mindful of and measure the establishment of coalitions, partnerships, and alliances with the members. After all, members are involved in solving problems, making decisions, and allocating resources. Team projects generate training opportunities and business for members. For example, cross-fertilization of marketing ideas can occur among members, or members can become political allies to lobby for funding and other areas of mutual concern.

Meeting Member Needs

Meeting the needs of key community business partners and members is an ongoing responsibility and is critically important in fostering goodwill and support for bureau programs and the delivery of marketing initiatives that fill member needs. Meeting those needs will yield additional revenue as well as marketing support that leverages CVB resources. According to the DMAI, the average U.S. bureau with a membership program generates approximately eight percent of its total income from membership and related partnership and alliance funding for specific projects.

Member Assessment Survey. The key to CVB leveraging is to assess member attitudes, business requirements, and interests to keep the bureau on track in delivering maximum benefits and producing new partnerships that build additional bureau resources for the future. That task is best handled through an impartial evaluation of members/partners that provides objective analysis of a CVB's needs and how the bureau is perceived in delivering them. It should be produced by questionnaire and delivered by either mail or Internet to provide projected information for documentation and follow-up. Specifically, this assessment can ensure good CVB performance by addressing the following areas:

- How well is the bureau meeting the expectations of members (increasing business, networking opportunities, cooperative advertising, promotional and marketing opportunities, industry updates, and global exposure)?

- What is the satisfaction level with the services rendered (receiving sales and convention leads, placement of brochures, listings, marketing partnership opportunities)?

- What is the bureau's overall rating (responsiveness, accountability, communications, value for money, and focus on mission)?

Major Alliances for Joint Marketing

Major alliances should be considered to produce new joint initiatives for principal stakeholders, including airports and credit card companies. Excellent models exist in Los Angeles, where the local bureau has forged an international alliance with the airport. And its past efforts with American Express to market regional leisure tourism through joint promotion of blockbuster art exhibits and long-running theater productions have produced significant, measurable economic returns to the community. Exhibit 6 lists some additional opportunities for building alliances.

Criteria for CVB Marketing Success

Three paramount criteria determine how a CVB works best from a marketing perspective. First, the bureau should deliver economic development benefits in fulfilling its core marketing mission. The results, or economic impacts, which are based on the incremental attraction of visitors through numerous market segments, are quantifiable results projected as a series of goals and reportable to bureau leadership, stakeholders, and other community constituents.

The bureau should also provide marketing excellence through its research, planning, execution, and evaluation and strive to deliver the highest standards of performance in the following areas:

- Economic impact results among market segments

- Successfully planned, designed, and executed marketing initiatives

- Reporting and accountability

Exhibit 6   Suggested Marketing Alliance Programs

- Co-op ad programs
- Annual meetings
- Convention sales
- E-commerce merchandise sales
- Event hosting
- Phone cards
- Print advertising
- Ticket sales
- Web site advertising
- Publication sales
- Restaurant information/reservations booth

Courtesy of MMMarketing.

- Long- and short-term planning
- Goal-setting, tracking, and delivery
- Staff and program performance evaluation
- Community partnerships and alliance-building to galvanize tourism industry interests, stretch resources, and leverage success

Finally, the bureau should be the recognized leader in the community for tourism marketing. Today's CVB should be well-regarded for its local leadership position. Stakeholders such as hotels, convention centers, attractions, cultural institutions, related businesses, and other associations should look to the bureau as the focal point for destination marketing, planning, coordinating community stakeholder efforts, research, and long-range vision. In other words, through the leadership of the CEO, the bureau's role is that of the industry voice, the inspiration, the chief lobbyist, and the chief cheerleader. It should also closely monitor and manage key marketing issues affecting the destination, such as the need for a convention center, expansion efforts, a new headquarters hotel, and other infrastructure requirements, visitor amenities, and service issues.

Endnotes

1. Peter F. Drucker, *The Practice of Management* (New York: Harper, 1954).

2. Philip Kotler, *Marketing Management*, Seventh Ed. (Englewood Cliffs, N.J.: Prentice-Hall, 1991).

3. John Boatright, personal correspondence with author.

4. For more information about branding, see Duane Knapp and Gary Sherwin's *Destination BrandScience.* An order form is included at the back of this book.

Chapter 4 Outline

The Role of Research at the CVB
The CVB Research Function
What to Research?
    Destination Research
    Tourism's Economic Impact
    Destination Brand Image
    Forecasting
    Secondary Research
CVB Performance Reporting
    Convention Sales Performance
        Reporting
    Travel Trade Sales Performance
        Reporting
    Marketing and Communication
        Performance Reporting
CVB Return on Investment
    Case Study Example

Competencies

1. Explain how CVBs use research to guide their strategic and operational decisions. (pp. 49–50)

2. Identify how the roles of research manager and research communicator operate within the organizational structure of a CVB. (pp. 50–51)

3. Identify types of research projects typically undertaken by CVBs and describe their relevance for the CVB. (pp. 51–56)

4. Explain the difference between tourism research and performance reporting, and explain how these efforts support and reinforce each other. (pp. 56–58)

5. Explain why CVBs should engage in regular performance reporting and describe the various performance measures and productivity metrics that are used to gauge a CVB's performance. (pp. 56–58)

6. Identify performance measures and productivity metrics for the areas of convention sales, travel trade sales, and marketing and communications. (pp. 58–70)

7. Explain how CVBs use return–on–investment information to quantify their impact on the local community. (pp. 70–74)

4

Tourism Research and Performance Reporting

By *Ruth Nadler Trojan*

Ruth Nadler Trojan is president and CEO of Nadler & Associates, a solutions-oriented tourism research and planning organization. She counts more than twenty years of experience in market research, with the last fifteen years focused on tourism research. Previously, she was vice president of research for NYC & Company (formerly the New York Convention and Visitors Bureau). A past chair and past president of the Travel & Tourism Research Association, she is regular guest lecturer at New York University's Center for Hospitality, Travel and Tourism Administration. She holds a B.A. degree from Washington University in St. Louis and an M.B.A from Fordham University.

> ### *What is research, but a blind date with knowledge.*
> ### *— William Henry*

A BLIND DATE. TOURISM RESEARCH. For many, one or the other (or both for that matter) can reduce even the most self-assured person to a state often characterized by nervous twitches, an uncontrollable desire to flee, or, at the very least, a glassy-eyed stare.

But, this is avoidable. This chapter will attempt to demystify tourism research by walking readers through some common tourism market research projects that a CVB may undertake and what makes the CVB research function successful. It will also review how performance reporting can assist CVBs as they wrestle with doing more with less, and documenting what they have accomplished with their stakeholder funding. As for demystifying blind dates, readers are on their own.

The Role of Research at the CVB

CVBs conduct research to gain insight and actionable information on their destination's visitor market, far beyond what anecdotal stories and any one individual's impressions and opinions can offer. The results of research guide the decision-making process of the CVB and the tourism industry of the destination on many levels. At the strategic and organizational levels, research greatly contributes to:

- Creating and implementing long-term marketing and operational plans.

- Setting organizational goals and policies.

- Developing and/or expanding a CVB's funding resources.

- Formulating a destination's tourism master plan.

- Determining the CVB's contribution to the local economy in terms of visitor spending, tax revenues, and jobs supported.

At the tactical and program-specific levels, research frequently offers guidance with more short-term and specific marketing and operational decisions a CVB may face, such as: What should the message be in the CVB's summer direct mail campaign? Which trade shows should the CVB attend? Where should the CVB advertise? Research also assists in individual and departmental goal setting and provides the CVB staff with tools to efficiently and effectively manage their time and other, usually limited, resources.

The CVB Research Function

Not all CVBs can afford to have a full-time person on staff to manage the research function. However, for research to meet the needs of the organization and the industry, the function itself should be centralized, with an individual clearly responsible for the direction and management of it. The continuity provided improves the likelihood that the research function will meet the needs of the organization, that the research will be of consistently high quality, and that the function will communicate with all other functions and levels of the CVB in a consistent and seamless fashion.

For this to happen, the CVB must have a corporate culture where research has a clearly defined and active role. The CVB's senior management must be committed to the use of research and acknowledge its role and value in creating and supporting an informed decision-making process.

Organizationally speaking, the research function must report to a senior-enough authority to ensure the research results are continually incorporated into the CVB's decision-making process. The research function must have extensive and open channels of communications to decision makers at all levels to guarantee that the research is relevant to their needs and that the research results are available and understood.

In its most simplified form, the CVB research process determines what the questions are and attempts to find the answers. To accomplish this, the successful CVB research function includes two major roles: research manager and research communicator.

Regarding the manager, the research function works with the CVB staff and other CVB stakeholders and industry partners to identify marketplace questions that the CVB and the tourism industry need answered. Having a clear sense of the current business issues and questions faced by the CVB and how they fit into the organization's overall business strategy will greatly assist the research function in setting priorities if and when it finds itself faced with more questions than available resources to answer them all. Also, including staff and stakeholders at this early stage of the research process greatly reduces the chance that the research results will be rejected and/or challenged because "I wasn't asked what I needed to know; the wrong questions were asked."

After this question-gathering step, the research function reviews and selects the research programs and vendors best suited to answer the research questions. Directing and managing the research programs is a core element of the research function, one which ensures that the programs remain focused and on target.

When the results from the research programs become available, the second overall responsibility of the function comes into play, that of research communicator. For many, research is an intimidating science, perceived to be filled with numbers and incomprehensible statistical methodologies and symbols such as $\Sigma, \Delta, \bullet, \infty$. Although that is not necessarily always the case, that perception is a challenge the research function must overcome if research is to play a useful role at the CVB. A truly successful research function acts as the bridge between the research results and their intended end-users.

The key to successful research communication is that the presentation of the results must constantly be linked back to the original question. Also, actionable conclusions based on the results should be developed and presented to end-users at all levels to further encourage the use of the research.

Exhibit 1 shows a sample function description for a CVB that has centralized its research function.

After the CVB makes the commitment to using research in its operations, it is encouraged not to manage its research programs in a vacuum. Developing a research advisory committee comprising representatives of the CVB's board, its membership, a local university, and local government can assist the CVB in defining its research program and, when funds are limited, leverage previously unknown funding sources. A further advantage of a research advisory committee is that it creates "ambassadors" who extend the CVB's ability to communicate, justify, and incorporate the results of the research program.

What to Research?

In its most basic form, the CVB research function oversees two fundamental tourism research topic areas. The first is destination research, which yields a multitude of data such as visitor profiles, image studies, and economic impact studies. The second area of interest is CVB accountability research, which measures the performance of various CVB operations and functions and forms the basis for CVB performance reporting.

It is useful at this point to clearly explain the difference between a performance indicator and a performance measure because these two terms are often used interchangeably. A *performance indicator* is a number (usually) that illustrates the performance of the travel and tourism industry or one of its industry sectors— hotel occupancy, airport arrivals, attraction attendance, restaurant employment— and is sometimes a by-product of destination research. A *performance measure* is a CVB-specific number quantifying the outcome of a CVB activity, for example, the number of conventions booked by the CVB, or the number of tour packages sold on the CVB's Web site.

Exhibit 1   Sample CVB Research Functions

FUNCTION SUMMARY: Develop, administer, and manage a comprehensive information and research program to deliver ongoing economic, marketing, and internal performance data required for strategic planning in support of the {name of CVB} objectives to designated internal and external audiences.

FUNCTION SCOPE: This position serves to define and lead a complete information management and resource program to deliver market and performance information to enhance fulfillment of {name of CVB}'s mission. Through strategic internal and external needs assessment, this position leads strategies and programs to provide consistent information critical to market and competitive analyses, performance, assessment, and strategic planning. This position interacts with all {name of CVB} departments at all levels and with key government and tourism industry principals to enhance and communicate {name of CVB} market research efforts. This position articulates and leads a commitment to service excellence to all external and internal customers of research services, from the president and CEO to front-line levels.

FUNCTION ACCOUNTABILITIES AND RESPONSIBILITIES

- Design, develop, and manage short- and long-term information and market research programs to monitor, track, analyze, and explain key trends and market conditions impacting the {destination} tourism industry.

- Direct ongoing performance reporting programs to provide accurate and timely assessment of {name of CVB} program effectiveness.

- Manage a complete research communications and publications program to effectively increase public and internal understanding of key {destination} tourism issues, opportunities, and challenges.

- Manage vendors to produce field research according to predetermined timelines and budget, including technical supervision, scheduling and deadlines, and evaluation of interim and final reports.

- Act as {name of CVB} liaison with government officials and tourism industry principals in developing cooperative market research programs.

- Direct and conduct annual research department planning and budgeting process in concert with {name of CVB}-wide efforts and objectives.

- Fulfills information and research-related projects and market analyses as directed by the {name of CVB} officers and board of directors.

Below are some of the more common destination research projects a CVB might conduct in support of its and the local tourism industry's programs and efforts. Later, the tenets of CVB performance reporting and the role of accountability research will be reviewed at length.

Destination Research: Visitor Volume, Market Share, and Profile Studies

Some of the most fundamental visitor marketplace questions a CVB must answer so it can function effectively as its destination's marketing organization include: How many visitors come to our destination? Who are they? Are we getting our fair share? The answers to these questions, usually only available through visitor research studies, assist the CVB in making some of its most basic, yet most important, sales and marketing decisions: To whom should we sell our destination? How do find we them? What should we tell them about our destination so they will come?

Aside from overall visitor counts and what portion of the total visitor marketplace the destination has achieved (known as market share), knowing which specific visitor market segments come to the destination is essential so the CVB can produce targeted marketing campaigns that will resonate with those segments. Key visitor market segments and those of particular interest to the destination's CVB and tourism industry may include:

- Domestic versus international visitors.

- Business versus leisure visitors.

- Overnight versus day-trippers.

- Niche markets: cultural visitors, seniors, families, gay/lesbian travel.

- Industry segments: visitors staying in hotels, visitors traveling on packages, visitors traveling in RVs.

The more information the CVB can gather about its visitors, the more likely the bureau and its industry partners will be able to successfully produce tourism products of interest to potential visitors and communicate them about in compelling ways. This information is also essential when identifying and developing appropriate partnerships and additional funding sources. Key visitor attributes can include, but are not limited to:

- Where the visitor lives (top points-of-origin).

- Visitor spending and spending categories.

- Mode of transportation.

- Demographics: age, gender, occupation, household income.

- Leisure activities while in the destination.

- Type of accommodations.

- Travel party size and composition.

- Length of stay.

- When the visitor came (seasonality).

- Purpose of trip.

- Trip information sources.

However, it would be cost-prohibitive for most CVBs to fund a research study that would provide attributes for all visitor market segments. Again, it is the role of the research function to detect existing and emerging trends and to maintain constant communication with the CVB's departments so it can prioritize the segments and attributes to be examined within the framework of the CVB's available resources.

Tourism's Economic Impact

How much money does tourism pump into the local economy? How many jobs are created? What does tourism generate in the way of tax dollars? Should the private and/or the public sector invest in tourism? For a CVB, these are some of the most important questions it will ever have to answer. But, as the umbrella organization for the local tourism industry, the CVB must answer these questions.

Typically, tourism impact studies produce two sets of industry data—direct and secondary (often called indirect). The secondary data illustrates the degree to which the visitor dollar moves along the chain of buying and selling among the tourism industry's businesses and employees until it "leaks" out of the local economy.

Direct data encompasses total visitor spending and spending by specific categories (lodging, transportation, eating and drinking, recreation and entertainment, shopping) as well as spending by key market segments. Also involved are payroll, tax revenues generated (local, state/provincial, federal), and total jobs supported and jobs by specific industry sector. Secondary data includes such things as indirect and induced spending, secondary payroll, secondary jobs, total economic impact, and economic multiplier.

A visitor impact study is arguably the most important research the CVB's research function can undertake. However, CVBs can be intimidated because it involves economic input-output models, subjective assumptions, multiplier effects, and so on. But they need not fear. Impact studies are increasingly being conducted and used by CVBs of all sizes, with many receiving assistance from local universities and/or state travel departments. There are also many reputable firms that specialize in tourism economic impact studies for local communities. Stakeholders who request this information, such as local government, tourism industry partners, and the media, are also becoming increasingly familiar and comfortable with impact studies.

Destination Brand Image

As with all consumer products, a visitor destination wholly depends on what the consumer thinks about it and how he or she feels about it, because this image of the destination determines whether the consumer becomes a visitor. For a CVB, knowing what visitors and potential visitors think about the destination is essential when developing tourism products and marketing campaigns.

Destination brand image studies typically assist the CVB and its industry partners in gaining insight on how visitors perceive the destination. Depending on the destination in question, image studies should be able to answer the following questions: Does the marketplace think of our destination as a desirable place for a vacation or a convention? Is the marketplace aware of our destination's available tourism products, attributes, and offerings? What are our perceived/real strengths as a visitor destination? What are our perceived/real weaknesses as a visitor

Exhibit 2   Consumer Agreement or Disagreement by Brand Statement

Q: Please Indicate your level of agreement/disagreement with the following statements:	Strongly disagree	Somewhat disagree	Somewhat agree	Strongly agree
A tourist can be entertained for days in [name of destination]	❑	❑	❑	❑
I would feel safe visiting [name of destination]	❑	❑	❑	❑
[name of destination] is a friendly place	❑	❑	❑	❑
[name of destination] is a great place to take children				
[name of destination] is a good value for the money	❑	❑	❑	❑
[name of destination] is a year-round destination	❑	❑	❑	❑

destination? Is our destination sufficiently different from its competitors in the mind of the marketplace?

The research methodologies available to answer these questions are far too numerous to review in detail, but they can range from written or verbal questionnaires to in-depth interviews to focus groups. They can be as simple as measuring the level of consumer agreement or disagreement with typical destination brand image statements, depending on the destination's offerings (see Exhibit 2). They can also be as elaborate as ongoing, multi-year brand image tracking studies that incorporate extensive consumer demographic and psychographic information, changes in lifestyles and social values, economic and global shifts, and competitive assessments. All of this information is then wrapped together to provide a comprehensive picture of consumers, travel, and where the specific destination fits into this mindset.

There is a strong link between destination branding studies and studies that measure the performance of a CVB's marketing efforts, such as advertising effectiveness studies. Both measure how the brand is performing and evolving in the mind of the consumer. They also can guide CVBs as they continuously fine-tune their marketing efforts, as well as the destination as a whole as it addresses its tourism product challenges and opportunities.

Forecasting

Unlike fortunetellers and seers, forecasting visitor activity and trends typically does not include using a crystal ball; rather, it is an attempt to estimate the most likely level of visitor volume and demand based on known information, including economic, market, and social conditions and circumstances.

Visitor forecasts can be as simple as estimating overall visitor volume and visitor spending at the destination for the coming year. Or, they can be more extensive:

One-year, two-year, or five-year series for overall visitor volume and visitor spending, plus a range of key visitor market segments, such as overnight versus day trip, leisure versus business, top international visitor-producing countries. And, depending on the CVB's needs, forecasts can be as elaborate as a series of scenarios for a given set of possible conditions, for example: What will visitor volume be next year if the exchange rate of the dollar declines 5 percent or 10 percent? What if the price of gas increases 15 percent or 20 percent?

Forecasting is useful for both short-term and long-term planning. It can assist the CVB in deciding how to shift marketing dollars from one market segment to another due to changes in current economic conditions. As a long-term decision-making tool, forecasting contributes to the development of tourism policies and products, such as guiding the destination's tourism industry in developing tourism offerings for emerging and shifting market segments, including aging baby boomers and the extended-family unit.

Secondary Research

In addition to primary tourism research conducted to answer specific questions, there is a wealth of pre-existing secondary research that measures and monitors tourism activity at city, state/provincial, and national levels. Sources for secondary data include government agencies, trade and professional associations, colleges and universities, periodicals, and link-compilation Web sites. For many destinations, this secondary data can partially answer some of the marketplace questions that the CVB cannot answer through extensive primary research due to funding limitations.

One of the most efficient ways a CVB can use the secondary tourism data available for its destination is in the form of a tourism barometer, which can monitor tourism-related activity for a destination on a monthly, quarterly, semiannual and/or annual basis. Common activity categories found in a tourism barometer, subject to availability, can include hotel room nights filled, hotel occupancy, airport arrivals, attendance at cultural institutions and/or attractions, hotel tax revenues, and tourism-related employment.

Tracking these categories throughout the year yields a sense of how the destination's tourism industry is faring. In addition, seasonal patterns emerge, assisting the CVB and the tourism industry in the timing of their sales and marketing campaigns and product offerings.

CVB Performance Reporting

Just as research positions the role of tourism in the local economy and offers insight into tourism product development, it plays an increasingly important role in how a CVB manages itself and its resources. It is an axiom that businesses, to succeed, should function in the most cost-efficient and cost-effective manner possible. Standards, best practices, and systematic approaches to organizational functions have been developed that provide companies in various industries with management tools to identify organizational strengths, weaknesses, and opportunities.

CVBs also benefit from systematic, organizational performance reviews. And, due to their unique funding sources, CVBs are often called upon to undergo external performance reviews by various local stakeholders. At times, these external audits/reviews may be done by firms lacking CVB knowledge and experience. In the past, the CVB community had no uniform approach to reporting performance to these audiences. As a result, CVBs would sometimes find themselves limited in their ability to articulate how they managed their resources, the results of their efforts, and, ultimately, their contribution to the local community in terms of return on investment.

In response to this need, the Destination Marketing Association International (DMAI) adopted and promulgated standard CVB performance reporting techniques in 2004. This portion of the research chapter will guide the CVB through the process necessary to implement actionable and credible performance reporting. Throughout, two questions should be asked on a regular basis: "Are we measuring the right things? Are we measuring these things right?"

The recommended performance reporting process currently focuses on three CVB functional areas: (1) convention sales, (2) travel trade sales, and (3) marketing and communication (direct to consumer). We will address each of these areas in detail in the following sections. To develop a performance-reporting program for each function, a number of actions and tools are needed. First, the purpose or mission for each function must be defined. From this mission flows operational definitions and measures needed to illustrate, in an accountable and auditable fashion, the function's (and eventually the CVB's) performance as measured against the mission. Once these elements are defined, performance reporting focuses on three basic measures: activity measures, performance measures, and productivity metrics.

An *activity* is a physical action taken by the CVB functional area that ultimately supports its mission, such as attending a tradeshow, conducting a familiarization tour, or writing and distributing a press release. Activity measures track these activities.

A *performance measure* is a measure that helps to define and quantify the results of the CVB activity. Implementation of this system of measures will yield actionable tools that the CVB staff can use for short- and long-term enhancement of its efforts.

A *productivity metric* is a metric that illustrates the relationship between the CVB performance and its resources. Typically expressed as a ratio (cost per lead, number of bookings per sales manager), productivity metrics assist the CVB in managing its resources in the most cost-efficient and cost-effective manner possible.

Many of the productivity metrics are designed with the intent that the CVB establish a benchmark year and recalculate these metrics regularly, for example, at quarter-end or year-end. By examining these metrics over time, the CVB can monitor its progress toward achieving desired resource efficiencies.

Quantitative measures are not the be-all and end-all when assessing and reviewing a CVB's performance internally and with stakeholders. Comprehensive narrative reviews of the CVB's key initiatives and programs must accompany the performance reporting and are strongly recommended. CVBs are encouraged to link the narrative reviews to the material contained in the accompanying performance report so the reader gains a fuller appreciation of the bureau's accomplishments and challenges.

Let's now turn to examining the three functional areas in more detail.

Convention Sales Performance Reporting

The fundamental mission of the convention sales function is to generate visitors (delegates), visitor (delegate) spending, and economic impact for the destination by booking events at the destination's hotels and convention facilities. From this mission, we must construct the operational definitions and measures needed. Exhibit 3 presents several operational definitions that cover the basics of the CVB convention sales function. Exhibit 4 presents a list of convention sales activity measures. Exhibit 5 presents a list of convention sales performance measures.

Convention sales productivity metrics approach measurement from various perspectives. There are personnel productivity metrics, repeat business ratios, cost productivity metrics, lead conversion ratios, and others as identified below. Personnel productivity metrics include such measures as:

- Number of leads per sales manager.

- Number of bookings per sales manager.

- Number of booked room nights per sales manager.

Repeat business ratios measure repeat business in a couple of ways. One measure focuses on repeat business in terms of the number of bookings, while the other focuses on repeat business as a component of total booked room nights. These two measures are calculated as follows:

$$\text{Repeat business bookings ratio} = \frac{\text{Number of repeat business bookings}}{\text{Total number of bookings}}$$

$$\text{Repeat business room nights ratio} = \frac{\text{Room nights from repeat business bookings}}{\text{Total booked room nights}}$$

Cost productivity ratios address the cost efficiency. The three cost productivity ratios listed below measure the cost efficiency of the CVB's convention sales function with respect to its key performance measures: leads, bookings, and booked room nights.

$$\text{Cost per lead} = \frac{\text{Convention sales function costs}}{\text{Number of leads}}$$

$$\text{Cost per booking} = \frac{\text{Convention sales function costs}}{\text{Number of bookings}}$$

$$\text{Cost per booked room night} = \frac{\text{Convention sales function costs}}{\text{Number of booked nights}}$$

Exhibit 3   Convention Sales Performance Reporting Definitions

Lead: An event inquiry by a corporation, association, organization, or independent meeting planner that includes a request for a minimum of 10 sleeping rooms per night (peak rooms) over a specific set or range of dates is forwarded by the CVB sales staff only to those hotels that meet the meeting planner's event criteria. A lead is more formalized than just exchanging or forwarding business cards to hotels. Lead is both a status level *and* the actual inquiry sent to the hotel(s) or convention center. For convention center events, if the CVB sends a lead first to the convention center for date availability and then to the hotel(s) for room blocks as a matter of policy, this process should be counted as *one* lead for reporting purposes. CVBs may have confidential or internal leads that are generated for performance reporting but are not distributed or published in an external document or calendar.

Bid: Proposal submitted by the CVB and/or hotel(s) to a planner that includes defined dates and room blocks. A bid is an activity, not a performance measure.

Tentative: Status assigned to a group or event after the bid has been submitted to the meeting planner, and the destination is waiting for a decision. The tentative status is only a trackable measure, not a performance measure.

Booking: There are two definitions of a booking, depending on where the event will be held:

- **Hotel Event Booking:** A future event contracted in writing by the event organization with the hotel. The CVB should receive a copy of the contract or a written communication from an authorized agent of the hotel that a contract has been signed. The communication should detail dates, space requirements, and estimated room blocks. The CVB should track estimated attendance and attendee spending for the event.

- **Citywide/Convention Center Event Booking:** Given the long time frame often involved in booking a citywide/convention center event, the booking process generally takes two steps:

    - Confirmed booking: A future event confirmed in writing (letter, booking notice) signed by an authorized agent of the event organization and the convention center (if applicable). The communication should detail dates, space requirements, and estimated room blocks. The CVB should track estimated attendance and attendee spending.

    - Contracted booking: A future event contracted in writing by the event organization with the event facility such as the convention center. The CVB should receive communication of this stage in writing from an authorized agent of the convention center.

Lost Opportunity: A potential event in the lead or tentative stage that was subsequently to be received by the destination. This does *not* include venue changes within the destination. The CVB should track the number of estimated room nights, attendance, and attendee spending, and the reason associated with the lost opportunity. A list of possible lost opportunity reasons should include but not be limited to:

- Dates not available at hotels

- Safety concerns

(continued)

Exhibit 3   *(continued)*

- Hotel room rates too high
- Meeting cancelled or postponed
- Lack of hotel interest
- Union or labor costs
- Dates not available at convention center
- Transportation or access issues
- Convention center costs too high
- National or international incidents
- No hotel adjacent to convention center
- Board preference or internal politics.

Cancelled Business: An event that was booked for the destination (a confirmed and/or contracted booking for a citywide/convention center event) that subsequently did not take place, either because the event itself was cancelled or it left the destination before taking place. The CVB should track the estimated number of room nights, attendance, and attendee spending, and the reason associated with the cancellation.

These formulas include the function's personnel, marketing and promotion, and administrative and general operations line item costs as defined in the *DMAI Bureau Uniform System of Accounts and Line Item Cost Allocation Worksheet.*

Lead conversion ratios measure, over a stated amount of time, the effectiveness of the CVB's lead-qualifying process and the likelihood that generated leads will book for the destination. These ratios are particularly useful because they can be calculated for each individual convention sales representative and for the convention sales function as a whole. There are two standard lead-conversion ratios—one that examines the booking rate and one that examines the rate of lost opportunities:

$$\text{Booking ratio} = \frac{\text{Number of bookings}}{\text{Total number of bookings} + \text{number of lost opportunities}}$$

$$\text{Lost opportunity ratio} = \frac{\text{Number of lost opportunities}}{\text{Number of bookings} + \text{number of lost opportunities}}$$

For example, assume that in the current year, a CVB generated forty-five bookings and forty lost opportunities and had forty-eight leads outstanding (from 133 leads that were generated sometime in the past). The booking ratio would be forty-five bookings divided by eighty-five (that is, forty-five bookings plus forty lost opportunities), or 53 percent. The lost opportunity ratio would be forty lost opportunities divided by eighty-five, or 47 percent.

If a CVB wishes to regularly report lead conversion, it should use a rolling twelve-month review of those leads generated in the past twelve months and compute the percentage that booked were lost or are still outstanding.

Exhibit 4   Convention Sales Activity Measures

- Number of bids
- Trade shows attended or exhibited
  - Number of trade shows
  - Number of co-op partners participating
  - Co-op monies generated
- Sales missions (with industry partners)
  - Number of sales missions
  - Number of co-op partners participating
  - Co-op monies generated
- Familiarization tours
  - Number of familiarization tours
  - Number of participants (event organizers only)
  - Number of accounts
  - Number of co-op partners participating
  - Co-op monies generated
- Number of sales calls
- Number of client site inspections
- Client events
  - Number of client events
  - Number of participants (event organizers only)
  - Number of accounts
  - Number of co-op partners participating
  - Co-op monies generated
- Sponsorships
  - Number of client events
  - Trade show elements or sessions
  - Monies spent
  - Number of people at sponsored events (customer-exposed impressions)
- Number of accounts with activity

A ratio known as the convention booking to room supply ratio measures the degree to which a CVB is booking rooms in the destination's convention hotels. It is calculated as follows:

$$\text{Convention booking to room supply ratio} = \frac{\text{Booked room nights (by-year production)}}{\text{Total (available) convention hotel room nights}}$$

There are also metrics that illustrate a CVB's convention sales performance (measured in room nights) relative to the destination's convention product (total room nights sold). These ratios are most useful when a CVB establishes a benchmark year and compares the measure for subsequent years. The metric below illustrates the relationship between a CVB's convention sales performance (measured in room nights) relative to the destination's convention product (total room nights sold).

Exhibit 5   Convention Sales Performance Measures

- Leads
  - Number of leads
  - Lead room nights (estimate)
- Bookings
  1. Hotel events
     - Number of bookings
     - Booked room nights (estimate)
     - Booked attendance (estimate)
     - Booked attendee spending (estimate)
  2. Citywide/Convention center events
     - Number of confirmed bookings
     - Booked room nights (estimate)
     - Booked attendance (estimate)
     - Booked attendee spending (estimate)
     - Number of contracted bookings
     - Booked room nights (estimate)
     - Booked attendance (estimate)
     - Booked attendee spending (estimate)
- Lost opportunities
  - Number of lost opportunities
  - Reason for lost opportunity
  - Lost room nights (estimate)
  - Lost attendance (estimate)
  - Lost attendee spending (estimate)
- Cancellations
  - Number of cancellations
  - Reason for cancellation
  - Cancelled room nights (estimate)
  - Cancelled attendance (estimate)
  - Cancelled attendee spending (estimate)
- Number of leads per trade show attended or exhibited by CVB sales staff
- Annual production: By-year production measures review the CVB's event bookings in terms of when the events will occur (regardless when the booking was generated):
  - Number of bookings
  - Number of booked room nights (estimated)
  - Number of booked attendees (estimated)
  - Booked attendee spending (estimated)

To ensure the usefulness of by-year production performance measures, CVBs should incorporate a standard practice to regularly update the room commitments and estimated attendance of future events.

Exhibit 5 *(continued)*

- Post-event measures
  - Room night pick-up (estimate)
  - Total attendance (estimate)
- Tentatives
  - Number of tentatives
  - Tentative room nights (estimated)

$$\text{Demand ratio} = \frac{\text{CVB booked room nights (by year production)}}{\text{Total meeting/convention room nights sold}}$$

This ratio should not be used for comparative purposes between CVBs given the wide variety of room inventories by industry segments among destinations.

Travel Trade Sales Performance Reporting

The mission of the travel trade sales function is, according to DMAI, "to increase leisure visitor volume, visitor spending and economic impact for the destination through the promotion and distribution of the destination's travel products to the travel trade." Exhibit 6 defines the key terms used in relation to the travel trade sales function. Exhibit 7 presents a list of travel trade sales activity measures. Exhibit 8 presents a list of travel trade sales performance measures.

Travel trade productivity metrics measure productivity from various perspectives. For example, personnel productivity metrics include such measures as:

- Number of leads per sales manager (hotel and non-hotel leads)
- Number of bookings per sales manager (hotel and non-hotel leads)
- Number of booked room nights per sales manager (hotel bookings only)

Various cost productivity metrics address the issue of cost efficiency. The three cost productivity ratios listed below measure the cost efficiency of the CVB's travel trade sales as a function of its key performance measures: leads, bookings, and booked room nights. CVBs are encouraged to establish a benchmark in the current year (or prior year if information is available).

$$\text{Cost per lead} = \frac{\text{Travel trade sales function costs}}{\text{Number of leads}}$$

$$\text{Cost per booking} = \frac{\text{Travel trade sales function costs}}{\text{Number of bookings}}$$

$$\text{Cost per booked room night} = \frac{\text{Travel trade sales function costs}}{\text{Number of booked nights}}$$

Exhibit 6   Travel Trade Sales Performance Reporting Definitions

---

Hotel Lead: A group tour or independent tour program inquiry from the travel trade that includes a request for hotel rooms over a specific set or range of dates forwarded by the CVB sales staff *only* to those hotels that meet the travel trade's criteria. A lead is more formalized than just exchanging or forwarding business cards to hotels.

Non-hotel Lead: An inquiry for a group tour or independent tour program not requiring hotel rooms from the travel trade over a specific set or range of dates is forwarded by the CVB sales staff *only* to those non-hotel tourism industry businesses that meet the travel trade's criteria. A referral is more formalized than just exchanging or forwarding business cards.

It should be noted that a lead is both a status level and an actual inquiry sent to the hotel(s) or non-hotel tourism industry business(es). CVBs may have confidential or internal leads that are generated for performance reporting but are not distributed or published in an external document or calendar.

Booking from a Hotel Lead: A booking confirmed in writing (letter, booking notice, e-mail) from an authorized agent (hotel, travel trade) or by documenting the tour's or program's presence in the travel trade's distribution channels such as a brochure, Web site, or special sales or marketing program. The booking must be the result of a CVB-generated lead. CVBs should include information on room nights, total visitors, and associated spending.

Booking from a Non-hotel Lead: A booking confirmed either in writing (letter, booking notice, e-mail) from an authorized agent or by documenting the tour's or program's presence in the travel trade's distribution channels such as a brochure, Web site, or special sales or marketing program. The booking must be the result of a CVB-generated lead. The CVB should include information on total visitors and associated spending.

These formulas include the function's personnel, marketing and promotion, and administrative and general operations line item costs as defined in the *DMAI Bureau Uniform System of Accounts and Line Item Cost Allocation Worksheet.*

The leads-to-bookings conversion ratio (for hotel leads only) measures, over a stated amount of time, the effectiveness of the CVB's lead-qualifying process and the likelihood that generated leads will book for the destination. This ratio is particularly useful because it can be calculated for each individual travel trade sales representative and for the travel trade sales function as a whole:

$$\text{Lead-to-bookings conversion ratio} = \frac{\text{Number of bookings from hotel leads}}{\text{Number of leads that did not book } + \text{ number of bookings from hotel leads}}$$

For example, assume that in the current year, a CVB generated 250 travel trade bookings from 378 travel trade hotel-only leads that were generated sometime in the past. The lead-to-booking conversion ratio is 255 bookings divided by 378 leads, or 67 percent.

Exhibit 7   Travel Trade Sales Activity Measures

- Trade shows attended and/or exhibited
  - Number of trade shows
  - Number of co-op partners participating
  - Co-op monies generated
- Number of accounts with activity
- Familiarization tours
  - Number of familiarization tours
  - Number of participants (travel trade only)
  - Number of accounts
  - Number of co-op partners participating
  - Co-op monies generated
- Number of sales trips
- Sales missions (with industry partners)
  - Number of sales missions
  - Number of co-op partners participating
  - Co-op monies generated
- Number of sales calls
- Client events
  - Number of client events
  - Number of participants (travel trade only)
  - Number of accounts
  - Number of co-op partners participating
  - Co-op monies generated
- Number of site inspections
- Number of developed suggested itineraries
- Number of packages developed
- Sponsorships
  - Number of client events
  - Tradeshow elements and/or sessions
  - Monies spent
  - Number of people at sponsored events ("customer-exposed impressions")

Marketing and Communication Performance Reporting

The mission of the marketing and communications function is, according to DMAI, "to increase visitor volume, visitor spending, and economic impact for the destination by developing awareness and preference." Exhibit 9 identifies some of the more common marketing activities a CVB conducts to fulfill its mission of generating visitor volume to its destination. Exhibit 10 presents a variety of marketing and communications performance measures.

Exhibit 8   Travel Trade Sales Performance Measures

- Leads (including confidential or internal leads) (* If the CVB engages in the listed sales or marketing effort)
  - Number of hotel leads
    - Lead room nights (estimate)
    - Number of visitors (estimate)
    - Visitor spending (estimate)*
  - Number of non-hotel leads
    - Number of non-hotel leads by member category
    - Number of visitors (estimate)
    - Visitor spending (estimate)*
- Bookings (including confidential bookings)
  - Number of bookings from hotel leads
    - Booked room nights (estimate)
    - Booked visitors (estimated)
    - Booked visitor spending (estimate)*
  - Number of bookings from non-hotel leads
    - Booked visitors (estimated)
    - Booked visitor spending (estimate)*

As a best practice, CVBs are encouraged to obtain destination-level visitor spending through destination-specific visitor research; otherwise, CVBs should use pre-existing secondary research from credible sources or pursue third-party sources.

The performance reporting discussed here focuses solely on the marketing and communications function's direct-to-consumer efforts. However, it should be noted that marketing and communications efforts can also span the spectrum of convention and travel trade segments and that many of the activity and performance measures and productivity metrics discussed below can be applied to them as well. CVBs are encouraged to monitor activity measures, performance measures, and productivity metrics for each program or niche market and on a total annual basis.

As a best practice, if a CVB spends a significant percentage of its budget on marketing efforts, it must then be prepared to invest in the research necessary to accurately and credibly measure the effectiveness of those efforts.

The ultimate measure of marketing productivity is the number of individuals whose visit to the destination occurred *clearly and significantly* because of the CVB's marketing efforts. CVBs *should not* use their destination's total number of visitors in conversion studies *as it is extremely unlikely that the CVB generated each and every visitor to its destination.*

Marketing and communications productivity metrics focus on various kinds of conversion studies. A conversion study determines the percentage of individuals responding to a specific CVB marketing effort (such as those who requested travel information or looked at package Web pages) who eventually visit the

Exhibit 9   Marketing and Communications Activity Measures

Advertising and Promotions
- Number of programs
- Total reach
- Total frequency
- Gross impressions
- Total value of media placed
- Paid media dollars
- Co-op media dollars
- In-kind or barter media dollars
- Unpaid media dollars
- Number of co-op partners

As a best practice, CVBs that advertise should conduct an audit of media placements to ensure that their media plan has been properly executed.

Online Activity
- Number of play-per-click keywords purchased per search engine
- Number of Web pages of content developed

Media and Public Relations
- Media trade shows
- Number of media trade shows attended
- Number of appointments
- Media missions
  - Number of media missions
  - Number of co-op partners
  - Number of media contacts
- Number of media and public relations calls
- Media familiarization tours
  - Number of familiarization tours
  - Number of journalists or media participating
  - Number of publications represented
- Press releases
  - Number of press releases issued
  - Number press releases distributed (including downloaded off CVB Web site)
- Number of media inquiries
- Number of media interviews
- Number of newsletters (included e-newsletters) produced
- Number of public service announcements (PSAs) produced
- Number of accounts with activity

Event Marketing
- Number of events supported
- Number of events produced

Exhibit 10   Marketing and Communications Performance Measures

Advertising and Promotions

Performance measures for advertising campaigns are typically determined by advertising-effectiveness studies. Performance measures for advertising campaigns typically include (but are not limited to):

- Advertising awareness (aided and unaided)
- Changes in a destination's brand image among target audiences over time
- Intent to travel to a destination

Inquiries or Fulfillment

- Number of brochure requests
- Number of consumer calls handled
- Number of coupons redeemed
- Number of people who register on the CVB's Web site to receive an e-newsletter, also known as "opt-ins"

Online and CVB Web Site

- Number of user sessions
- Number of unique users
- Number of repeat visits
- Click-throughs to the CVB Web site
- Number of specific page view counts
- Number of click-throughs to member and sponsor Web sites
- Number of Web coupons redeemed
- Average length of session
- Number of search engine referrals
- Web site ranking in the search engine's search results

Media and Public Relations

- Placements
  - Total number of placements
  - Domestic versus international placements
  - Broadcast versus print placements
- Number of impressions (circulation)
- Advertising equivalency (dollars)

Bookings

- Online and toll-free hotel reservations
  - Number of room nights booked
  - Rooms-booked revenue
  - Rooms-sold commission
  - Average length of stay
- Online ticket sales, such as attractions and tours
  - Total tickets sold
  - Tickets-sold revenue
  - Tickets-sold commission

Exhibit 10   *(continued)*

- Packages
  - Total packages sold
  - Packages-sold revenue
  - Packages-sold commission
  - Number of room nights booked

destination. One of the chief faults of conversion studies in the past was that they failed to exclude individuals who had already decided to come to the destination before they contacted the CVB. As a result, conversion study results tended to overstate the number of visitors generated by the particular CVB marketing effort under review. Modified conversion studies that address this issue can assist the CVB in determining the productivity of its marketing efforts, as can other research methodologies. As a best practice, CVBs are encouraged to work with market research professionals to begin to implement a research program that will determine the number of visitors generated by their marketing activities.

As a starting point, CVBs can initially focus on inquiry conversion studies, advertising-effectiveness research, online booking conversions, and package-purchase studies.

Inquiry Conversion. These studies measure the conversion of inquiries produced by the CVB's marketing efforts to generated visitors. Inquiries can include individuals who went to a particular Web site address in response to a specific marketing effort or who requested visitor information (guides, maps, etc.) via phone (this does not include individuals who called and were redirected elsewhere). Inquiries can also include Web site user sessions of a certain minimum length or user sessions for travel-specific pages.

As a best practice, CVBs should incorporate in their initial program setup a step where three pieces of information are collected from the inquirer: (1) how they got the phone number and/or Web site address (also known as lead source); (2) whether the consumer already decided to come to the destination before he or she contacted the CVB; and (3) recontact information (and securing permission to recontact for a follow-up survey). This information will assist the CVB in ultimately determining whether the inquiry turned into a visit to the destination and whether the visit was generated by the CVB's efforts. The recommended formula for calculating the inquiry conversion ratio is as follows:

$$\text{Inquiry conversion ratio} = \frac{\text{Number of visitors generated by the CVB's marketing effort(s)}}{\text{Number of inquiries generated by the CVB's marketing effort(s)}}$$

Advertising-Effectiveness Research. A conversion study for inquiries generated by a particular advertising campaign is limited in that it does not account for visitors generated by the campaign who did not contact the CVB. To gain a full accounting of all visitors who were generated, CVBs that advertise should conduct customized advertising effectiveness research studies. These studies can also be used to measure other key advertising performance measures including aware-ness, destination image and perception, and intent to travel.

Online Hotel Booking Function Conversion. A group of ratios is used to look at conversions from online booking functions. The first measures the ratio of people who look at the booking date/availability page in relation to the number of people who visit the Web site's home page:

$$\text{Overall look-to-look ratio} = \frac{\text{Number of page views for the online hotel booking date/rate availabity page}}{\text{Number of users to Web site (homepage)}}$$

The second ratio expresses the number of actual bookings in relation to the number of people using the homepage:

$$\text{Overall look-to-book ratio} = \frac{\text{Number of bookings through online hotel booking function}}{\text{Number of users to Web site (homepage)}}$$

The third ratio measures the rate at which people who look at the booking date/availability page actually book through the online function:

$$\text{Look-to-book ratio} = \frac{\text{Number of bookings through online hotel function}}{\text{Number of page views for the online hotel booking date/availability page}}$$

Package Conversion. For Web-based package conversions, two conversion ratios are offered. The design of the CVB's package Web pages will dictate the use of one or the other:

$$\text{Package purchases per main page visit} = \frac{\text{Number of CVB-offered packages purchased}}{\text{Number of page views for the initial package Web page}}$$

$$\text{Package purchases per pricing/availability page visit} = \frac{\text{Number of CVB-offered packages purchased}}{\text{Number of page views for the package pricing or availability Web page}}$$

As a best practice, CVBs should conduct follow-up research with package purchas-ers to determine average out-of-pocket expenditures.

CVB Return on Investment

CVBs use standard business return-on-investment (ROI) approaches to quantify their financial impact on local communities for convention and leisure travel. ROI formulas examine the return from the investment made by an organization, conceptually represented by the simple ROI formula below:

$$\text{Return on investment} = \frac{\text{Amount of return (income)}}{\text{Amount of investment (expense)}}$$

For a CVB, the amount of return is typically what the CVB returned to the destination (visitor spending, economic impact, tax dollars), *clearly and significantly generated* through its sales and marketing efforts. The amount of investment can also vary, based on which stakeholder requests the information.

Because ROI requests come in many forms, there are three ROI formulas that a CVB can choose to use to cover most of these requests. One of these examines ROI at the CVB level and two examine ROI at the functional level. When measuring their ROIs over time, CVBs should consistently use the same ROI formula to ensure that comparisons over time are meaningful.

The ROI formula that focuses on the entire CVB is the return on the total operating budget. Calculated as follows, this ratio represents the sum of visitor spending generated by the CVB's convention sales, travel trade sales, and marketing and communications functions in relation to the CVB's total operating budget:

$$\frac{\text{Return on total}}{\text{operating budget}} = \frac{\text{Visitor spending generated by the CVB's efforts}}{\text{Total CVB operating budget}}$$

The two ROI calculations that address the three specific functional areas all use the same basic formulas. The primary difference between the two versions for each functional area is that one calculation considers only the given function's direct operating budget, while the other includes both the direct and indirect operating budgets of the function. Although slight terminology differences may occur by functional area, the two basic formulas for ROI by function are as follows:

$$\frac{\text{Return on functional area}}{\text{direct operating budget}} = \frac{\text{Visitor spending generated by the CVB's efforts by functional area}}{\text{Direct operating budget for the functional area}}$$

$$\frac{\text{Return on functional area direct and indirect operating budget}}{} = \frac{\text{Visitor spending generated by the CVB's efforts by functional area}}{\text{Direct and indirect operating budget for the functional area}}$$

As an example, applying the first formula above to the convention sales function would give us the following calculation:

$$\frac{\text{Return on convention sales function direct operating budget}}{} = \frac{\text{Attendee spending generated by the CVB's convention sales function}}{\text{Convention sales function direct operating budget}}$$

Regardless of which functional area we wish to address, to calculate these figures, we need to define the terms used in the equations. With regard to the denominators, CVBs are encouraged to use DMAI's *Bureau Uniform System of Accounts and Line Item Cost Allocation Worksheet* for guidance on direct and indirect operating cost line items. CVBs must ensure the allocation methods are the same when comparing ROIs between bureaus. With regard to the numerators, what is "visitor spending" (or "attendee spending" when we speak of the convention sales function). For convention sales, attendee spending is defined as total estimated attendance × daily attendee spending × average length of stay. This definition further requires us to define or identify total attendance, daily attendee spending, and average length of stay.

Total estimated attendance is the attendance for events booked by the CVB in the time period for which the ROI is being calculated, regardless when the meeting will take place. Only booked events where the CVB generated the lead and/or confidential lead can be included.

With regard to daily attendee spending, in the absence of destination-specific attendee spending and length of stay information, CVBs can use the results of DMAI's *ExPact Study*. The study is based on surveys of eighty-six participating bureaus, 12,920 delegates, 1,286 exhibiting companies, and seventy-seven event organizers. Among the key findings were the following:

- Delegates spend on average of $945 per event or $266 per day. The average length of stay is 3.6 nights. The average for delegate spending increased 36 percent from 1998 to 2004, while average length of stay increased 15 percent.

- 77 percent of all delegate spending is accounted for by lodging (48 percent) and food and beverage (29 percent).

- Direct spending contributed to the local economy per exhibiting company: $6,753; per event organizer: $454,673.

- Per-delegate spending by association or event organization: $96 per event or $22 per day. Food and beverage is the largest share of event organizer expenditures.

- The study found that for the average event, delegates stay in a designated hotel 81 percent of the time.

Applying the functional ROI formulas to the travel trade sales function, we define visitor spending as total booked visitors × daily visitor spending × average length of stay. "Total booked visitors" includes only those visitors for which the CVB generated the lead and/or confidential lead (hotel and non-hotel leads). Booked visitor counts are estimated because actual post-trip figures are not collected. In the absence of destination-specific visitor spending figures and average length of stay information, CVBs should use pre-existing secondary research from credible sources.

Applying the functional ROI formulas to the marketing and communications function, we define visitor spending as total generated visitors × daily visitor spending × average length of stay. Total generated visitors is the number of visitors directly generated by the CVB's marketing efforts—a figure arrived at through the various studies described earlier under marketing and communication productivity metrics, including advertising campaign effectiveness, inquiry conversion studies, and package purchasing studies. In the absence of destination-specific visitor spending figures and average length of stay information, CVBs should use pre-existing secondary research from credible sources with appropriate footnotes and caveats. For generated visitors traveling on packages, a recommended alternative and conservative approach, if custom research is not available, would be to use the package purchase price.

Case Study Example

Let's look at a sample situation to see how the ROI calculations would be calculated. Assume that the Harmony Convention & Visitors Bureau's operating budget for the year in question was $7.0 million. Its funding and functional area budget breakouts were as follows:

>Public Funding (solely from hotel tax): $5.0 million
>Private Funding (member dues, sponsorships,
> co-op, in-kind, etc): $2.0 million
>Convention Sales Function
> Direct: $1.6 million
> Indirect: $400,000
>Travel Trade Sales Function
> Direct: $1.2 million
> Indirect: $300,000
>Marketing and Communications Function (direct to consumer only)
> Direct: $3.0 million
> Indirect: $500,000

By measuring its activity, performance, and productivity in the manner recommended earlier in this chapter, the Harmony CVB was able to identify $375.0 million in visitor spending that was *clearly and significantly* generated by its sales and marketing efforts, broken out by functional area as follows:

- Convention sales function: $160 million in attendee spending

- Travel trade sales function: $75 million in visitor spending

- Marketing and communications function: $140 million in visitor spending

The ROIs for the Harmony CVB and its functional areas can be calculated as follows:

$$\text{Return on total operating budget} = \frac{\text{Visitor spending generated by the CVB's efforts}}{\text{Total CVB operating budget}}$$

$$= \frac{\$375.0 \text{ million}}{\$7.0 \text{ million}}$$

$$= \underline{\underline{53.6}}$$

Return on functional area direct operating budget $=$ $\dfrac{\text{Visitor spending generated by the CVB's efforts by functional area}}{\text{Direct operating budget for the functional area}}$

For convention sales $= \dfrac{\$160.0 \text{ million}}{\$1.6 \text{ million}}$

$= \underline{\underline{100.0}}$

For travel trade sales $= \dfrac{\$75.0 \text{ million}}{\$1.2 \text{ million}}$

$= \underline{\underline{62.5}}$

For marketing and communications $= \dfrac{\$140.0 \text{ million}}{\$3.0 \text{ million}}$

$= \underline{\underline{46.7}}$

Return on functional area direct and indirect operating budget $=$ $\dfrac{\text{Visitor spending generated by the CVB's efforts by functional area}}{\text{Direct and indirect operating budget for the functional area}}$

For convention sales $= \dfrac{\$160.0 \text{ million}}{\$2.0 \text{ million}}$

$= \underline{\underline{80.0}}$

For travel trade sales $= \dfrac{\$75.0 \text{ million}}{\$1.5 \text{ million}}$

$= \underline{\underline{62.5}}$

For marketing and communications $= \dfrac{\$140.0 \text{ million}}{\$3.5 \text{ million}}$

$= \underline{\underline{40}}$

Chapter 5 Outline

Competencies

1. Describe the elements of a typical communications plan. (pp. 78–80)

2. Describe the features of a good news release, and explain the steps involved in writing one. (pp. 81–82)

3. Describe the ways in which electronic communications with media outlets are different from more traditional forms of communication. (pp. 83–84)

4. Compare and contrast the elements and planning procedures of individual and group press trips. (pp. 84–88)

5. Describe the ways in which CVBs can physically take their message to the media. (pp. 88–89)

6. Explain why it is important for a CVB to have a crisis communications plan, and describe the steps to implement such a plan. (pp. 89–90)

7. Describe the tactics a CVB should use when dealing with media interviews. (pp. 90–95)

8. Describe communication methods CVBs can use with members, employees, and stakeholders. (pp. 95–98)

5

Communications

By *Danielle Courtenay*

Danielle Courtenay is vice president of public relations for the Orlando/Orange County (Florida) Convention and Visitors Bureau. She develops long-range strategy and directs the day-to-day global public relations efforts of Orlando staff and eight international offices in the tourism and convention and meetings arenas. Responsibilities also include crisis communications and community relations. Former vice president of an advertising/ public relations firm, she has served on numerous public relations–oriented committees at the state and national levels. She holds a B.A. in public relations from Auburn University and an M.S. in marketing communications from Florida State University.

COMMUNICATIONS IS THE ONE OF THE CORNERSTONES of destination management. Many programs may have succeeded, but they were not fully effective if no one knew about them. Communications activities encompass many aspects of a convention and visitors bureau (CVB), including global publicity, member communications, community relations, crisis communications, issues management, government relations, internal communications, and marketing support. No matter how a CVB chooses to organize its departments or divide responsibilities, it should ensure that it has a knowledgeable person to oversee, develop, and implement activities for all of these aspects. This chapter will examine media relations, crisis communications and issues management, member communications, internal communications, and stakeholder communications.

Publicity's Value

Publicity for the destination is a powerful and cost-effective marketing tool. The generation of positive feature stories and reports by credible media outlets provides a third-party endorsement by trusted sources of information. According to the Travel Industry Association of America, 61 percent of travelers read about travel or destinations in the media and 34 percent said the travel media influenced their travel decision.

Publicity, although powerful, is most effective when integrated into the overall marketing plan or coupled with marketing programs. This integration can extend marketing reach by expanding a campaign, lengthening a campaign, or filling in the gaps when paid media programs or promotions are not possible. The foremost strength of publicity is in branding the destination in its current positioning or in repositioning the brand. It can also influence consumer behavior by moving them to request information, convincing them to buy packages or pack-age elements, and increasing Web hits. Because many media outlets have long lead times ranging from six months to a year, the timing of program announcements is crucial. Conversely, with the Internet one can generate news or create interest almost instantly. Striking a balance between short-term and long-term media exposure is a strategic decision that should relate to a CVB's overall publicity goals.

Creating a Plan

Many communications tactics will be integrated into the overall CVB business and marketing plan, but if the communications department is charged with developing a stand-alone plan, the direction and detail it provides will help ensure that communications programs are targeted and meet the CVB's needs. According to the Public Relations Society of America, a standard communications plan includes the following:

- *Mission or Purpose*—The overarching reason that the organization came into existence; a visionary statement that can guide the organization's planning for many years.

- *Goal*—Usually, a more specific expression of a mission or purpose. Often related to one aspect of the mission or purpose, it is commonly described as the desired outcome of a plan of action.

- *Situation*—A review of strengths and weaknesses and a competitive analysis.

- *Objectives*—Specific milestones that measure progress toward achievement of a goal. Objectives must address the desired result in terms of opinion change and/or behavioral outcome, not in terms of communication output; designate the public or publics among whom the behavioral outcome is to occur; specify the expected level of accomplishment; and identify the time frame in which those accomplishments are to occur.

- *Strategy*—A general, well-considered plan. Strategies do not indicate specific actions to achieve objectives. There can be multiple strategies for each objective.

- *Target Audiences*—A definition of whom the program is meant to influence, including media outlets, the political community, and consumers.

- *Message*—A clearly defined communication of the program concept.

- *Tactics*—The specific activities conducted to implement strategies of a public relations program. Public relations help an organization and its publics adapt mutually to each other. Communications is an element of this adaptive process, featuring tactics and tools that involve the use of selected personnel, time, cost, and other organizational resources. Tactics achieve the objectives and, in turn, support the goals that have been set to carry out the CVB's mission or purpose.

- *Measurement*—Defined method of measuring results against objectives.

- *Budget and Timeline*—Specific account of human resources, outsourcing, and other expenses to implement tactics with a detailed outline of when tactics will occur and who is responsible for each tactic.[1]

Database Maintenance

A quality database is a crucial element of a successful publicity plan. Whether the organization chooses to maintain the database in-house, outsource it, or subscribe to a service, capturing information on the clients—the media—is essential. It is important to regularly update contact information and that all contact information is captured. The news media continually stress the importance of public relations professionals knowing the publications before making contact with them. Include in the database such items as the specific name of the travel section; the method by which a journalist prefers to receive information; past articles written on the destination; the date of a journalist's last visit; what he or she did on a previous visit to the destination; and, of course, personal information. This will develop continuity when working with journalist contacts. As important as this element is to a successful program, it is also very time-consuming to maintain a national and international database in-house. Several companies specialize in public relations databases, and the CVB can subscribe to such a service. The advantage is that maintenance is all handled through the company. The disadvantage is that the databases are not customized to tourism.

Measurement

Two constant challenges that a CVB faces are ensuring that all of its constituents understand its impact, that is, the return on investment it generates, and measuring results of this impact. DMAI has developed recommended performance and activity measures to which all CVBs should adhere.

The most traditional method to measure publicity is to assign a circulation and advertising equivalency value to each of the articles, Web hits, and broadcast segments. This method works well for general reporting, and the information can be obtained through numerous clipping and analysis services on local, state, and national bases. When composing the measurement report, CVBs should use a standard economic impact model rather than a multiplier when it comes to the circulation or advertising value. There is not an industry standard for the multiplier, so it is likely more time will be spent defending the multipliers than highlighting good work. If obtaining the detailed information is unnecessary, CVBs can also track general exposure by utilizing Internet search engines such as Google. Regardless of how the information is tracked, to make the information more meaningful to the overall efforts, the CVB's communications department can group clips in its report by campaign or marketing initiative. This allows the publicity for integrated campaigns to be directly related to the campaign it is supporting. A useful section to include on the clip report is "CVB Generated"—that is, did the clip directly result from a CVB activity such as a press release, a press trip, providing information or interviews, or other means? By tracking this information, the communications department can informally track the effectiveness of the publicity tactics it employs. The information can also be used to determine which topics or aspects of the destination seem to most interest the journalists involved.

Target Publications and Geographic Penetration

CVBs can also track target publications and geographic penetration. At the beginning of the year or a campaign, identify publications in the forefront of the marketing efforts. This can be done in conjunction with the CVB's advertising agency or marketing department. Employing the same demographics and psychographics, or lifestyle indicators, used to determine advertising buys, have the agency or marketing department select the top twenty, fifty, or other predetermined number of markets in which they would buy advertising if they had a limitless budget. These become a target list. Add the top media outlets from the top ten or twenty markets and a solid list that is directly related to the destination marketing efforts results. Be patient if the decision is made to take this direction. These publications are usually harder to reach and may require targeted pitches and months or years of relationship building to obtain placement.

Just as advertising and promotions can be tracked when it comes to generating calls and sales, so can public relations. This can be accomplished by assigning a certain toll-free line or extension to CVB publicity staff so calls can be tracked. For the Internet, assign specific extensions in Web addresses that may lead to a special "splash" page only promoted through publicity efforts, such as site name/campaign name. In this way, public relations tracking can be done by linking a specific call or Web hit to a specific staff member.

Media Relations

One word encapsulates a successful media relations program—relationships. Inherent in the term media relations is a bond derived from mutual respect. In customer service, perception is reality and the customer comes first. Media relations is important to a CVB because media output influences customer perception. No matter how good the communications relationship is with journalists, always maintain professionalism and remember that nothing is really "off the record." An important goal of a successful program is to establish the organization's and communications personnel's credibility with the media. This can be achieved by sending media outlets relevant information, providing information in a timely manner when asked, being available to comment on positive and negative stories, and providing alternative sources if the CVB is not the proper source. But this does not preclude the personal touch when working with the media. For instance, send journalists personal thank-you notes when they produce great stories, send them birthday cards, and remember their favorite pastimes and the names of their family members or pets.

Media relations in international markets has one main item in common with domestic needs—success is still built on relationships. Many of the tactics still work in most international markets, but may have to be modified. For some markets, sending releases in English is fine, but for others translation of materials is essential. Countries use different formats for video and images, so when entering a foreign market find out what they are. Time differences can complicate communications, meaning electronic communications may play an even greater role in the media relations mix. Most important, do not forget about customs and cultural differences in etiquette and protocol.

Communications professionals should always put themselves in the journalist's shoes. When calling to pitch or suggest a story, first ask if the journalist has time to talk. If it is a bad time, ask for a better time to call, or ask if it would be more convenient if the information were sent via e-mail.

The CVB should always consider local media as one of its most important customers. Other titles or outlets may have the glamour and glitz, but the local media can make or break an organization through repeated reporting on bureau activities.

News Releases and Press Kits

News releases are the standard tool used to communicate with journalists on topics such as what's new, special events, marketing programs, research results, and destination attributes. The release should be used as a follow-up to a pitch or a means to keep the media informed. The CVB should not depend on a story used directly from a release. Media representatives receive hundreds of news releases daily from civic, social and cultural organizations; foundations; corporations; and government agencies. Many of these are not used because they are incomplete, improperly targeted, or arrive after deadline. Do not expect an editor to use a release unless it is really newsworthy or presents an unusual angle to a story.

A concise and properly structured news release is the key to getting your news in the media and building credibility. The standard method for writing a news release is the "inverted pyramid," which prioritizes information in the story. In this era of information overload and short attention spans, the headline and lead may determine if a story is considered or not. The first paragraph or two of a news release is called the lead. It should include the most important elements of the story, also known as the five Ws—who, what, when, where, and why—as well as how and how much, if significant. The details that follow elaborate on this information in declining order of importance. If the story's length must be reduced, eliminating the last and least important paragraphs can best shorten it.

News Release Mechanics

Follow the step-by-step process outlined below when preparing a news release, whether submitted by postal service, e-mail, or fax.

- *Format:* Type only on one side of the paper. Double space, use upper and lower case letters, and frame the copy with generous margins. Indent each paragraph five spaces.

- *Upper Right:* In the upper right corner under contacts, list the CVB press contact's name, e-mail address, telephone number, fax number, and the CVB's Web site. Having that information readily available assists journalists when they need more information.

- *Release Instructions:* Unless it is essential that the story not be used until a specific time or day, always type "FOR IMMEDIATE RELEASE" and type the date the news release is written under this line.

- *Content:* Keep the release as short as possible, employ clear and direct prose, and of course, always use good taste. Most releases run one to two pages long. For punctuation and usage, employ a recognized style guide such as the *Associated Press Stylebook* or Strunk and White's *Elements of Style*. These reference manuals are readily available in bookstores. If there is more than one page to the release, write "MORE" at the bottom of the page and "-2-" on the top of the second page. To avoid interrupting the flow of a release, do not split a paragraph over two pages. The release should be concluded with an end mark, such as "###" or "-30-."

- *Proof:* When the news release is completed, be sure to have it proofed by a senior CVB staffer. Mail, fax, or e-mail it to arrive on or before media deadlines.

Publicity Photos

Graphics can add greatly to a story and increase the potential of it being published. Send photos that are active, feature people, and tell a story to increase the chance of a release being used. Each publication will have its own specifications and interests. The communication department's goal is to make it easy for the media outlet to use the image. This can be accomplished by providing prints for the editor's review, and offering a multitude of formats to meet the needs of art directors. In all instances, make sure a photo caption and photographer credit are included with each image. According to the *Associated Press Stylebook*, the caption's job is to describe and explain the picture to the reader. The challenge is to do it interestingly, accurately, tastefully, and succinctly. A good caption clearly identifies the people, event, or location; gives the when, where, and what; and helps tell the story. In addition, a good publicity photo can replace a release when all that is needed is a caption. For instance, select a quirky photo such as Santa in beachwear on a jet ski to highlight the great weather and holiday, forward a shot of a celebrity enjoying the destination, or capture the wackiest element of a local festival.

Preparing a Press Kit

Reporters may want a complete set of background information on the destination and the CVB. This can be as simple as a letter with a news release and fact sheet or more extensive such as a press kit. A typical press kit might include a destination overview, as well as information on accommodations, attractions, history, culture, and activities. Destination fact sheets should include pertinent telephone numbers. Also include a CVB corporate backgrounder and a list of CVB services and information sources. Do not hesitate to suggest story angles, and consider inserting short (fifty- to five-hundred-word) separate descriptions for the leisure and business sides of the destination for quick use in directories, listings, and guides. Remember to include contact information and a business card. Because editors increasingly are using Web sites for research and digital content, make sure the media section of the CVB's Web site is up to date with a press kit, releases, and high-resolution images.

Other Media Communications

Broadcast Copy

The basic rules for newspaper and magazine copy apply to radio copy, with one big exception—radio copy is written to be heard, not to be read. It must still be accurate and cover the important information, but in a brief, conversational, and informal way. Consider how an announcement can be worded to fit into a station's format. Easy listening stations sound different from rock music stations. Keep it short and simple because a listener may hear the announcement only once and must understand it the first time.

Electronic Communications

The growth of the Internet has generated many new communication tactics. Because this is relatively uncharted territory at this time, it is difficult to provide comprehensive insight into what will be the best uses of the Web and electronic communications in the future. Because electronic communications are read quickly, the writing style must be suitably modified but still follow traditional grammar rules. Messages should be short and to the point, and all electronic communications should include a contact name, telephone number, and address. It is a good idea to ask journalists what format they prefer and note this in a database. In addition, many media outlets and freelancers will not accept attachments, so it is best to paste the information into the screen or provide a link to the information that can be housed on the CVB's Web site.

E-mail Pitches. Some journalists prefer to receive an e-mail rather than a telephone call to suggest a story. In these cases, make sure the subject line creates sufficient interest to encourage them to open the e-mail. Take steps to ensure it will not be filtered out as spam. Keep the pitch succinct and customize the message to each person receiving it.

One method of continuous communication is to provide a regularly scheduled update on the destination through an electronic newsletter or e-mailed tip sheet. To minimize the burden on reporters, limit the subjects covered to three to five items per issue or sheet.

Online Press Rooms. Each CVB should have a Web site or an area on a Web site specifically devoted to the needs of the news media. As this communications channel continues to grow, so does its use by journalists. The location as well as quality of a CVB's media relations site is important. The site should be visible on the destination's home page and heavily marketed. The CVB's communications team should check to see that the site's address is included on letters to the editor, press releases, e-mail tags, voice mail messages, business cards, and any other material that may be distributed to the media. Because most journalists use the site for research, post all material that may be helpful in as many languages as possible and practical. The site should include full press kits, press releases, lists of significant dates, claims and recognition for the destination and the CVB, press trip dates, requests for individual press trips, and any other materials that may affect the media. Place dated information in an archive section so journalists can access it if necessary or desirable. In addition, strengthen the Web site with links to other related areas such as research, calendar of events, other destination entities' media Web sites, and suitable images. The CVB also should clearly post the communication team's contact information, including areas of specialty, e-mail addresses, and telephone numbers. Posting a photo of each team member so that journalists can put a face with a name is a nice touch. And remember that the Internet should complement media relations efforts, not replace them.

Press Trips

Whether the CVB calls the tactic press trips, familiarization tours, or site visits, there is no better way for journalists to write stories on a destination than by experiencing it firsthand. These trips give them a chance to see the area, broaden their scope of knowledge of the destination, talk to experts, and formulate multiple stories. Both group and individual trips can be effective.

Group Trips

Organizing a group trip allows the CVB to expose multiple journalists to key messages at the same time and efficiently use resources. Such trips are useful because they present the opportunity to develop a strong relationship with the journalists, venues are more likely to do special programs for small groups than individuals, journalists discover various angles from the other participants, and a sense of camaraderie is usually developed. The drawbacks are that many top publications do not want to travel with other publications, some cannot accept complimentary trips, and one person can positively or negatively influence the other journalists. Of course, with any event, preplanning will determine how successful the trip turns out to be for the destination. A checklist for planning a group trip is shown in Exhibit 1. Below are the basic questions that the CVB publicity representative should answer to start the planning process.

- *Purpose:* Is the trip to support a specific initiative or message or is it for overall branding?

- *Date:* Is it more advantageous for the trip to occur in high season when participants can experience the destination in full force, or when it is less crowded? Should it be planned around a key special event or meeting? The choice will depend on the purpose of the trip. Keep in mind that if journalists are invited primarily to experience an event, the coverage will most likely promote the event for the following year.

- *Duration:* The important item here is to be cognizant of the amount of time the writers and photographers are out of the office. Members of the domestic media tend to like shorter trips and usually are willing to include a weekend.

Exhibit 1   Checklist for Group Press Trips

Set dates for press trip.
Obtain flight schedules.
Draft itinerary.
Add descriptions to itinerary.
Submit itinerary with descriptions to partners.
Compile invitation list.
Draft invitation copy.
Find e-leads (sales inquiries based on Internet marketing) for accommodations.
Conduct site inspections for accommodations.
Find e-leads for transportation; reserve rental van.
Confirm accommodations.
Follow up with journalists who did not respond to invitation.
Get waiver signed by participants.
Type list of journalists.
Confirm itinerary with hosts.
Invite appropriate CVB members, community leaders, etc., to a meal function if
     appropriate.
Fax confirmed itinerary to transportation company.
Send confirmation e-mail to journalists.
Fax detailed itinerary with directions to transportation company.
Draft welcome letter.
Prepare welcome kits that include:
        Welcome letter
        Press kit
        List of hosts
        Journalist itinerary
        Gift in gift bags
Deliver welcome kits to hotel.
Request cell phone, pager, car, and camera.
Request cash advance.
Pick up cell phone, pager, car, and camera.
Pick up cash advance.
Pick up snacks and drinks.
Obtain sunscreen, rain ponchos, and other trip supplies.
E-mail staff with phone numbers.
Execute press trip.
Act as liaison during trip.
Send thank-you letters to journalists, hosts, and partners.
Prepare after-action report.

International groups tend to be more flexible and usually can stay longer. At times, trip duration is also determined by airline schedules.

- *Theme:* Presenting a specific theme such as history, what's new, luxury, or "girlfriends' getaway" will attract journalists' attention quicker than just having the destination as the theme. When selecting a theme, consider the marketing campaigns the CVB is conducting. One of the campaigns may provide a natural theme, and in turn the press trip can be better integrated into the overall marketing campaign.

- *Target:* When putting together the invitation list, make sure to invite only media outlets that fit the theme of the trip and can accept group trips. Some outlets cannot accept sponsored press trips and will not accept freelance articles based on a complimentary trip. Others may be able to attend group trips, but editorial policy dictates that they pay a media rate. It is wise to know their policies and only add to the invitation list those who can accept trips. Consideration should also be given to not mixing broadcast and print outlets. Both have very specific needs, such as photographers desiring to shoot in the early morning or late afternoon, radio and television outlets needing live interviews, and print journalists wanting more in-depth interviews. If possible, try not to put competing outlets together unless it is a niche trip dealing with topics such as meeting trades or family. Also consider whether journalists will be asked to sign a liability waiver protecting the CVB from legal action. Some may decline due to this policy.

- *Itinerary:* Make sure the itinerary supports the overall theme of the trip down to the choice of accommodations and selection of dining options. One approach may include only elements that the general public can experience; another may provide more insight such as a behind-the-scenes tour showing how a ride operates or how animal specialists do their thing. Provide time for the journalists to explore venues on their own, conduct interviews, and gather photos or other artwork. When scheduling, build in time for the accommodations to be highlighted, time to relax, and enough time to get from location to location, including gift shop stops, snacks, and breaks. Be sure to give journalists an itinerary before they leave home that includes dress requirements for each day/event so they know what to pack.

- *Materials:* Ask the journalists if they would like to receive media materials ahead of the trip and offer to ship items they collected during the trip. Be prepared to provide supporting information and images for each location on the trip. Many CVBs provide disks of digital images or offer a site from which photos can be easily downloaded.

- *Extras:* Be flexible. International journalists love to see how residents live. They may request to visit a neighborhood, grocery store, or other "everyday" locations. Provide essentials such as suntan lotion, drinks, snacks, rain ponchos, and umbrellas that may be needed during the trip.

- *Follow-up:* Send thank-you notes to all the journalists and the venues that hosted them. Track whether the stories have run. Stories may be delayed for extended periods of time due to editorial requirements. If this occurs, offer to provide updates on the place visited. As the stories are produced, send another thank-you to the journalists. If the trip included freelancers, it is a nice touch to send them a copy of the article because they may not know all the outlets in which their story has run.

Individual Trips

An individual journalist trip may better serve the organization's purpose or time-frame than a group trip. These trips work especially well for broadcast outlets, photographers, and top-tier publications. Prior to starting the initiative, determine the parameters. Will the CVB provide airfare, rental car, all meals and activities or just a portion? Will the trip be fully escorted or will a CVB representative join the journalist for only parts of the itinerary? Will the journalist be allowed to bring a guest or family? If guests are allowed, what portion of the costs will the CVB cover? Answering these questions up front can mean more effective management of the process, and the department can avoid damaging its relationship with the media outlet or creating a budgetary issue for itself.

The same parameters can be used when journalists initiate the request to visit a destination, with one additional step—qualification. Although most people who contact the CVB are professional working journalists, there are always a few individuals who may try to take advantage of the CVB's resources or those of its members. Therefore, it is important to have a system in place to qualify journalists before hosting them at the destination. Steps for qualifying journalists can include:

- Looking in the CVB's media database for past interaction.

- Having the journalists fill out a trip request form with pertinent information such as expected publication date, trip dates, assistance needed, whether they will be filming, and so forth. By sending this form, the news organization immediately establishes credibility, and many times this step can weed out bogus journalists.

- Looking in the publication or on the publication's Web site to confirm that the requestor is listed as an editor, writer, or photographer.

- Asking freelancers for a letter of assignment from the editor of the outlet for which they are writing or photographing.

- Checking directories of organizations such as Society of American Travel Writers Association, Midwest Travel Writers Association, British Guild of Travel Writers, and National Association of Black Journalists.

- Calling the CVB nearest the writer's or photographer's home to see if it is familiar with the journalist in question.

To efficiently and effectively assist individual journalists, the Orlando/Orange County (Florida) Convention & Visitors Bureau, Inc., has developed a "Journalist VIP Passport." Its members offer journalists and guests complimentary services such as admission to attractions, food and beverages, and recreation opportunities. The passports are assigned to qualified journalists and allow them to plan their itinerary, but leave a lot of room for flexibility. For the CVB publicity team, the passport is a system for hosting individual journalists that can be embellished with additional items if necessary to fit a particular story angle.

Going to the Media

Taking the destination to journalists is another tactic for developing media relationships. This involves conducting meetings with or without CVB members, or planning a reception, event, or meal to showcase the destination in the journalists' own city.

Individual Meetings

By meeting journalists one-on-one, the CVB media representative has their undivided attention and can really determine their needs and interests. Although a story may not result, the return on this activity may be inclusion in future stories, participation in future press trips, and quick awareness of the CVB as a resource when journalists need information or quotes. When planning a trip, check dates of industry conferences they may be attending or covering, deadline days, time of year, and purpose. Before making the appointments, plot media outlets on a map to make sure you are using your time wisely. Most journalists will only grant a meeting of fifteen to thirty minutes, so be conscious of their time. Also, if the meeting will include CVB members, make sure the journalist is prepared for the number of guests. Many journalists hold such meetings in their offices, which do not accommodate large groups.

Media Events

In some markets, the best way to reach journalists may be to host an event to bring media representatives to one location. This enables more media outlets to be reached at one time and provides more publicity opportunities for members. However, this approach can be costly, and media attendance at events is never guaranteed. When planning an event, pick a theme that reflects the CVB's message. This theme can then translate into every aspect of the event, including the invitation, location, food, take away, and follow-up. To help boost attendance, look for locations that are centrally located and are a draw on their own, such as a brand new museum or a restaurant where it is difficult to get reservations or one that journalists typically would not frequent.

Satellite Media Tours and Video News Releases

To round out the publicity, a CVB can implement a broadcast strategy as part of its overall publicity plan. In addition to pursuing on-air opportunities, the CVB may have a story to tell that can be proactively pushed to the stations. Basically, there are two broadcast tactics that enable the destination to package the story and have it picked up by stations rather than convincing the stations to produce the package. The first is to produce a video news release that includes a general story, interviews, raw b-roll (an extended video news release to issue to television stations from which they can put together their own version), unedited footage with natural sound, and suggested script.

The second is to plan a satellite media tour. Satellite media tours are a series of pre-booked, live, one-on-one interviews that place a CVB spokesperson on television from one convenient location. The key for both of these tactics is to strike a blend between getting an organization's message across and making the program noncommercial. One satellite media tour that did this successfully touted "edutainment"—mixing education and entertainment to keep children learning over the summer break. The tour was timed for the end of the school year and focused on learning by using the destination's attractions as examples. The spokesperson was an astronaut who brought credibility, celebrity status and an appealing on-air personality to the project. The tour was timely and trendy.

Pursuing either of these strategies can be expensive. If the CVB is a novice at building these types of programs, it is recommended that a company specializing in them be brought on as a partner. The company will assist in developing the angle, shooting the b-roll, training the spokesperson, pitching the story, and, in some instances, reporting.

Issues Management and Crisis Communications

One of the most important strategic decisions that communications professionals must make is how to handle an issue or a crisis. Due to the nature of CVBs, issues can pop up regularly, and how they are handled can have a positive or negative effect on the organization. Common issues that CVBs deal with include funding, alternative uses of the resort tax, tourism development and growth of the community, commitment to the community, and budget usage. Strategically, the organization must determine if it is ultimately better to push for coverage or resolve the issue without any play in the media. For example, further tourism development can be a hotly debated issue in destinations with fragile environmental conditions, such as communities along the coast, or with special social or demographic conditions, such as second-home or retirement communities. The decision regarding media coverage may be based on the involved players, the severity of the issue and whether the CVB is private or public. If a CVB is public, it may be subject to more disclosure laws than a private entity and therefore will not have a choice on what the media has access to regarding the issue. On major issues, it is wise to engage the CVB board to make sure that members agree on whatever position is taken. Once a position has been determined, talking points should be developed and distributed to key media contacts to ensure a consistent message.

Some of the common crises CVBs deal with are natural disasters such as hurricanes, brush fires, flooding, tornadoes, and other weather phenomena, as well as man-made occurrences such as violence against a visitor, terrorism, and defective products. The worst mistake is to think that "it won't happen here." Every organization should have a crisis plan that covers operations, communications, and back-up systems, no matter how simple or complex. The plans can be intertwined or separate depending on what is most user-friendly for the organization. Once the plan is developed, have it reviewed by an expert or an outside entity to make sure that it is complete and accurate. After a final plan is created, training and meetings are needed to ensure that the CVB is ready to implement the plan. It is a good idea to meet with all departments and employees who will be involved in the program to make sure the system is fully understood and the necessary back-up exists. Meetings should also be held with any affiliates that are a part of or will be affected by the plan. These meetings will mean better cooperation if the destination or the CVB is faced with a crisis. The media might also be considered in this process. Having media meetings before a crisis gives the organization a chance to let the media know what role the CVB will play and what the organization can and cannot provide. This approach allows the bureau to avoid having to set the parameters while in crisis mode. Once the plan is final, if appropriate, run a drill for staff and outside parties. The appendix to this chapter deals at length with crisis management.

Media Interviews

Media interviews are a great tactic for the CVB to present its own views on a topic or promote the destination's attributes, whether the interviews are on-camera, during a television talk show, during a radio show, or in person or via telephone with a print reporter. If positioned correctly, the CVB can be seen as the resource for information regarding the destination and the local tourism industry. To effectively perform this role, the CVB should adopt a media policy for the organization clearly indicating that all media calls should be forwarded to the communications team. By doing this, the CVB can be protected from and provide better service to journalists. It is then the communications team's responsibility, with the appropriate executives, to determine if the CVB is the correct entity to speak on the topic; who within the organization will serve as the spokesperson; the length of the interview; and the date, time, and location of the interview. The public relations contact then can make the arrangements with the journalists, thus avoiding telephone "tag" and catching a spokesperson off guard. This direct contact by the communications team also allows for staff to learn more about the story and what supporting information he or she may need directly from the journalist, thereby optimizing the CVB representative's time during the interview. It is also the communications representative's responsibility to provide a reporter with any follow-up materials discussed during the interview, correct spelling of the spokesperson's name, his or her title, and additional contacts if desired or necessary. Whether the CVB is called for a reaction to a topic or proactively seeks media appearances, the following steps are generally the same.

Step 1: Choose Your Organization's Spokesperson(s). The president, CEO, or director of marketing/sales of the CVB will be the most likely choice for a spokesperson at one time or another, especially in crisis situations. For more specialized interviews, consider tapping research or sales personnel. Informal or formal training should be provided for all individuals placed in the role of spokesperson.

Step 2: Develop Key Message Points. After deciding on spokesperson(s), develop the key strategic message points to be mentioned in any interview. These points are the invisible outline the spokesperson(s) will follow in an interview. A spokesperson may add to or subtract from the points or add personal anecdotes to help illustrate them based on the time he or she has available. The spokesperson(s) should be supplied with a list of key points and other background information. It is important for the spokesperson(s) to know what has previously been shared with the media before they meet journalists face-to-face so they are well-prepared.

Step 3: Prepare Spokesperson(s) for Interviews. Know the message. It is important to determine what should be said to reporters and relayed to the public before your spokesperson appears in an interview. Even the most intelligent and articulate spokesperson can make a stronger impression if he or she comes across as dynamic and positive, and speaks with conviction.

General Tips for Interviewing

It almost goes without saying—prepare in advance. For example, if the situation involves television, watch the program on which the spokesperson will appear, taking special note of the anchor's or reporter's interviewing style.

Remember, interviews are granted, and neither the CVB nor any other organization is obligated to grant them.

Understand the audience. Tailor the remarks for the audience involved. But remember that with the increase in news-based Web sites, interviews can reach a much broader, even global audience.

Determine what the interviewer is ultimately looking to report. It is not appropriate to expect him or her to reveal specific questions in advance, but try to find out what the general topics or themes will be before the interview takes place.

Plan for the worst. Imagine the most embarrassing, difficult question to answer, then rehearse exactly how to respond, being careful to incorporate at least one of the key points in the response.

Find out where the interview will be held, either at the studio or on location. This not only involves planning travel time, but also can offer an opportunity to suggest an alternative location better suited to delivering the CVB's message.

Set a specific amount of time—such as fifteen minutes—for the interview. This allows the interview to be ended if it is not going well without seeming hostile or awkward.

Find out if other guests will be on hand (for example, a consumer advocate or a competitor's spokesperson). This will provide a better indication of the focus of the interview. During the interview, avoid arguing with any of the guests. The CVB's spokesperson should present key points in a calm, authoritative manner, no matter what happens.

At the outset, confirm whether to look at the camera, reporter, or another location during the interview.

Determine appropriate dress for the interview, taking into consideration the interview's location. Also, provide in advance the correct spelling of the spokesperson's name and title.

Tell the spokesperson to speak in clear, simple, conversational English. Do not lapse into tourism industry jargon.

For broadcast, keep answers to no more than fifteen seconds; ten to twelve is even better. Practice timing answers to develop a sense for this length of time. Also remember that it is not a spokesperson's responsibility to fill "dead air." In other words, do not ramble.

Be positive and upbeat, smile, and remember that the spokesperson is in control of the responses and is the expert. The real audience is the viewer or reader, not the interviewer.

Television Interviews

When on television, total appearance is what counts the most. Some experts believe that a message on television is ten percent words, thirty percent voice, and sixty percent nonverbal communication. A person's appearance and body language could spell the difference between success and failure.

Wear comfortable clothes and preferably solid colors, but avoid wearing shirts or blouses that are bright white, which may reflect glare, or that have busy patterns or designs that might appear to vibrate on the air and distract viewers' attention. Do not wear flashy ties or jewelry, and avoid dangling jewelry that might reflect light or make noise. Also, do not wear glasses unless the interviewer cannot be seen without squinting. Keep in mind that contacts may start to dry out from the hot lights.

Wear makeup. Most stations usually do not provide it, unless the interview is in a studio.

Make sure the set is comfortable. Be especially attentive to the microphone and chair. If it's a swivel chair, ask the stagehands to lock it to avoid possibly swaying in it during the interview.

Speak in sound bites.

Remember to maintain good posture and avoid unnecessary gestures. Sit erect, with legs crossed and arms folded in your lap or comfortably resting on the arms of the chair. Hold your head still instead of nodding while the interviewer is asking a question.

Keep in mind approximately how much time is left during the interview to make sure all the key points are covered.

Radio Interviews

As in television appearances, the voice counts in the delivery of the message. The person being interviewed should sound upbeat, believable, and interesting. Radio audiences often differ from television audiences, with certain formats or programs attracting very specific listeners—teenagers, older adults, minorities, and so forth. Some radio shows, such as call-in programs, involve direct interaction with the audience, which calls for a spokesperson who knows the information without hesitation and can provide impromptu answers.

Telephone Interviews

Print and radio reporters are the most likely media personnel to request a phone interview because it saves time and the reporter can directly enter key points into the computer while the interviewee is talking. When speaking with reporters on the phone, make sure the phone connection is clear and of high quality, especially if the interview is for a radio broadcast. If the connection is bad, arrange to hang up and agree on a call-back time and system. Using a phone's speaker or hands-free feature is fine for print interviews. However, using a speakerphone is not recommended for radio interviews because it distorts audio quality.

Silence other sources of noise in the room from which the interview is being conducted; forward all calls and close the office door. Talk into the receiver in normal, conversational tones.

Know in advance whether the interview is going to be live or taped, and if taped, whether it is to be edited. If it is going to be edited, consider answering in short sound bites—snappy answers between ten and twenty seconds long.

Print Interviews

Prepare for newspaper and magazine interviews in the same fashion as broadcast interviews, and remember that print interviews are often heavily edited. An exception is articles that reprint conversations with a reporter word for word.

If there is a controversy or the CVB has had issues with the reporter, tape the interview in case questions arise about quotes or information used in the printed story. Also, do not be facetious and do not joke, which can give the impression of arrogance or dishonesty.

When in doubt about a fact or when more time is needed for a response, tell the reporter that the information will be obtained and provided shortly.

Online Interviews

Some reporters have started e-mailing questions or chatting in real-time via computer instant messaging or non-delayed communications for an interview. Although this method appears to be more relaxed and informal, the communications team should prepare as diligently for this type of interview as for any other. Because of the medium, be ready for the story to appear immediately as opposed to having time to discuss the results with key constituents.

Tips for Handling Media Questions ————————————

Although the communications team may proactively seek coverage of the organization, CVBs are often asked to answer questions posed by reporters, sometimes at a moment's notice. Always take the opportunity, when getting a call from a reporter, to strengthen the position of the organization as a resource. Keep the following tips in mind when a reporter calls:

- Be responsive. Take the call promptly and provide what information is available. Reporters are often on deadline and need immediate access to information and quotes to finish a story.

- Assume everything that is said will be captured in print or on tape. Ask the writer to clarify the objective of the story before answering questions.

- Offer the writer a bio of the spokesperson with correct spelling of name, title, and responsibilities, if appropriate.

- Avoid industry jargon. An articulate, clear response probably will be quoted.

- Localize the response. Tie answers to other local, statewide, or national newsworthy subjects or events. Tailor the message to an interesting current trend, or otherwise provide a "hook."

- Offer to arrange interviews with people affected by the story.

- Offer the CVB office or the visitors information center as a visual backdrop if it is in a convenient location.

- Provide a local expert who can comment on breaking national stories.

- Provide contact names and phone numbers for added insight or further questions.

- Make good on promises; get follow-up information to reporters before deadline.

- Provide visuals in formats requested by media outlets.

- Anticipate reporters' needs.

If a reporter begins to challenge you or probe for sensitive information, here are some techniques to help maintain control:

- Place the key points at the beginning of each response.

- Do not argue against a reporter's point of view. Rather, state the response positively without repeating the argument or mentioning competitors at all.

- If the reporter asks a question to which the CVB does not want to provide a response, handle it with honesty. Do not feel compelled to give out confidential information. Simply explain that such information is proprietary or confidential.

- The reporter may ask the same question multiple times in multiple ways—stick to the original answer.

- Do not answer hypothetical questions or speculate. Avoid guesswork and answer the reporter with something to the effect of, "That is a hypothetical question, so it is impossible to know what the outcome might be. But let me tell you exactly what did happen when we..."

- Avoid negatives. Do not answer with "No, we don't think..." Rather, say "We are developing an innovative program to..." Approach each question in a positive way.

- Do not let the reporter put words in your mouth. If a question is worded in a way that is negative to the organization, do not repeat it in the response, even to deny it. For example, if a reporter asks questions about the reason he or she thinks the area hotels are looking deserted, do not respond with "I wouldn't want to use the word 'deserted.'" Instead, say, "We believe the industry is on the upswing because of..."

- Use anecdotes to dramatize or illustrate key points.

- Be relaxed and candid. Spokespersons typically know more about the subject than the person asking the questions because they were selected due to their expertise. For this reason, use responses that the organization wants to convey instead of letting a journalist force or influence an answer.

- Be brief. Simple facts stated succinctly are best. Providing complicated answers increases the chance of a spokesperson being misquoted or the information being taken out of context.

- Credibility is crucial. Always provide accurate, factual answers.

Nonmedia Communications

Member Communications

In member-based CVBs, keeping the members informed about the organization's programs and providing updates on the destination are benefits of belonging to or supporting the CVB. The best communications plan includes multiple touch points through a wide variety of outlets. When developing such a plan, conduct a communications audit to identify ongoing and special communications. Once the audit is complete, create a calendar that includes type of communication, date distributed, and topics in a succinct format for use within the organization. As a part of the communications plan, determine which aspects will be delivered via traditional mail and which via e-mail. When dealing with electronic communications, remember to account for various formats and the members' capabilities to receive messages. In addition to communication, providing a full-service, well-rounded program is important to maintaining a healthy relationship with the members. Although timing and the needs of each CVB will determine the tactics, below are some factors to consider.

Networking events provide opportunities for member-to-member communication for the sole purpose of exchanging business ideas and networking. Educational events, on the other hand, whether during breakfast, a luncheon, or a seminar, provide opportunities for members to broaden their skills or learn about a new direction the CVB may be taking.

For the CVB's annual meeting, determine the necessary events of the meeting, such as installation of officers, then establish a theme that can be carried on each year—for example, celebrating successes, customer service, or elevating business.

Another intraorganizational communication tool is a periodic printed or electronic newsletter that provides research updates, new conventions booked, results of programs, introduction or updates on CVB initiatives, and the latest on community issues.

Create a standard format across the organization to provide leads for convention and tourism business, as well as for requesting information for journalists, for press releases, or to sign up for programs. Offer to customize the leads each member would like to receive. Regarding special alerts, develop a format for sending out breaking news or requesting the local tourism industry to act on an issue on short notice.

Finally, provide a scheduled time that new members or new employees of existing members can learn about CVB operations and how they may most benefit by working with the organization. An extension of this would be to provide specialized orientations for areas such as convention services, research, or travel industry marketing.

Internal Communications

Employees make a CVB successful. They are the assets of the organization and help build the image of the destination. It is as important to communicate with internal staff as it is with members, consumers, meeting planners, or travel agents. Regardless of the type of information—new campaigns, CVB issues, or destination updates—the employees should be first to know details of the programs. The goal of an internal communications plan should be that CVB employees are never surprised by a story in the media, asked a question from a client that they have not been advised how to handle, or made to feel that they are the last to know.

There are really two facets to internal communications. The first regards programs being rolled out in the marketplace or issues in the community. The second involves CVB policies. Due to the complexity of CVBs, often the two are intertwined. As plans are developed and timelines established for new programs or policies, building communication within the CVB is crucial. This can be as simple as an e-mail announcing the program, a memo from the president or appropriate management staff member, an all-staff briefing, or introducing the information via departmental meeting. If a major program is being launched, make sure it is clear when the information can be released outside the organization. As a follow-up to a program introduction, take time to e-mail any media coverage or post it in a central location such as a break room or on a CVB intranet.

Encourage employees to use existing tools for updates that are being distributed outside the organization in addition to tools created especially for them. A few ideas include distributing all news releases internally, copying employees on e-newsletters to meeting planners and travel agents, encouraging them to read member newsletters, and giving everyone in the organization a copy of new CVB publications when available. Also, all CVB staff, including new hires, should know the organization's policy on how news media inquiries will be handled. The most succinct method is to require that all media calls be directed to the communications department. This allows the department to schedule a time, brief the spokesperson, pull background information, and ensure that the information is accurate.

Stakeholder Communications

Within any destination, there resides a group of companies or people with close ties to the organization. These may be the political leaders who determine funding, key businesses that support the CVB, or leaders of sister organizations such as chambers of commerce, economic development commissions, and hotel/motel associations—all of whom the CVB relies on or partners with to ensure success. Stakeholders vary within each community, but inclusion in the group should be defined by funding issues, value to the industry, third-party endorsers, and destination partners. Educating stakeholders about the value of the tourism industry and the work the CVB does is a never-ending task.

The most important aspect of stakeholder communications is proactively cultivating important relationships. First, develop a list of the CVB's stakeholders, then determine the best way to reach them. It may be that one-on-one briefings are the optimal way to start a relationship. Follow up by inviting them to CVB events, sending regular correspondence by mail or e-mail, adding them to the member newsletter list, or getting involved in their business or civic endeavors. A key opportunity among this group is to position the CVB as a resource on tourism issues, as well as the channel to reach the local tourism industry. Often, non-hospitality businesses do not know how to reach the tourism industry, and the CVB can establish a critical connection to those key groups with very little resource allocation.

As a part of the CVB organization, the board of directors is at the forefront when it comes to communications. One of the goals of putting together the CVB's board should be to reach out to traditional and non-traditional tourism businesses. This mixture gives the CVB a much broader perspective and the ability to reach industries it may not have had access to without a representative on the board. Having a diverse board also assists in communicating the value of the CVB internally and externally.

For the board to be an ally and a champion for the CVB, it must be well-informed. The board should be alerted immediately of any issues, stories, or broadcasts that may occur involving a controversial issue. In addition, board members need to be well-armed with information to tell the CVB story. Communicating with the board can take many forms. At the beginning of the year or term, set aside time for an orientation on board members' role in the organization, the role of the CVB in the industry and the community, and any challenges or issues the CVB or tourism industry is facing. To better prepare them, provide position statements, talking points, or question-and-answer sheets on complex or controversial issues. Also, supply regular updates on the progress of the organization during board meetings or through regular highlight reports to the board or by e-blasts.

A convention and visitors bureau is no longer the effective, but occasionally insular, organization quietly going aboutitsbusinessoffillingbedswithheads. Instead, the contemporary CVB can act much like a private corporation, with a keen awareness that success depends upon perception shaping and image building. Positive images are not only directed toward potential visitors, but also toward potential partners and sponsors, as well as toward the local community upon which the organization depends for support. The contemporary CVB must be as communications savvy as it is technologically adept, because ultimately it is the message that is received, rather than the medium. Y et communications has also become highly technical with sophisticated database maintenance and satellite media tours.

At the heart of communications, however, is a clear, consistent message about the CVB's goals, objectives, and accomplishments. T his message is conveyed through a good communications plan, news releases, press trips, and interviews.

In addition, good communications is crucial in times of crisis, acting as a link between partners such as lodging facilities and airlines and the public. In the future, communications should assume an even more important place among the CVBs functions as the world becomes smaller, the number of media outlets increases, and CVBs continue to produce knowledge and information that is economically important locally, nationally, and internationally.

Endnotes

1. Courtesy of Public Relations Society of America.

Appendix

Case Study in Crisis Management: Management Lessons Learned from 9/11 and Its Aftermath

By *William A. Hanbury*

*William A. **Hanbury** is president and CEO of the Washington, D.C., Convention and Tourism Corporation. WCTC is the metro area's primary marketing organization and is responsible for the economic health of a $10 billion hospitality industry employing 260,000 individuals. Hanbury also serves as the president of the American Experience Foundation, a not-for-profit organization advancing arts, culture and history in the nation's capital. Hanbury holds a master's degree in public administration from Harvard University and a bachelor of arts from Wilkes University.*

I sat in a major traffic jam on Route 395 in southwest Washington, D.C., and the entire western horizon was consumed in smoke. Since I was following the live radio coverage of the World Trade Center Towers disaster, it was obvious the nation's capital was now also under attack. I was caught in a mass exodus of workers attempting to use the Metro system and city's highways as the media reported another plane was about to crash into downtown Washington, D.C. The offices of the Washington, D.C., Convention and Tourism Corporation (WCTC), where I worked three blocks from the White House, were immediately evacuated. All I could think about was getting my children out of their schools and seeking the shelter of my home.

Through the chaos of that day, I eventually retrieved my children from their schools and returned home. Like all Americans, I helplessly watched TV as one of the saddest days in American history unfolded before us. I grieved for the victims and felt sincere admiration for the heroes of 9/11. As reports of the gallantry on Flight 93 began to emerge, I was indebted to the passengers who decided to "let's roll" and take matters into their own hands. In all likelihood, these brave individuals helped prevent further loss of life in Washington that day.

In the first hours of 9/11, I never could have imagined the depths of the economic damage caused by the events of that day and the subsequent business crisis that followed during the fourth quarter of 2001. I also did not realize at the time that our organization would eventually be primarily responsible for dealing with both the tragedy and the business free-fall that evolved.

This is the story of the important management lessons learned from a small group of marketing and communications professionals associated with WCTC and major institutions of the nation's capital. These individuals devised a strategy to initiate a recovery from the most serious economic crisis ever to confront the American hospitality industry. Through a series of marketing and communications initiatives, WCTC returned Washington, D.C., to a new "normal," put people back to work, and restored the capital's image as a premier destination.

It is to be hoped that our experiences will serve as a model for other organizations as they prepare for the next inevitable safety and security emergency. Effective management of these crises can limit widespread negative publicity, thus minimizing the damage to a company's image and revenues.

Not Prepared and Not Properly Staffed

As the new CEO of the WCTC in 2001, I was leading an organization entrusted with maintaining the economic health of the region's largest employer: the travel and tourism industry. This sector of the economy employs more than 200,000 workers and has an area-wide annual financial impact of $9 billion.

At the time of the 9/11 attacks, WCTC was not organizationally prepared to handle even a small crisis, let alone the largest economic crisis in the history of the nation's capital. WCTC had been in existence for less than five months, the result of a merger of two underperforming entities that formerly shared the responsibility of marketing Washington, D.C., as a convention and tourism destination.

We were in the throes of a complete reorganization—from human resources and administrative systems to information technology and communications. Although we had accomplished some personnel changes in the first five months, several key individuals whom I had recruited to the organization had not even arrived, or had just come on board. Dawn Poker, our new executive vice president, had been on the job a total of six days on September 11.

This Ain't No Hurricane

As an initial response to that tragic day, we convened a meeting of our senior staff and key volunteer leadership on the morning of September 12. The Pentagon was still burning. It was obvious the capital city was in for a difficult time and we needed to discuss our response to the events of the previous day. We were unaware then that Washington had already started a dramatic economic decline that would not be completely reversed for almost two full years.

During the meeting, we coordinated a conference call with our newly-hired consultants from Burson-Marstellar's crisis management team. Also on the call was our new vice president of marketing and communications, Victoria Isley, who was not due to begin her job until October 1. She was relocating from Tampa, Florida, and had been responsible for that city's crisis communications during several hurricanes along the gulf coast.

We listened intently to Victoria's expert recommendations about our future communications to the public about traveling to Washington, D.C. At one point, Reba Pittman Walker, executive director of the Washington Hotel Association, reminded everyone, "This ain't no hurricane" and we shouldn't assume we would be responding in a similar manner. The response was that, "While the tragic events may be vastly different, the evaluation steps and processes are the same." Reba's comment eventually became a motto often repeated as our team spent several extraordinary months dealing with what seemed like a never-ending series of improbable and dramatic events.

Our challenges were only beginning with the tragedy of 9/11. Over the next two years, the capital's economy and the WCTC management team dealt with the economic aftermath of 9/11, anthrax incidents, increased threat levels, a major national recession, war in Afghanistan and Iraq, snipers, the snowstorm of the century, SARS, and in the end—yes, even a hurricane!

With a true sense of esprit de corps, several individuals built a strong collaboration of both public- and private-sector partners, which was unrivaled by any previous civic cooperative venture. In a community known for its lack of collegiality, they found the financial and in-kind partners necessary to eventually deliver a strong and convincing message that Washington was a welcoming, safe, and accommodating city. In addition, the lessons learned by the management group were extremely beneficial in the post-9/11 environment as the nation's capital faced one crisis after another throughout 2002 and 2003.

Rocked to the Economic Core

Washington, D.C., and New York City were rocked to the economic core by the events of 9/11. Although the human and physical damage was much worse in New York, Washington was strapped with an economic decline deeper and longer than that of New York City. The White House, the Capitol, and Reagan National Airport were all shut down. The situation was further exacerbated by the bio-terrorism scare from anthrax that erupted in October 2001. On a nightly basis, the White House and Bush administration officials complicated matters by proclaiming Washington as the "number one terrorism target" in the world. The traveling public responded by eliminating the nation's capital as a preferred convention and tourism destination.

In the weeks immediately following 9/11, the economic damage was staggering:

- Reagan National Airport remained closed and 10,000 workers were idled as the Secret Service and federal authorities assessed the danger of continuing flights in close proximity to the White House and the Capitol. Even when the airport reopened, its "lift" capacity was only at twenty-four percent three months after 9/11.

- Metro hotels, which normally enjoy annual occupancy rates of eighty percent in September and October, were running below thirty percent. These rates continued throughout the fourth quarter of 2001.

- Area restaurants experienced major layoffs and a dramatic downturn in revenues—more than fifty percent in some cases.

- More than 17,000 restaurant and hotel workers were either out of work or were having their hours severely curtailed.

- The esteemed institutions of the Smithsonian experienced record-low attendance. Visitation plummeted fifty percent below normal for the fourth quarter of 2001 and the first quarter of 2002.

- Hundreds of conferences, seminars, and tour programs were canceled by associations, school districts, and travel companies.

- Federal agencies stopped convening conferences and training activities in the region, and even congressional staffers were urging constituents not to travel to the capital.

- The hospitality industry was losing more than $10 million a day, a trend that lasted for more than one hundred days with a total economic loss of $1 billion to the region's economy.

Setting the Rules for Crisis Management

From our first meeting after 9/11, our management team established several operating mandates that we adhered to throughout months of adversity.

First and foremost, we all considered establishing these mandates very serious business. As soldiers carried automatic weapons and streets remained closed around the White House and Capitol, we had a sense of urgency that was not defined by the clock. With so much at stake economically, team members did not have to be convinced to work long hours and remain focused on the task at hand. In fact, there were times in the first weeks after 9/11 when I demanded that exhausted staff members go home and rest.

We typically worked whatever amount of hours it would take to accomplish pressing tasks. Eighteen-hour days were common. With the bottom dropping out of the hospitality economy and with the global media pronouncing Washington as "shut down," we had to balance messages of safety with messages of reality, and let the world know we were open for business. In the first few weeks after 9/11, we were receiving up to twenty media inquiries per day, all with a negative angle. We weren't thinking about placing positive stories; rather, it was a full-time job for our staff and Burson-Marstellar just to refute misinformation concerning safety, access, and security in the capital city.

As history shows, our medical, law enforcement, and military "first responders" provided extraordinary service following the attack on the Pentagon. However, the business and political communities were slow to respond as the region's economy began to unravel. With empty hotel rooms and deserted restaurants throughout the metropolitan area, it became almost mandatory for the WCTC to lead the economic recovery. We considered ourselves to be "economic responders"—those individuals on whom the community was relying to lead the post-9/11 business recovery.

WCTC wanted to make sure the entire community was issuing coordinated, accurate responses to all media inquiries and a defined approach to outgoing communications. We recruited District of Columbia government officials, the hotel and restaurant associations, the Board of Trade, the Greater Washington Initiative, area chambers of commerce, and regional economic development agencies to partner with us in this initiative almost immediately after 9/11. Eventually, all these organizations presented a coordinated approach to the economic recovery efforts, including the reopening of Reagan National Airport, and future marketing/communications initiatives. This collaborative spirit continued as the region dealt with other emergencies throughout 2002 and 2003.

Implementing a Tactical Plan

Within forty-eight hours after the World Trade Center Towers and the Pentagon were attacked, we had at least six people working full time on our response. In the first few days, I am not certain if we accomplished anything significant, but at least we were doing something. WCTC was actively engaged, and this provided an encouraging sign to our business community and political constituents. Some of the tactical steps we initially took included:

- WCTC immediately set up a hotline for stranded travelers, uneasy meeting planners, and tourism group leaders. With the airport shut down, several thousand travelers were stranded in D.C., and we provided them with hotel referrals and information updates.

- Our newly-designed Web site instantly became a valuable tool, providing travel and security information updated on an hourly basis.

- Within twenty-four hours of the attack, we used a recently-created stakeholders' e-mail list to send daily updates. This also proved a valuable tool and a new method of communication to stakeholders, civic leaders, and clients as the crisis continued. In fact, this stakeholders' e-mail list saw service repeatedly as D.C. dealt with crisis after crisis throughout 2002 and 2003.

- WCTC and its partners worked with the Pentagon Victim Assistance Center to supply food for on-site rescue workers and complimentary accommodations for immediate family members suffering losses in the terrorism attacks.

- We led the development of a community task force, in close cooperation with Washington Mayor Anthony A. Williams, which included a wide range of civic, business, labor, and political leaders. The members divided into working groups and eventually achieved substantive results.

- Along with other regional business groups, WCTC rallied the business community to get Reagan National Airport reopened. The closure had an immediate and severe economic impact on the entire region's economy. Reopening Reagan, which serves sixteen million passengers annually, became an economic and symbolic necessity. The public perception of D.C. as unsafe and "closed for business" continued until the airport was again operational. In fact, the reopening of the airport was an important step in restoring the entire nation's faith in flying.

- In an effort to mitigate the cancellations of conventions and tour groups, we called hundreds of clients in the first two weeks after 9/11. Even Mayor Williams participated as we attempted to dispel misinformation and assure meeting planners and group leaders that the capital was safe and open for business. As a result of this effort, only one major citywide convention center–based piece of business was canceled.

- Burson-Marstellar, in close cooperation with WCTC's communications department, was most helpful as it managed our public relations initiatives and the refuting of misinformation. We eventually developed a series of positive stories and met with editorial boards as our communications initiatives expanded.

- WCTC initiated ongoing communications to the Congress and 180 foreign embassies, urging members to reduce negative messages to their constituents and encourage travel to the capital.

- WCTC, in conjunction with the mayor, met three different times with White House staff members about the economic effects of the crisis on the city. We encouraged the White House to deliver positive messages about travel to the capital and to reopen key tourism assets, thus eliminating the perception that Washington was a closed city. Also, we requested that the White House support us by encouraging federal government conferences and meetings in the capital region, minimizing disturbances to local commerce by street and building closures, and toning down other highly visible security measures.

- WCTC worked with school and educational groups to lift field trip restrictions placed on the nation's capital. Eventually, WCTC worked with First Lady Laura Bush on a major media event welcoming out-of-town school groups to the reopened White House. This step was crucial to reconnect Washington to the commercially important and symbolic student and youth travel market.

- Because the downturn of the travel economy was such a compelling topic in the fourth quarter of 2001, we took advantage of a series of speaking and media opportunities. From CNN to travel industry venues, there were ample national forums to articulate our story.

- We also took advantage of a series of free advertisements offered by convention and tourism industry publications.

The "Come. Be Inspired" Marketing Campaign

Following 9/11, the news media constantly conveyed the powerful image of a burning Pentagon. At every turn, it seemed the nation's capital was under siege and at the center of a dramatic and challenging international crisis. Throughout the fourth quarter of 2001 and the first quarter of 2002, a series of bio-terrorism events and frequent warnings of terrorism allowed the media to continue to project an image that Washington was unsafe for travel.

WCTC management felt that only when these negative images subsided could we turn all this destructive attention into a positive thing. For most Americans, Washington's familiar national landmarks and institutions carried an inspiring message. No other American city evokes a stronger sense of patriotism than does Washington, D.C.

Our marketing team worked in conjunction with our advertising agency, Eisner Communications, to develop an innovative marketing plan titled: "Come. Be Inspired." It was targeted to Americans who were looking for ways to show their patriotism. The campaign was designed to inspire citizens to visit the famous sites and institutions that best symbolize freedom and democracy in a time when those concepts were under assault. However, our path to fully implementing this marketing plan had many obstacles.

For one, Washington was immediately compared to New York City. Within ten days after 9/11, New York was aggressively on the TV airways with a huge media campaign encouraging travel there. The Big Apple would eventually spend more than $25 million in public dollars on this campaign. We didn't have access to large public-funding resources. Instead, we were required to raise financial and in-kind resources from a wide range of public and private sources.

During this time, WCTC was highly criticized for not launching our recovery advertising campaign as soon as possible. However, we were determined not to spend any money until the American public was more receptive to an invitition to visit Washington and the rhetoric from federal officials toned down.

We closely monitored polling data and followed the good intuition of our marketing team before launching our advertising campaign well into the first quarter of 2002. This aspect of the campaign required enormous discipline on the part of WCTC. Had the national campaign been launched with full force in October, much of the investment would have been wasted. There were still too many negative messages being communicated by the federal government and in the aftermath of the bio-terrorism attacks. Instead, we initiated the advertising campaign in late February 2002 as America was beginning to travel again and the terrorism threat level was diminishing. The campaign played the defining role in returning Washington, D.C., to near normal business levels by the late spring of 2002.

We raised or received in-kind marketing support of approximately $10 million for this effort. Significant support came in the form of television public service announcements, but the campaign also encompassed a full range of marketing activities: newspaper, Internet, direct mail, public relations, niche marketing, and promotional activities.

The "Come. Be Inspired." marketing campaign was developed to rebuild visitation to our key artistic, cultural, civic, and historic institutions and thus positively affecting regional hotels, restaurants, retail outlets, and travel service companies. The campaign was broadly divided into two segments.

Phase I—Be a Tourist in Your Home Town. Phase I was a locally focused campaign in metro D.C., which we defined as north of Richmond and south of Baltimore. Because our airport was closed and people had not resumed air travel, we attempted to draw people from more local markets. This program began in early October and lasted through December 2001.

WCTC and its partners wanted to find a way for people who called the capital region "home" to experience the city's inspiration firsthand. We wanted Virginia and Maryland residents to visit and entitled the promotion: "Be A Tourist In Your Home Town." This initiative was launched in October, less than five weeks after the initial terrorism attacks and just prior to the anthrax scare. The Washington Metropolitan Transit Authority provided free passes to visitors. Restaurants, hotels, and attractions offered special promotions as added value for local residents to rediscover the arts, culture, monuments, and spirit of the nation's capital. This program gained very extensive regional and national publicity and got people comfortable with returning to our key tourism assets.

Another promotion during Phase I was "Washington Restaurant Week," an idea we borrowed from New York City. This program was intended to attract regional citizens back to D.C. restaurants by providing substantial discounts on top-notch restaurant offerings. More than seventy restaurants participated in the event, which was deemed a huge success—increasing restaurant revenues from fifty to two hundred percent.

Phase II—Come. Be Inspired. In February 2002, WCTC launched the regional and national phase of the "Come. Be Inspired." campaign. It had a major television component using the cast of "The West Wing" television show and Mayor Anthony A. Williams as talent. These ads were both purchased and given free airtime by the NBC network in a public service announcement format. Warner Brothers Studios generously provided the creative and production expertise at no cost.

In addition, the campaign extensively used newspapers, magazines, direct mail, public relations, and Internet-based educational activities.

The campaign's primary message was to remind American citizens and international visitors that Washington's artistic, cultural, and historic institutions were open for business. Citizens and international visitors could return to the nation's capital to best display their patriotism and love for democracy.

As a continuation of the TV campaign, we produced another commercial later in the spring of 2002 that was also well-received. For this ad, EUE Screen Gems donated a huge portion of the creative and production costs to produce a very effective ad featuring notable celebrities, political leaders, and First Lady Laura Bush. Also, the major networks provided significant advertising placement time at no cost to WCTC, and the ad received extensive play throughout the nation.

In the end, the campaign was considered a success. Hotel and restaurant revenues returned to near normal levels by summer 2002. The Smithsonian and other tourism demand generators saw substantive upturns in attendance. Student and youth travel began to return to the capital. The community as a whole felt that there was an acceptable level of economic recovery by the fall of 2002.

Lessons Learned for the Next Inevitable Crisis

Terrorism and natural crises have been, and will continue to be, a threat to the normal operations of businesses worldwide. These low-probability, but high-impact, events can disrupt operations and cause significant financial losses. Managing crises caused by these events requires thoughtful coordination of all stakeholders and sophisticated recovery plans.

In early 2002, as other crises emerged for the nation's capital, the WCTC expended significant organizational resources to write and put into practice a Crisis Management Plan. The plan has been used repeatedly since it was written and updated several times as additional best practices were discovered by WCTC.

The crisis plan was specifically designed to adequately prepare the WCTC staff and the Washington community for a crisis or disaster. It allows us to respond in a coordinated fashion to extraordinary working conditions and economic results of an emergency. In the initial stages of a crisis, WCTC's main responsibility is to coordinate and disseminate accurate information to the media, visitors, local businesses, and our civic stakeholders. A secondary responsibility is to assess what role we should play in the economic response to a crisis. This role can change based on the depth and scope of a particular event.

We consider crisis situations to include natural disasters, terrorism attacks, serious crimes, highway closures, outbreaks of communicable or dangerous diseases, political protests, chronic negative media attention, riots, and any other emergency that could harm the region's commerce.

The crisis plan is familiar to every WCTC employee, and each individual has assigned responsibilities under the plan. The plan includes detailed information and instructions in the following areas:

- *WCTC Crisis Response Team*—The team's personnel are deployed depending on the type of crisis and they respond in proportion to the level and severity of the crisis. The crisis plan established internal advisory codes as to the severity of an emergency.

- *WCTC Employee Network*—This establishes a human resource outreach plan to contact all staff to determine their personal needs and capacity to work during a crisis.

- *Industry Info Network*—It establishes a telephone and Internet-based communications network to determine the status of conditions and act as an information resource for businesses, media, civic leaders, and consumers.

- *Evacuation Procedures and "Sheltering in Place"*—This defines evacuation procedures and "sheltering in place," which the WCTC staff is capable of implementing for up to three days.

- *Emergency Communications Access*—This establishes internal phone communication procedures for both cell and land-based lines. In addition, computer and fax technology are addressed in this section of the plan.

The crisis plan is an important physical document (called the "football") that is carried by senior managers when on business travel or when a crisis advisory is issued. It contains extensive task details on how to proceed in a crisis; telephone and electronic contact information; city, federal, and law enforcement contacts; media affairs information; driving instructions to our off-site office location; details on WCTC's evacuation rallying point for employees; details on the Homeland Security Advisory System; and information on actions in the event of a chemical, biological, nuclear, or radiological attack on the nation's capital.

Beyond just having the crisis plan "on the shelf," WCTC actively keeps the plan updated and ready to implement. We take the crisis plan very seriously throughout every level of the organization.

Our crisis plan places significant emphasis on media and message dissemination. Several members of the WCTC staff are media trained and have extensive media experience. Having dealt with a series of crises that received unprecedented news coverage, WCTC considers itself ready to deal with almost every level of media attention.

Our media plan includes prepared statements concerning various potential emergency scenarios. Topics that have been fully vetted and are common knowledge to senior WCTC personnel include elevated threat levels, stranded-visitor procedures, terrorism-generated negative economic impact, accurate travel information, as well as answering questions about safety and security.

The crisis plan has been used repeatedly since its inception. For example, it was of invaluable assistance to the WCTC management initiatives surrounding the sniper attacks in the fall of 2002, a major winter storm, elevated threat levels initiated by the Homeland Security Department, the SARS crisis, and in response to Hurricane Isabel.

Transition to Economic Recovery

When emergency conditions have subsided, it is important for CVB management to move quickly to the recovery process. Lessons WCTC learned as economic responders included three important steps:

- Internal and external communications must be coordinated. Managers must reach out to all of the organization's stakeholders to ensure proper forums for sharing information and providing efficient communication channels. The Internet can play an invaluable role in advocacy and full participation of stakeholders.

- The general public and all clients must be reassured. Managers must practice full information disclosure with the public, the media, and customers. Internet sites should be coordinated and updated with timely and accurate information.

- Recovery marketing and product repositioning cannot be accomplished until these first two steps are well underway. Also, the target audiences need to recover from the initial shock of the crisis. Reallocating or finding new personnel and financial resources will, in all likelihood, be necessary to implement recovery marketing. Normal marketing plan action and traditional funding streams will doubtless prove insufficient.

Concluding Thoughts

This case study provides a framework of key steps in managing response to, and recovering from, a crisis. It is meant only as a template and not an exhaustive checklist of crisis response and recovery efforts. Individual companies and organizations must adopt their own set of procedures in order to have an effective initiative. Familiarity with crisis conditions and training in all aspects of crisis response and recovery will better enable CVB managers to handle future crises. Furthermore, resiliency and a positive, cooperative attitude hasten recovery. No matter how serious the crisis, the damage is reduced and the recovery accelerated when managers are fully prepared and when stakeholders cooperate.

In Washington, D.C., we often discuss the "glory and burden" of marketing the nation's capital. We have the glory of hosting inaugurations, state visits, embassy events, and the full range of federal government activities. But, we also have the responsibility when our nation is in crisis. The 9/11 attacks and the ensuing events best represent this responsibility. It is only prudent for management to be well prepared for the next crisis, not only in Washington, but in any location where terrorism or an emergency is a possibility.

Chapter 6 Outline

CVB Marketing Tactics
    Convention Centers
    CVBs and Headquarter Hotels
    Visitors Information Centers
    Attractions
    Products Created by the CVB
    Packages Combining Products
    Transportation and Accessibility
CVB Product Marketing
    The Product Life Cycle
Community Visioning

Competencies

1. Discuss the four Ps of marketing and explain the ways in which they do and do not apply to CVBs. (p. 111)

2. Describe the unique challenges CVBs face when marketing conventions and hotels. (pp. 112–115)

3. Explain how CVBs can create their own products and how this is beneficial to the destination. (pp. 116–118)

4. Explain the dilemma faced by CVBs marketing the diverse elements of a destination. (pp. 118–119)

5. Describe what happens in each stage of the product life cycle. (p. 119)

6. Explain the importance of community visioning and describe its benefits to a CVB and its destination. (pp. 119–122)

6

Product Development

By *Cole Carley*

Cole Carley is executive director of the Fargo–Moorhead Convention & Visitors Bureau, which promotes the metropolitan destination of Fargo, North Dakota, and Moorhead, Minnesota, and draws funding and governance from both. A former DMAI board member, he helped establish the North Dakota Tourism Alliance Partnership and has served as president of both the Minnesota and North Dakota associations of convention and visitors bureaus. He attended St. John's University where he earned a B.A. degree in English.

IN THE CIVIC SYMPHONY that is a convention and visitors bureau (CVB), participants gather at the request of the conductor. Sometimes they show up, sometimes they leave early, sometimes they play the same notes, and sometimes they play different ones. They have been known to play together in harmony and create inspirational music, but they also can sound discordant and out of tune. This is an uncommon orchestra because, unlike most others, its members do not have to play the selected song or heed the directions and tempo of the conductor unless they desire to do so. It is also unusual in that each of the performers works for another orchestra.

Both consultants and educators dealing with tourism frequently make mention of the "tourism team," in which the CVB is linked with virtually every facet of the community to pursue its mission of marketing that community as a destination. It is a relationship that exemplifies the principles of interdependence, much like members of an orchestra or choir who can only really succeed by counting on each other. To change metaphors, as baseball legend Casey Stengel said, "It's easy to get good players. Getting them to work together, that's the hard part."

CVBs are the facilitators and matchmakers of tourism commerce seeking to unite buyers and sellers in a happy and profitable relationship. The classic "four Ps" of marketing are place, price, product, and promotion. It is generally acknowledged that CVBs have no real control over place, price, or product, and only partial control of promotion. After all, no one reports (in the chain of command sense) to the CVB, and the CVB reports to almost everyone. In fact, the real "four Ps" of CVBs are probably persistence, professionalism, persuasion, and promotion. It is such a curious mix of marketing and politics that the function of CVBs might be described as bowling blindfolded with a group of other people. You throw the ball, you hear it hit some pins, and they tell you how you did.

But, at its heart, a CVB is a marketing organization, and all organizations involved in marketing need products to sell. Ask a real estate company what its most important activity is and the answer may surprise you. You might expect to hear "selling houses," but what you will probably hear is "getting listings."

111

Without their own listings, realtors are just selling other companies' houses, usually at a lower commission rate. The same is true for retailers, as well. Given the choice between buying too much merchandise and too little, they will usually err on the side of having too much inventory. No inventory means no sales.

It is true, too, for tourism. As destination marketing organizations, CVBs are always looking for new things to promote and new ways to promote them. For years, they have spent most of their time, effort, and money on promotion. Increasingly, however, local tourism entities find themselves in a leadership position concerning the creation of tourism products in their communities. This is unusual, of course, because CVBs have little, if any, control over the people and organizations that may ultimately underwrite tourism products and projects. This chapter will examine a partial list of products the contemporary CVB promotes, such as:

- Convention centers

- Headquarter hotels

- Visitors information centers

- Attractions, events, and cultural offerings

- Packages combining products

- Transportation/accessibility

- Services

Naturally, the destination itself is the umbrella product marketed by the CVB, but the destination is composed of the various venues, events, and experiences that it offers.

CVB Marketing Tactics

CVB marketing tactics are many and varied and include online meeting planner guides with links to convention centers and convention hotels, as well as printed versions with photos, floor diagrams, seating capacities, convention center services, and so forth. Meeting planners can also fill in a CVB's online request for proposal (RFP) or submit their own via e-mail. The RFP contains all the information that meeting planners need to communicate to the destination about the event. Other approaches involve sifting through databases of meeting planners and events, making sales calls to meeting planners and association executives, soliciting local residents who may be members of organizations that could meet or compete in their home cities, and working trade shows and expos. Last but not least is advertising in publications targeted to meeting planners and association executives.

Convention Centers

CVBs began by selling meetings. The first recorded instance of convention marketing occurred in Detroit during the last years of the nineteenth century. In 1896, a group of business owners hired a sales representative to go on the road to sell Detroit as a meetings destination. They apparently noticed that an increase in visitors paralleled an increase in revenue.

Convention marketing is usually the largest budget item and point of emphasis for CVBs because, unlike in the leisure segment of tourism, several progress points can be specifically identified and quantified with relative ease. A CVB's activities and their economic impact can be tracked in its number of sales calls, formal presentations, and meeting planner site visits as well as the projected number of rooms booked for a meeting. Recognizing the value of meetings, cities all over the world have invested billions of dollars in meetings infrastructure.

The largest expenditure a community makes for accommodating conventions is the convention center. This is usually a publicly owned facility built to supply a venue for conventions. It ranges from thousands to millions of square feet in size. Convention centers are usually constructed following a feasibility study that illustrates the potential for meetings revenue to the city, as well as methods of funding the construction and maintenance of the facility. CVBs may be asked to participate in—sometimes even lead—the efforts to acquire a convention center. Then, seeking a return on that investment, the destination frequently turns to the CVB to market the convention center along with its other products.

Selling conventions involves several classic sales steps combined with some factors that make the CVB convention sale unique. Four aspects of the selling experience pertain specifically to convention bureaus. First, the CVB sale is usually an educational and promotional process involving an event that is going to occur anyway; not the introduction of a new product that might take money away from other priorities or the bottom line. The meeting will happen; *where* it will happen is the variable, not *if*. The CVB is not, therefore, trying to get the customer to spend more money on a brand new product; it is trying to persuade the customer to move the meeting to a particular location.

Second, if one loses the sale, one can't sell another, possibly smaller or cheaper product, also called a "switchpitch," because there is only one meeting and it is going somewhere. This is a winner-takes-all proposition with the losing players out of the game for another year or longer. One exception to this is that with larger associations, there may be other, smaller meetings of a regional, committee, seminar, or board nature that one conceivably can acquire by having been in on the pitch for the bigger product.

Third, CVBs are constantly searching for new business because they can retain very little. If a convention comes to a city, it will probably move on to another next year, and the CVB will be faced with filling the vacancy the move will create. If, on the other hand, some convention business does stand a good chance of repeating in the community, the hotel that hosted the meeting will probably have its own sales force pursuing its return. Once the CVB sells the business, hotels frequently take over from there and the CVB moves on to pursue new clients. Experienced marketers know that new business takes much more time, effort, and money to create than repeat business.

Fourth, the timeline from the sale itself to "consumption," or hosting the convention, usually is measured in years. Some conventions are scheduled and sold years ahead of time, and CVBs will find themselves bidding for a meeting that will not arrive in the community for three to five years or more. This sometimes means that convention centers and hotels are being booked when ground has not even been broken to build the structures.

Just as there are some aspects particular to convention sales, there are some classic sales elements, too. Prospecting, research, face-to-face pitches, problem-solving, client education, feature and benefit analysis, closing, paperwork, follow-up, and still more follow-up are common to most sales situations, and they are vital here, as well. CVBs also use trade shows, promotional products, printed and electronic meeting planner guides, familiarization tours, advertising, and sponsorship of association activities in their marketing of conventions and convention centers.

CVBs and Headquarter Hotels

In North America, funding for CVBs frequently comes at least in part from a lodging tax; that is, a sales tax on rooms levied by a city and collected by its hotels from their guests. Lodging taxes originated in larger cities and were then adopted by state legislatures, enabling other cities to create this source of funding for tourism marketing. Consequently, hotels have always been CVBs' closest marketing partners. Hotels can also contain their own convention or meeting facilities. One of the first goals of any CVB is to put "heads in beds," or fill hotel rooms by marketing the city and its meeting facilities, events, and attractions. Most hotels have their own sales staffs and most national hotel chains have national and international sales offices throughout the country, if not the world. The function of a hotel's local sales staff is to solicit business within the trade area of the property. The CVB therefore usually starts its marketing efforts outside the local geographic trade area. The CVB's goal is to attract travelers, either individually or in groups, who are not normally inclined to go to that city.

Although they must be careful to be impartial about promoting individual hotels, CVBs will sometimes strongly support efforts to attract hotels to form part of a convention and lodging complex. These hotels will either adjoin or be in short walking distance of the convention center. A successful convention facility must have at least some hotel rooms that are easily accessed by delegates, and convention center hotels are frequently part of the master plan for new or expanded meeting venues in a destination.

For CVBs, the value of successfully marketing overnight stays is twofold. First, increased overnights mean increased lodging tax revenue, and that equals funding perpetuation for the CVB. Second, the real economic value of visitors comes with a stay of one or more nights. People staying overnight necessarily spend more money on food and beverages, shopping, transportation, and other things. People driving in for the day, on average, spend much less. It is no wonder, therefore, that "heads in beds" is the first goal of any CVB.

The CVB must maintain strict impartiality in the promotion of hotels. The perception of favoritism between the CVB and any hotel will erode the relationship and credibility of the CVB with the hotel community. The marketing of hotels is also where the bureau and the lodging property part philosophical company. The CVB is selling a city; the hotel is selling room nights. The CVB *cannot* care where people stay in the destination; the hotel *has to* care. In addition, any property partiality shown by the CVB is not only professional suicide, it borders on illegal, especially where the use of public funds is concerned. One of the first lessons a new CVB employee learns is to promote hotels as a group, not individual properties. Favoritism can be fatal.

Hotel marketing tactics closely resemble those mentioned for convention centers:

- Online hotel/motel guides with complete information about hotels, amenities search engines, links to hotel sites, and links to booking engines

- Hard copy of hotel/motel guides and/or inclusion of same information in the meeting planner guides and visitors guides

- Sales calls

- Trade shows/expos

- Destination packages that combine hotel rooms with other local tourism products

Visitors Information Centers

Experienced marketers understand that the easier they make it for potential customers to do business with them, the more they will sell. Shopping centers and supermarkets have long known that the amount of money spent by a customer is directly proportional to the time spent at the store. CVBs that help "sell" a destination by supplying a wealth of information about its tourism products will want to have at least one, and probably several, points of information dissemination conveniently available to the traveler. Visitors information centers started as little more than additions to rest areas or as small temporary buildings located in parking lots. They have matured into larger facilities that also frequently provide a revenue source for the CVB through sales of souvenir merchandise or event tickets. Increasingly, such centers are also the product of partnerships with private businesses that provide the CVB with space. Many CVBs incorporate an information center into their office location. Doing so can provide convenient information opportunities for the visitor as well as save money by combining office space and staff with public space. The fully functional visitors center will have staff on hand to make suggestions to travelers and sell them on the idea of extending their visit to the destination.

A CVB's marketing tools here might include appropriate multiple signs pointing out visitors centers. This usually involves close relationships with state highway and city street departments. Another is notation of visitors information centers on all maps of the destination. Highway billboards offer opportunities, as do signs, flyers, table tents, or other displays at local hotels, restaurants, retail stores, gas stations, and shopping centers. In today's digital age, there probably will be information on the CVB's Web site regarding visitors information centers in addition to the information found in hardcopy visitors guides.

Attractions

Visitors come to a destination because of its activities or because of a particular event. These are usually referred to as attractions. The dictionary defines attraction as "something that attracts or is intended to attract people by appealing to their desires and tastes." Events or venues of inherent interest to a visitor include museums, amusement parks, zoos, themed restaurants (sometimes called "eatertainment"), festivals, and more recently, places to shop. When marketing attractions, CVBs usually endeavor to illustrate how specific attractions make the destination special using superlatives like first, biggest, newest, oldest, original, and only.

Twenty years ago, not many people believed that shopping was a major activity for visitors. That was before the Mall of America. At its opening in the summer of 1992, the mall's founders boasted that they would attract forty million people, as many visitors as Walt Disney World. They were right, and they did it the first year.

Look at a map of a major theme park and notice how much space is devoted to retail merchandise. People are frequently surprised when they hear that the Hard Rock Cafe makes more money selling shirts than selling sandwiches. Check the proliferation of factory outlet malls and "big box" retailers. It is obvious that the Travel Industry Association of America is correct when it notes that the top activity of visitors to a destination is by far shopping. Places to shop, therefore, must be included near the top of any list of tourism attractions.

In this case, the CVB must present clear, accessible, detailed attractions information on its Web site and in its visitors guide, and there should be links from the CVB Web site to attractions' Web sites. Publication of an attractions guide is a good idea, as are participation in and promotion of a local attractions association. Advertising specific attractions, where affordable and appropriate, furthers marketing goals. Also consider creating destination packages that combine attractions with other local tourism products.

Products Created by the CVB

Great marketing involves creativity somewhere in the mix. Because of competition and demands of the industry and stakeholders, creativity should become second nature to the CVB—for marketing purposes as well as survival. Attractions and tours can sometimes be devised by inventive bureau employees keeping a creative eye on the community and knowing what visitors want. In rural areas, for instance, farms or other outdoor settings may be utilized for agricultural tourism or bird-watching. Creative combinations of elements can lead to interesting tour ideas that can be marketed to tour operators and travel agents. Here are a few examples from the upper Midwest:

- *Europe Without A Passport:* A regional offering of ethnic attractions, festivals, and businesses combined with a captivating story that tied tour elements to their countries, such as a Greek restaurant or a museum housing a Viking ship.

- *The Adventure That Lewis and Clark Missed:* Part of Lewis and Clark's Voyage of Discovery traversed the western section of North Dakota. A CVB in the eastern section of that state assembled a tour of historical attractions to capitalize on the Lewis and Clark promotion.

- *Seeing Stars:* People could view stars at both a local planetarium and a local restored movie theater showing vintage films.

Creativity and cooperation can generate a virtually endless array of interesting ways to combine local attractions, festivals, and even nontraditional elements that can be marketed to individual visitors as well as to the travel trade.

To market in this arena, brainstorm ideas to assemble "virtual products" by combining components and themes. Include these products on the Web site, in the group tour planner, and on the spouse/guest tour list for upcoming conventions. Create interesting brochures or single-sheet flyers to mail, fax, or e-mail to travel trade prospects, and advertise if affordable.

Packages Combining Products

Recently, CVBs have started packaging two or more tourism products in their destinations to increase both the quality of the visitor's experience and the time spent. This is one of the few ways of marketing the destination in which the CVB can control the process and the product by assembling a package of lodging, meals, entertainment, shopping coupons, or whatever works best.

This is occasionally done as a source of revenue, with the CVB acting as a type of travel agent and taking a cut from the price of the package. Other times, it is simply a new way to market the destination. A local travel agent or destination management company may also create the packages as a commissionable product to sell. This idea probably originally came from observing the cruise industry where the guest has a single charge for accommodations, basic food, and some entertainment. Cruising has grown steadily over the past decade, and packaging destination products is modeled after its marketing technique. It can also serve as a unifying factor in the diverse tourism industry.

CVB marketing tactics here might entail advertising in consumer publications or other mass media, putting available packages on an easily accessed section of the CVB Web site, and printing flyers to display at consumer tourism expos and at visitors information centers.

Transportation and Accessibility

In a business that depends on people traveling, ease of getting to a destination is not just a feature, it is a necessity. The perception, let alone reality, of inaccessibility can be a major marketing obstacle in the competitive and perception-sensitive field of tourism. This is especially true of smaller cities where some travelers might associate transportation with horse-drawn carriages, sled dogs, or barnstorming biplanes. If potential visitors do not *think* they can get there by jet or freeway, they may not even check the options. Destinations perceived as rural or remote must emphasize the ease of getting to their city, assuming that it is indeed easily accessed. In addition, airports constitute a significant portion of a city's infrastructure, and usage charges can, in turn, be plowed back into the airport to reinforce the quality of service and the perception of modernity.

Rental car companies, especially the large international brands, are another part of a complete transportation package. They are usually present at most airports with frequent flights and at more locations in larger cities. Include transportation information on the CVB Web site and in the meeting planner guide. If the destination is relatively small, consider emphasizing its accessibility. Put links to air, ground, and rail transportation vendors in the community on the CVB's Web site.

CVB Product Marketing

A CVB's products are things that serve travelers, in whatever form, while they are visiting a destination. Like traditional products, they need to be improved, updated, and supplemented. As mentioned previously, however, CVBs have no real control over most of the products they promote. They are, in this sense, like an advertising agency that is hired to sell a product or service. The agency may give advice on the various aspects of marketing the product, but in the end the products themselves belong to their client(s).

Of course, when an entity such as a CVB has no real control over the products it promotes, the idea of product development becomes problematic, or at least challenging. It is frustrating to be held responsible for the success of something over which one has no control. Accountability without authority is the CVB product marketing dilemma.

Because CVBs have no real money of their own, especially to develop expensive things like attractions or convention centers, they must depend on the rest of the destination to provide the products. They can merely motivate, persuade, cajole, argue, plead, coax, or otherwise prevail upon a community's residents and leaders to create the products that constitute the CVB's wares.

A destination, through its products and the visitors' interactions with them, must ultimately produce the outcome of positive customer experience. Private businesses are in a better position to control the conditions that affect the totality of that experience. The CVB, conversely, must make marketing promises that someone else has to keep. If a destination plan that many stakeholders have helped create exists, there is a mechanism in place to help ensure that the promises are kept.

Corporations collectively spend billions of dollars annually for market research and product development, known as R&D. They use research to help guide their direction, additional research to help develop new product concepts, more research to test the product at various stages of development, even more research to develop tactics for product launch, and still more research to determine the product's success or failure and how to tweak it for continued profitability. The successful business constantly asks itself: What is working? What is not working? What do we do about what is not working?

The CVB, because it does not own the product(s), cannot pursue much of this process. Because it frequently operates with public funds, it must work in the open, unable to take advantage of the succeed-in-public/fail-in-secret luxury that private corporations have in product development. Again, because of lack of ownership, the CVB must depend on people and organizations inside the destination to underwrite the development and assessment of the products.

The Product Life Cycle

The process does not end with successful product/destination development. There must be continuous assessment of the need to update, refurbish, change and enhance the products and their marketing because the public perpetually wants new activities, new options, and new destinations. This leads to what is known as the product life cycle.

The product life cycle consists of four stages: introduction, growth, maturity, and decline. In the introduction phase, awareness of a new product is developed as it is distributed in a limited market. Once the product reaches the growth stage, it is promoted to a wider audience and brand recognition is established. Eventually the product reaches maturity, and market competitors emerge. At this point, firms strive to differentiate their product from others. In the final stage of the cycle, sales decline and the firm must decide whether to keep promoting the product.

Decline, fortunately, is not necessarily inevitable. The product can experience rebirth instead of decline if the company (or in this case, the destination) is able to recreate the product by adding new features or using innovative marketing.

The life cycle theory has been applied to destinations for nearly twenty-five years. It was first described by R.W. Butler in his 1980 article, "The Concept of the Tourist Area Life Cycle of Evaluation and Implications for Management."[1] Las Vegas has recently attempted a rebirth by changing its marketing outlook completely. For several years, the Las Vegas CVB portrayed the city as a family destination with the addition of family attractions so parents would bring their children to the city as a family vacation. More recently, research indicated that this approach needed changing, so the CVB reached back to the initial appeal of the city—sin. During 2003, casinos in Las Vegas added "adult" stage shows, and the marketing slogan became "What happens here, stays here."

Using the life cycle system, products or destinations could endlessly reinvent themselves as long as innovation and marketing funds and ideas are consistently available.

Community Visioning

As we have seen, just as a destination has products, the destination itself *is* a product and must continually, relentlessly reinvent itself. Restaurants add new themes or dishes, hotels add guest amenities, theme parks add rides, attractions add new features, and all of them must remodel and refurbish. Lacking ownership, the CVB must depend on its relationships and networks to convey the necessity of updating existing products or services.

For a moment, consider the destination as a huge theme park resort. Common to both the resort and the destination are certain essentials: entertainment (attractions), lodging, food and drink, retail shops for souvenirs, and customer service centers. But there is also a common infrastructure: roads, paths, parking lots, some transportation, water, waste disposal, electricity, signage, and communications. The advantage for the theme park resort is that its owners can plan meticulously for these elements and their placement. They can also allow space for expansion and growth and ensure that that growth is planned and placed properly. They can make certain that the brand is reinforced again and again as the visitor encounters the various park services because, of course, the theme park resort is targeted toward the single aim of visitor enjoyment that produces revenue for the owners.

A city destination is another matter. While it needs all the above and more, it is still a city with residents as well as visitors, and its "owners" are those residents and their elected officials. The placement and development of services, infrastructure, and other elements must first satisfy the people who pay the taxes that sustain the community. City participation in the creation and maintenance of visitor services and products must also address how those things will serve the resident public. How well a city and its residents reinforce any brand promises made on their behalf will depend on how well the residents understand and appreciate both the brand promises and the economic value that visitors bring. Once again, leadership and communication go to the top of the list of essential CVB abilities.

As a result, more and more CVBs are requesting, imploring, and sometimes demanding to be a part of the process that ultimately produces the elements they must promote. Of course, that assumes that there is a step-by-step process when, in fact, there frequently may be none. Tourism product development can be random and haphazard as independent businesses, special interest groups, and city governments all move ahead on their own, without looking at the whole destination's development from the "30,000-foot level." Some CVBs are going even further and taking the responsibility for organizing the community visioning process.

Community visioning is an exercise in strategic planning that, in this case, centers on a product plan for tourism. Typically, it would bring together representatives from lodging, retail, food and beverage, attractions, city government, civic leadership, the business community, other tourism venues, transportation, and infrastructure. Working with a facilitator or consultant, the group would meet several times to consider such issues as the plan's:

- Long- and short-range implications for the local tourism industry.

- Cataloging of current tourism products and services.

- SWOT analysis.

- Potential tourism products and services.

- Effect on infrastructure.

- Effect on environment.

- Tie-ins to historical and cultural segments.

- Economic effect.

- Social effects for the destination's residents.

- Baselines and methods for measuring success.

As veteran tourism educator Don Anderson puts it, "Essentially, a vision statement is a concise and realistic word picture of a tourism organization or destination at some future time, which determines the overall direction...it is related to a mission statement since a vision is something to seek, while a mission is something to achieve."[2]

The community visioning process can have several beneficial effects. It can raise awareness in the destination about the value of tourism and convert nonparticipants in tourism into allies or partners of the CVB. The process also can lay out a logical, step-by-step plan for achieving greater success as a destination. If such a plan does not already exist, this is a huge outcome.

Through research in the visioning process, the CVB and the community may be able to define or affirm the destination brand. This is more than a brand name; it is a collection of the perceptions customers have toward a product.

The visioning process can demonstrate the value of a CVB's knowledge and contributions to the city's economic well-being and identify potential funding sources for future product development. It also can provide a "place at the table" or basic respect for the CVB in future destination planning, even with elements that may not directly involve tourism.

This effort can provide valuable research about the community and its visitors that the CVB might not have been able to afford on its own, and the CVB may be able to use the outcome as a road map for future marketing plans and budgets.

Whatever the outcome, the result should be a workable plan that is relevant, useful and actually *gets used*. The last thing any city needs are SPLOTS (strategic plans languishing on the shelf).

Following the community visioning process, the destination must act. The community and the CVB must facilitate the plan's metamorphosis from strategy to tactics, from vision to reality. This is also the most difficult phase of the community vision plan. It is easy to dream about great physical or procedural innovations to improve the destination; it is more difficult to make the transition from buy-in to build-in. Ideally, the vision process should have a concluding component that ensures follow-up. Because this may be a multi-year project, there should be interim check points and baselines to determine progress. This is also when the CVB shows its true ability to lead because someone inevitably must lead and be the "keeper of the vision." The leader must be constant and consistent in holding the core values and tactics high for all to see. It is easier to follow people who know where they are going. This is not about dependence or independence, but interdependence—the knowledge that "if we did not have each other, none of us would have much of anything."

This is also a time for the CVB to show that leadership can transcend authority. Although the CVB is not in a position to control development in its destination, it can nevertheless strongly influence development through the use of traits CVBs have always used to accomplish their goals: leadership and communication. Because of those two elements, CVBs have frequently been able to claim a place at the table of destination development and success. Despite the lack of actual power, CVBs worldwide have demonstrated that their willingness to step up and speak up for their stakeholders can put them in positions of perceived power and real influence. This is because CVBs realize that power equals responsibility and that sustained power demands leadership. Exercising leadership in this way is a subtle process that requires political savvy. It involves balancing intention with persuasion, courage with courtesy. Also essential is the ability to communicate clearly, as well as knowledge of the people and organizations with whom one communicates. It is like leading a brass band through a minefield. The timid need not apply.

Leadership must not be confused with management. Management is something one does with things that are under one's control, often involving inanimate elements such as budgets, technology, and physical resources rather than people. Management is a function of efficiency while leadership is a function of effectiveness. Managers direct; leaders beckon. It is best to lead people and manage things.

Finally, all community tourism product development is, incrementally, destination development. Any product in the destination is already or becomes a part of the destination brand and visitors' overall perception of the destination. It is essential that new product development reinforce the destination brand promise that the CVB makes in its marketing efforts. Like an orchestra, tourism in general and CVBs in particular rely on interdependence. Destination marketing and product development are a group experience. One can only harmonize by playing well with others, just as the members of an orchestra or choir can only really succeed by counting on and complementing each other. More sound and a greater variety of music can be performed and enjoyed by the members of an orchestrated organization playing together and with the proper pitch.

Endnotes

1. R.W. Butler, "The Concept of a Tourist Area Cycle of Evolution: Implications for Management of Resources," *Canadian Geographer* 24 (1980): 5–12.

2. Don Anderson, quoted in Destination Marketing Association International, CDME course materials, Purdue University, West Lafayette, Ind., 1997.

Chapter 7 Outline

Statistics on Travelers' Use of the Internet
Situation Analysis for Destination
    Marketing Organizations on the Web:
    The Threat of Disintermediation
Best Practices Adoption
    Analyzing Existing Web Sites
Developing an Interactive Program Strategy:
    Addressing the Web Site
        Developing an Action Plan for
        Web-Site Building
        Planning Design for Online Branding
        Targeting the Customer Online
        Addressing Navigation
Building the Web Site: In-House or
    Outsource
        Choosing Vendors and Technology
        Evaluation Tools
        The Project Management Cycle
        E-CRM Database
        Back-End Database and Content
        Management
The Strategic Internet Marketing Plan
    Writing the Internet Marketing Plan
    Ongoing Online Marketing,
        Communications, and Research
E-Team and Staffing (Strategy and Tactical
    Teams)

Competencies

1. Describe how the Internet has changed the way that travelers obtain travel destination information and services. (pp. 125–126)

2. Identify the threats to destination marketing organizations from online competitors and outline ways in which DMOs can position themselves to reach a greater share of online consumers. (pp. 126–128)

3. Describe features of effective CVB and DMO Web sites, including design, navigation, customer relationship management, search engine compliance, technical considerations, e-commerce, and performance tracking. (pp. 128–136)

4. Explain the factors to be considered when building a successful destination Web site. (pp. 136–138)

5. Describe the pros and cons of working with in-house staff or outsourcing Web design and management tasks to outside agencies. (pp. 138–141)

6. Describe components of a strategic Internet marketing plan, and identify ongoing online marketing, communication, and research tasks necessary to a successful Internet marketing plan. (pp. 141–144)

7. Identify possible new staff positions that could assist a CVB or DMO with managing Internet technologies and programs. (pp. 144–145)

7

Technology

By *Leah Woolford*

Leah Woolford is CEO and founder of USDM.net, which handles Internet marketing and Web technology for DMAI and has more than 150 clients nationwide. Logging nearly a dozen years of experience in Internet strategic planning for business development, online marketing, and technology, she has worked with state tourism offices, CVBs, and other travel industry organizations. A frequent speaker in her field, she has authored several Internet destination marketing articles and publications. She studied visual design, advertising, and mass communications at Stephen F. Austin University and graduated from Texas Academy of Art with a degree in design communications and marketing.

In THIS CHAPTER, readers will learn how Internet technologies have made an impact on the travel and tourism industry and how today's destination management professionals use the resulting innovations in technology, communications, marketing, and consumer behavior.

The Internet is the fastest-growing communication tool ever devised. It took radio broadcasters thirty-eight years to reach an audience of fifty million, television thirteen years, and the Internet just four years. Technology has evolved from simple desktop computers processing and storing information to highly portable computers interacting instantaneously and continuously with a worldwide network of computers to access and share documents, digital images, databases, audio, streaming video, and human experience.

Portability, speed, and consumer expectations have been further enhanced by high-speed access, wireless access, handheld portable access by PDA or phone, location-specific information driven by global positioning satellites, database-driven content and marketing, video streaming, and much more.

In less than ten years, Internet technologies and electronic commerce have dramatically transformed a worldwide marketplace and consumer behavior, creating entirely new business enterprises online and shifting tens of billions of dollars in revenue streams. Nowhere is this more evident than in how travel information and services are delivered to consumers. Travel now accounts for more commerce online than any other industry, including computers, books, and music. According to a July 2004 PhoCusWright, Inc., report, an estimated $52.8 billion was spent online for travel in 2004 compared to $39.4 billion in 2003. These expenditures represent trips booked over the Internet by leisure travelers and business people making their own arrangements. The percentage of travel booked on the Internet continues to rise, and will compose one-third of travel bookings by the end of 2006, compared to 20 percent in 2003 and 15 percent in 2002.

Almost every week, one can find an article in *The Wall Street Journal*, the *New York Times*, or *USA Today* reporting online leisure travel statistics from various surveys conducted by reputable research, travel industry, and marketing organizations (such as the Travel Industry Association of America, Forrester Research, Inc., PhoCusWright, Inc., Jupiter Research, and eMarketer.com). For destination management professionals, the Travel Industry Association of America (TIA) is an excellent resource for research and information about the travel industry. TIA offers numerous research subscription packages and reports, and many CVBs are members of TIA. Its research department's annual report on *Travelers' Use of the Internet* examines current use of the Internet for travel planning and booking among several market segments, and is a very useful tool for destination marketers.

Statistics on Travelers' Use of the Internet

The following statistics are from the TIA 2003 edition of *Travelers' Use of the Internet*, and are reprinted here with permission of TIA.

- As of July 2003, half (54 percent) of 211 million American adults age 18 or older currently use the Internet at home, work/school, or both.

- Most (84 percent) of these 114 million adults who use the Internet indicate they are travelers, meaning they have taken a least one trip of fifty miles or more away from home. This translates to a U.S. market of 95.8 million travelers who use the Internet, or online travelers.

- A majority (67 percent) of these 95.8 million online travelers say they have consulted the Internet to get information on destinations or to check prices or schedules. This translates to 64 million online travel planners, or 30 percent of the U.S. adult population.

- Nearly all online travel planners say that at least one trip was planned online for pleasure, vacation, or personal purposes, and nearly half of those planning trips online say they do most or all of their travel planning on the Internet.

- Of particular note to destination marketers are the most popular types of Web sites used for travel planning. Among the 64 million online travelers, 66 percent use online travel agency sites (such as Expedia, Travelocity, or Priceline), 67 percent use search engines, and 55 percent use destination Web sites.

Clearly, the impact of Internet technologies—from Web sites to e-mails to online searching to e-commerce—on travel consumer behavior and purchasing is enormous and merits a serious shift for CVBs in travel marketing focus, budgets, and strategies.

Situation Analysis for Destination Marketing Organizations on the Web: The Threat of Disintermediation

Disintermediation is essentially "removing the middleman." The term is a popular buzzword describing many Internet-based businesses that use the Web to sell products directly to customers rather than going through traditional retail channels.

Destination marketing organizations (DMOs) are faced with a similar disintermediation threat from an online travel industry that is trying to displace them as the traditional and official DMO.

Although CVBs and other DMOs are strategically positioned in the early stages of the travel planning and buying process and can provide (through their local relationships) current content and detailed information on the destination, new Web sites and often much-better-financed online competitors (online travel agencies such as Expedia and Travelocity) are leveraging their content network and supplier deals to lure travelers to their sites for this same kind of travel planning information and online booking.

The online travel agencies, in particular, have spent tens of million of dollars to build their online brands and drive traffic to their Web sites. They enjoy large traffic and consumer loyalty because they provide robust booking capabilities, great rates, and easy online reservations. However, they often lack the detailed content, such as information on local events and attractions, which the traveler is seeking and which the CVBs and DMOs can deliver.

Hotel Web sites, while also lacking in detailed destination content, now offer the guaranteed lowest price on a room reservation—competing more evenly with the travel agencies to which they once sold their excess inventory at much lower rates only to see their own brand undersold by an online competitor.

Even the meeting-planner segment of the travel industry (the most coveted prospects for CVBs due to their ability to book many rooms or even citywide conventions) are being lured by new online meeting-planner ventures to Web sites to compare venues, "hot dates and hot rates," and no-commission housing services. In addition, the Internet's easy availability of competitive hotel room pricing and booking has caused "delegate attrition." Meeting delegates are booking cheaper rooms online at the meeting or convention hotel instead of through the room inventory blocked out by the meeting sponsors.

DMOs still have strategic advantages, but they must assert their rightful place and position themselves firmly as the official representative for their destination to all market segments. Destinations can do this by taking a leadership role in the technology development and online marketing of the destination through strategic planning and execution. While online travel companies are focused on profitable business models and gaining market share, it is critical that the DMO allocate realistic budgets to meet goals and expectations in this increasingly competitive environment.

To this end, an examination of a DMO's strengths, weaknesses, opportunities, and threats is helpful. Among a DMO's strengths are the following:

1. Travel planning on the Web is already popular with consumers, thus alleviating any challenges or delays from consumer adoption of a new technology.

2. Research shows that many online travel planners visit destination Web sites when planning.

Among its weaknesses:

1. CVBs lack brand awareness among online consumers.

2. Private sector competitors have better marketing budgets than CVBs.

DMOs also have important opportunities:

1. Because they are often established, sanctioned, and funded by city governments and hotel room taxes, DMOs are positioned in a leadership role to provide travel information and maintain the position of the official travel portal for the destination—as the comprehensive, designated, local resource.

2. By taking its rightful place as the official portal site, the DMO can further leverage existing travel partner relationships to raise co-op marketing funds, generate revenue from online bookings and advertising, and provide a platform for travel partners to enhance their own online presence, programs, bookings, and revenues.

The threats to any DMO include:

1. Not acting aggressively enough to meet competitive goals.

2. Reacting to unnecessary "gee-whiz," clever technology items one would like to have, resulting in untrackable budget dollars.

3. Not capturing the Web site visitor.

In all segments, letting any online exposure go untouched is a mistake. The power of suggestion, the motivation of incentives, and the careful evaluation of behaviors increase the prospects of converting a Web site visitor to a room night booked, a package sold, or a user registered.

Best Practices Adoption

The reality of decreased and threatened budgets for DMOs has slowed the adoption of best practices for Web sites and Internet marketing. Yet the need for examining and implementing best practices for both what today's online travel planners and bookers expect and what other competing DMO Web sites are offering continues to grow. DMOs must continually update their own online content and the entire Internet consumer experience and keep up with the expectations for Web site design, navigability, online booking, search engine presence, and more. They also must keep pace with what competing destinations offer online—in terms of content, value, convenience, and consumer-friendly technical ease. The dramatic increase in consumers' use of the Internet for travel planning and booking, combined with the increased responsiveness from online media over more traditional offline media, should compel DMOs to look hard at converting a larger portion of their technology, printing, and traditional media budgets to their online initiatives. Consumer demand, improved efficiencies, and stronger returns are compelling reasons to change long-entrenched DMO budgets and habits.

DMOs must benchmark and set standards of excellence for Internet initiatives. Implementing a best-practices approach to destination Internet marketing can begin with an analysis of the existing CVB or DMO Web site, particularly in relation to other travel Web sites and to contemporary consumer online behavior and expectations.

Analyzing Existing Web Sites

Because of the technical and interactive aspects of a Web site versus a print or broadcast medium, the "look and feel" design of the Web site is not nearly as important as are vital technical aspects. Web sites must have much more than aesthetic appeal.

A thorough Web site analysis from a qualified third party is an absolute must. The analysis should examine design, navigability, customer relationship management (CRM), technical compatibility, search-engine compliance, third-party technologies (hardware, software, applications), e-commerce (online booking and advertising), tracking and reporting, and success metrics.

Some professional Internet marketing companies can provide a routine Web site technical analysis, but CVBs and DMOs may want to consider using the Destination Marketing Association International (DMAI) designated alliance partner for Internet marketing and technology—USDM.net. Its Web site analysis includes CVB industry-specific best practices standards, and it reports on how a bureau's Web site compares to those of other CVBs with a similar market and budget.

Here are some issues, strengths, and weaknesses to consider regarding a CVB Web site.

Design Analysis. The home page and interior pages should be evaluated by a general score concerning the design and layout on a scale of 1 to 10, with 10 being the best. Some highlights of typical strengths of Web site design include:

- Bright, tourism-related colors, and well-chosen branding images.

- Good, strong content on the portal site.

- Navigation bar in a consistent place and easy to identify.

- The information presented in a pleasing format and relatively easy to read.

- Database-driven content with robust search capabilities.

 Weaknesses include:

- Lack of visual call to action. At the most basic level, calls to action tell site visitors what they can accomplish on that page, and encourage them forward in the conversion process. The Web is a personal medium and should provide a visual, emotional tie with consumer.

- The branding of the destination is lost with too many small images instead of a few large, striking branding images.

- The navigation and arrangement of copy are not clearly positioned for call-to-action purchasing. Copy is too long and hard to read.

- The site does not visually sell anything in particular. If one is not familiar with what to do, it is very difficult to plan a trip completely.

- The interior of the site continues to be a portal only. One can easily lose his or her place when the information is displayed exactly the same and the pages have text links within each one.

Navigability. The home page for a CVB or destination Web site is absolutely critical. This is the first impression that brands the destination. By what they see on the page, such as style and imagery, users should immediately have an intuitive response to, sense of, and feeling about the destination. The home page should deliver a compelling reason to visit.

A key element is the navigation bar, which must be user-friendly and provide clear direction to the principal contents of the Web site. When consumers reach key content pages on the Web site, they should find valuable information rather than fluff. Colorful but useless copy will not make consumers return to the Web site. And remember, they also should be encouraged to seek a way to complete a transaction.

The navigation bar, which should be found on every page of the Web site, ought to include buttons or text links that can be clicked to go directly to all pages of the site. Overall, the navigation bar must contain basic descriptive terms to help users find the content they seek. The navigation should first identify the visitor type (leisure traveler, meeting planner, group travel, etc.) followed by sub-navigation for each visitor type section.

Every destination Web site must contain basic categories of information of interest to the travel planner. Graphics can help reinforce the site content. The Web site user should think of a CVB's Web site as the *only* travel source for the destination's information and return to the site repeatedly. Essential information categories include attractions, accommodations, dining, and shopping, as well as itineraries, maps, and driving information. Other key elements include search capabilities that return relevant results and "scanability," or the quality of being quickly read and digested. Long pages that require a lot of scrolling are tedious and alienate site visitors.

In addition, a compelling call to action improves response by helping attract and prompt the reader. "Win a Trip to Atlanta," "Register Here to Receive eNewsletter," and "Book Hotel Rooms Online" are excellent examples of good, strong calls to action that ultimately help close the sale.

Begin with the end in mind. If a DMO Web site offers online booking—and it should—make sure that offer or booking-engine window appears front and center on the home page. Do not bury it inside and make qualified buyers wait or search to do business.

Customer Relationship Management. A relationship is the total of all points of communication and interaction between an organization and its customers and prospects. At the most sophisticated level, customer relationship management (CRM) will provide dynamic content based on the visitor's preferences, geography, and profile information. At the most basic, such a system should facilitate the expected dialogue between the visitor and the Web site; that is, the CRM software should respond correctly and appropriately to the visitor's queries and searches.

Automatic responders to Web site forms reassure the visitor that his or her action was successful, or note that required form fields need to be completed. For example, when the vacation guide request form is filled out online, the respondent should see the message, "Your request for information will be answered in a timely manner. Thank you for your interest in [destination]."

Of course, every such thank-you page presents the opportunity to offer another sign-up prompt, a link to another special page, and a "click here to return" link.

Acknowledging online that a transaction occurred is worthwhile, but e-mailing that acknowledgment is even better. Why? Because clearly and specifically identified and targeted information streamlines CRM. The leisure visitor, meeting planner, tour operator, or media person visiting a destination Web site appreciates the bundling of relevant information in its own convenient section that is clearly labeled and easy to find from the main home page.

Allowing, and prompting, Web site users to "opt" in (exercise the option to give their permission to include them in future e-mails) for information via e-mail is a practical and valuable way to gather information about the Web site user, as well as build the registration database for the Web site. Incorporating the use of forms for e-newsletter subscription on the visitor's guide request sign-up is good, but prompting visitors elsewhere on the Web site works better. For example, on a Web page about area golf courses or restaurants, the Web site content manager might include text that prompts the visitor to register to receive occasional special offers by e-mail.

Displaying a Web site's terms of use and privacy policy should be included as a link on the bottom of every page. Privacy and permission issues gained the weight of federal enforcement when the CAN-SPAM Act became law on January 1, 2004. The legislation mandates new requirements for e-mail practices in an effort to reduce unwanted and unclear e-mails, including clear and specific instructions and function for (1) "opting out" (that is, being removed from the list for future e-mails), (2) valid subject lines and headlines, and (3) a physical address of the sender.

Personalization of the Web site experience enhances customer relationships. This can be as simple as allowing visitors to register their preferences on a form so they can receive an e-newsletter customized to their interests (golf, cultural events, festivals, etc.) or as sophisticated as a database-driven Web site with content and pop-up prompts customized to the preferences of the repeat visitor. Imagine visiting a Web site that greets one with, "Hello Michael. Welcome back! Last time you visited us, you looked at our festivals pages and our golf specials. Click on these links to quickly see updated information. We're glad you're here and hope you register for the free summer family vacation we're offering to special visitors."

Technical Compatibility. An attractive Web site with useful content is not adequate. The site must be programmed so the visitor can easily interact with it to obtain trip-planning information and easily book travel online. Basic technical design flaws can make the best-looking site difficult to use from the consumer's point of view. This section evaluates some of best-practices technical requirements identified in numerous focus groups with leisure online travelers and points out the most common errors designers make that can frustrate the consumer to the extent they leave the Web site.

Among the top requirements, the Web site must be multi-browser friendly, allowing users of AOL, Netscape, or Microsoft's Internet Explorer Web browsers to view the site. Web site users should also be able to successfully submit inquiries to receive additional information via e-mail such as e-newsletter sign-up.

A "Contact Us" link should be found at the bottom of each page. This is extremely important in gathering feedback from consumers, for answering questions about the site and destination, and for expressing opinions.

Another aspect involves search results. A search conducted in top search engines (for example, Google and Yahoo) using popular phrases such as "Attractions" and "Events" should produce relevant results on the DMO's Web site relative to the searches performed. Improvements can be made to incorporate more popular terms.

One of the most common technical problems is printing of information that runs off the edge of the printed page. This can be corrected with proper page programming. The CVB's Calendar of Events is a key area that visitors would print. The use of a print-friendly icon should be added for maximum effectiveness.

In the realm of quality assurance, a bureau should always check for broken links, missing or skewed images, or typos on the Web site.

Concerning screen size, the Web site should fit an 800-by-600 screen resolution without horizontal scrolling. If excessive vertical scrolling is needed for internal detail pages, consider sectioning this data out in a more manageable format.

The presence, ease, and efficiency of the search function should appear on most key areas of the site and not be buried at the page bottom.

In regard to download time, if its Web site does not download in less than fifteen seconds, through a standard phone line, a CVB likely has lost the prospect. Also, allow content to load first so consumers can read while images load.

Search Engine Compliance. Among the 64 million online travelers cited earlier in the TIA survey, 66 percent use online travel agency sites such as Expedia, Travelocity, or Priceline; 67 percent use search engines; and 55 percent use destination Web sites. This one statistic underscores the vital importance to DMOs of search engine compliance and search engine ranking.

Consider the fact that large commercial travel sites were early adopters of Web technology and commerce in the travel category and have spent tens of millions of dollars on their Web sites, their branding, and the driving of traffic to their sites.

Destination Web sites, on the other hand, are typically hosted by CVBs and other DMOs that are late adopters of online commerce, have had modest budgets for Web site development and technology, and continue to have limited online budgets for driving traffic.

The intrinsic nature of their Web site content (often superior to travel sites in level of detail, accuracy, and currency about the destination) has helped destinations maintain a third-place popularity behind travel sites and supplier sites among consumers researching online. Still, search engines are more popular than travel sites for online planning, and thereby offer DMOs a strategic advantage for competing against large, well-financed travel sites that seek to displace them as the destination travel booking source for consumers.

Having the destination Web site of a DMO or CVB get listed and ranked highly (top ten search results) in key search engines is literally worth a fortune in marketing value and should, therefore, be a vital part of the technical requirements, ongoing marketing tactics, and a major portion of the marketing budget.

A Web page's ranking and listing in a search engine is largely determined by the relevance of that page's content to the search term. Search engines get their listings from Web masters who submit pages for inclusion, but most often by sending out automated search mechanisms (called "spiders" because they crawl across the World Wide Web) to go to each Web site, follow every link, and index what they find in the engine's results. These spiders collect and categorize Web page content according to their specific programmed formulas, also called algorithms.

Because search engine ranking is so important and valuable, an entire specialty service of "search engine compliance" has evolved. The phrase refers to those steps taken for Web pages to "be in compliance with the search engine algorithms" that categorize, list, and rank Web page content into their directories. These ranking algorithms vary among search engines and address many points in an effort to provide relevant results to search terms.

Here are a few considerations for search engine compliance from USDM.net's "65-point Checklist" for SEO (search engine optimization, or the editing of a Web page's content and format so it will be compliant with how that search engine examines, scores, and ranks the page) and SEM (search engine marketing, or the purposeful creation of specific Web pages and submission of those pages to search engines for ranking). Regarding obstacles to the search, the Web site should not utilize frames (a feature supported by most modern Web browsers that enables the Web author to divide the browser display area into two or more sections), redirects (a redirect is a page that, once someone accesses it with a web browser, literally redirects that person to a final destination page), or Flash (a tool for creating interactive and animated Web sites) because they hinder the search process for the search engines. Text links or robots (programs used to gather Web pages for indexing), however, can invite or allow the engines to "spider" the site freely.

Web site hierarchy, as the term suggests, helps structure the site. A few sub-folders can enable the search engine to easily read through and index the interior Web pages. Each page name should be named after the most relevant topic of the page.

Another factor to consider—the number and quality of links to the Web site improve indexing of the site in the search engines. Once search engines find specific pages, they will rate them based on certain specific criteria, and each search engine's parameters vary. Key elements such as title tag, keywords in the source code, and descriptions—including execution of keywords appropriately—are critical to success.

Optimizing Web pages for search engine compliance is an entirely new field of marketing specialization. Marketing pages are defined as interior Web pages providing focused information on popular destination topics as referenced by search behavior for the destination—for example, events, attractions, and lodging.

If a person using a search engine enters a destination name and a specific tourism topic such as attractions, for example, he or she should be able to go directly to the page on the destination's Web site that discusses this information. Marketing pages can provide valuable entry points to a CVB's Web site.

Third-Party Technologies. Today's sophisticated Web sites either employ or interface with third-party technologies—hardware, software, or applications not directly owned by the CVB or the Web site visitor, but by a third party who agrees to allow others to license the technology to perform specific needed functions, such as displaying event calendars or maps, booking hotel rooms, or providing searches on the Web site. Whenever one sees those little pop-up screens with a lot of copy and the prompt to click to "I agree…," one is often encountering and agreeing to a third-party technology owner's licensing agreement. Information technology and Web managers need to make sure these third-party technologies are compatible with all other operating systems they are using. Sometimes, special interface programs need to be programmed to allow complete linking across technologies. A programmer must be familiar with all the technologies involved that he or she is attempting to link. This may require an outside programmer hired temporarily on a contract basis.

E-Commerce and Web-Site Advertising. Selling online to visitors to a CVB's or DMO's destination Web site—ranging from air, lodging, and car rentals to vacation packages, attraction tickets, and more—is one kind of e-commerce. Advertising can also be sold to the sponsoring CVB or DMO travel partners and others wishing to reach the Web site's online audience and thereby boost their e-commerce presence on visitor-targeted Web sites.

Many DMOs currently have some form of e-commerce on their Web sites. Some outsource their online hotel bookings to third-party travel sites (and consequently see little or no revenue themselves). Others use outside booking engines with a revenue-sharing program. Some drive their own online package sales. Many combinations are available given so many disparate booking engines.

The goal is to offer the consumer dynamic destination booking that enables Web site visitors to browse, compare, and purchase online, while at the same time supporting the multiple booking channels, most notably those of the destination's local hotel properties, whose bed taxes support most North American CVBs' budgets.

Web site advertising can deliver online revenue streams advantageous to both the CVB and the advertiser. Ads should be deliverable to key pages on a destination Web site with linking, tracking, and reporting of impressions (total number of times ad was displayed), "click-thrus" (total number of times someone "clicked through" from a link to the advertiser's page), and, where possible, conversion to sales. Quarterly reports to advertisers and sponsors help them appreciate the targeted exposure and increased traffic to and sales through their own Web sites. Maximizing advertising and co-op marketing opportunities to travel partners should be a written goal in a CVB's or DMO's strategic Internet marketing plan, and one implemented through tactics on the destination's Web site, in its e-newsletters, and via selected online media campaigns. The secrets to ongoing success are strategic planning, careful tracking, and accurate, regular reporting.

Performance Tracking and Measurement. As a communications and marketing medium, the Internet provides superior tracking and analysis potential because it runs through a network of computers that count every interaction. Every visitor to a destination Web site, every page viewed, every link clicked, every e-mail opened, and every response can be measured, if proper tracking and reporting methods are in place.

For purposes of analyzing Web site traffic, "hits" are no longer the standard measure of site traffic and "page views" are quickly becoming obsolete as HTML Web pages are replaced by database-driven Web content. Tracking unique visitors is still an important metric, but it is just the beginning.

For proper customer relationship management, a destination Web site manager will want to track, in the organization's online database, registered users and their preferences, requests for the visitors guide, and requests for the e-newsletter. Also, tracking people who decline to receive e-mail from your organization has now become mandatory under the federal CAN-SPAM law.

For search engine optimization and maintenance, Web site managers will want to track link popularity, search engine positioning and ranking, and much more.

A CVB's stakeholders, board members, travel partners, and advertisers will be interested in additional e-commerce metrics related to return on investment regarding the Internet marketing budget, online sales in booking channels, and advertising budgets on the Web site. Advertising impressions, "click-thrus," and conversions are important to advertisers. Hotel-booking-engine page views, pricing inquiries, sales, and look-to-book ratios (that is, percentage of how many people looked at a price versus purchased a room reservation) are important to lodging partners.

Many DMAI members have adopted the following best-practices metrics for performance tracking and measurement developed by USDM.net:

- Visitors in "pace report" format by month and year-to-date. This reports data in time frames that allow comparison of month-to-month, quarter-to-quarter, year-to-date, and year-to-year, enabling management to analyze if the pace of the reported visitor activity—such as inquiries, Web site registrations, visitor guide requests, and hotel reservations—is ahead of or behind previous months, quarters, or years.

- Branding impressions in pace report format by month and year-to-date.

- Advertising page impressions per advertiser, per campaign by month and year-to-date.

- Increase in registered users pace reporting by month and year-to-date.

- Increase in special-interest categories of registered users.

- Opt-out rate of all registered-user categories (of interests such as special deals and packages, arts and culture, historical attractions, golf, festivals, and so forth).

- Advertising and sponsorship "click-thru" rate.

- Visitors guide requests by month and year-to-date.

- Destination planning guide requests by month and year-to-date.

- Look-to-book ratios (the number of people viewing reservations divided by the number of people who actually booked, or made, a reservation) for each booking engine (online application that facilitates a booking process) in the booking channel (that section of the Web site that presents all of the booking engines, whether connected to a single hotel, a CVB's database of selected inventory, or other available reservation systems' databases).

- Look-to-book ratios for packages purchased.

- Search engine positioning and ranking.

- Link popularity.

- Online marketing campaign response, conversion, and return-on-investment metrics.

- Raised awareness to the CVB's travel partner Web sites.

To accurately report the many metrics that should be measured month-to-month, quarter-to-quarter, and year-to-year in a travel-industry standard pace report, the links, databases, and even outside vendors such as Internet service providers must be carefully managed to avoid corrupt or incomplete data. When a DMO or CVB contracts with any qualified third party to assess its Web site and Internet program, a comparison of these metrics for its program should be made against other CVBs of similar market size and bureau budget. Also, the assessment should report on all of the technical and marketing issues presented in this chapter.

Developing an Interactive Program Strategy: Addressing the Web Site

Almost as quickly as millions of people have embraced the Internet as a new communications tool, online consumer behavior has continued to evolve in usage patterns and expectations, arguably at a rate faster than many CVB or DMO budgets and resources can adapt to.

High-speed Web access is now the norm, and today's online travel consumer expects a more interactive Web site, no longer being satisfied with yesterday's online brochure.

Today's best-practices DMO is updating its Internet program to become the interactive program consumers want. The difference on the Web site is a change from being an information channel to becoming a deliverable product for the consumer. Electronic customer relationship management (e-CRM) is at the heart of the interactive program. Marketers can bring the consumer to the Web site and programmers can deliver information, but the e-CRM strategists help manage and maximize the consumer experience. Technology assists, but is guided by an interactive plan.

Developing an Action Plan for Web-Site Building

Understanding the potential diverse target market segments—leisure travelers, business travelers, meeting planners, convention attendees, tour operators, and others—enables one to plan for the varied needs and reactions that these audience segments will have. The bottom line goal is some sort of conversion of Web site visitors to registered users, booked accommodations guests, requests for proposals, or media inquiries.

The action plan should determine the desires and expectations of the various destination Web site visitors. If the DMO does not know what those are, it should ask its Web site visitors. For firmer information, ask them again later in focus groups when presenting the first draft of the proposed Web site for the visitor's review and comments.

Once a CVB determines the desires and expectations of its audiences, it can implement a plan to rebuild its Web site with content, navigation, and site functionality that fit the differing needs of each audience segment. Clearly define the mission and critical items, then plan to launch the site in phases, remembering that timing is key to capitalizing on seasonality and impact is crucial to overall goals.

Planning Design for Online Branding

Developing the design and online branding of the destination's Web site dictates that a CVB adjust its destination brand to accommodate each online segment. The online message should adapt to the expectations of each online segment's consumers, not to the organization's latest advertising campaign. The interactive nature of this medium means that the DMO would be wise to focus on each customer segment's specific needs over its own. The marketers should put themselves in the customer's shoes and continually ask, "What's in it for me?" In other words, the successful destination Web site design and branding should be guided more by what the consumers want to do online than what you want to say.

Targeting the Customer Online

The goal with visitors and meeting attendees is to motivate. The goal with meeting planners is to accommodate. The goal with small-group leaders is to administrate. A bureau should recognize these segment differences and deliver what they respectively want.

A few mistakes to avoid when segmenting audiences online include:

- Fulfilling your needs before theirs.
- Not providing them what they expect.
- Leaving the general navigation up for a segment audience to see.
- Not tracking their behavior.

Addressing Navigation

Web site section navigation is fine-tuned and the vernacular changed to appeal to each segment, and it varies by each destination's research of its segment audiences' needs. Below is a sample of a typical basic navigation outline:

- Home page

- Visitor information (accommodations, things to see and do, events, specials, sports, arts and culture)

- Resources

- Book accommodations/packages

- Search

- Meeting planners

- Groups

- Press and media

Building the Web Site: In-House or Outsource

There are two implementation options for building the destination Web site: outsource it or use in-house staff. If a bureau outsources the effort, it should consider hiring an agency that understands the tourism business and has demonstrated results online. The benefit of this option is that the process can be pain-free and enjoyable, reduce bureau staff time, and produce a site with measurable returns on the investment. The risk is hiring the wrong company, a move that can prove costly and ineffective.

If the bureau chooses to utilize in-house staff, it should consider whether current staff can handle the development portions or whether additional staff are needed to undertake the project. The benefit of this option is that bureau staff possibly knows the destination product better than an outside agency does. But there are some risks. One, it could mean time taken from other projects and a deadline to complete this one. Also, experience with only this destination could build in bias and skew the approach for potential visitors. And staff may be incapable of applying best-practice standards from multiple destination projects.

Either way, using in-house staff or hiring Web page developers not experienced specifically in Internet marketing and tourism means greater risk to the project. Often, the company that can provide a thorough assessment is one qualified to implement changes.

Choosing Vendors and Technology Evaluation Tools

One consideration is whether the bureau should choose multiple consultant/vendor partners for each tactic or select a sole-source provider. In choosing the former, the CVB must evaluate and be responsible for choosing a qualified partner for each tactic online. Thus, the bureau's strategy team must commit to thoroughly educating themselves so they can challenge and measure each partner's results and work properly. The benefit is the bureau might "bargain shop" this way and save some budget through separate programs, but responsibility for meeting goals will ultimately rest in-house. The risks are that multiple companies the bureau hires may have differing, even incompatible philosophies or methods, causing the CVB to squander valuable time evaluating small pieces and programs that may need replacement later. The most frustrating risk from going with multiple providers, however, is the lack of accountability as multiple providers point fingers of blame at each other when failures occur.

When considering a sole-source provider, make sure this firm can demonstrate from start to finish the successful management and fulfillment of complete Internet programs for destinations. A DMO also must be ready to commit to a true partner; a sole-source provider will want full accountability for results and must be close to the staff and goals.

A DMO would benefit from one accountable source for all pieces of the program. If new technologies are desired, the provider will negotiate costs and assume responsibility of the programs. The bureau can leverage the firm's experience and successes to catch up to and move ahead of competition in the most expedient fashion. Proficient sole-source providers are endorsed or recognized by national trade associations, such as DMAI.

The risk, as with choosing any consultant, is that the provider must have people and methodologies the bureau trusts. Some Web site development companies claim to be capable of doing it all but often lack true strategy or best-practices knowledge for tourism or marketing. At a minimum, negotiate a consulting and management contract from a sole-source provider to manage solutions and assume risk. This choice is critical to success.

The Project Management Cycle

A phased approach and documentation process form the foundation for clear and concise management of any complex project. The phases of Web site construction, as defined by USDM.net for best practices, are detailed below.

In the pre-project phase, all the relevant documentation and materials necessary to understand the goals and objectives and the scope of the project are gathered. Timeline and budget frameworks are completed in this phase. Pre-project team members include an executive sponsor, client strategist, creative director, and technology director.

The objective of the next phase—planning and documentation—is to detail the deliverables and expectations of the project from both the CVB and the outside provider, construct the documentation for each detailed phase of the project, and obtain agreement on the scope of work and the deliverables from both parties. Planning and documentation team members from the CVB side include the executive sponsor, senior client strategist, meeting planner strategist, creative director, technology director, project manager, and account manager.

A kick-off meeting that includes most of the project team serves as a forum for project managers to transfer project information to all team members and for executive sponsors to answer any questions for the team. Proper preparation by project managers allows these meetings to run efficiently and create excitement.

Subsequently, each project phase will have associated milestones for review and approval. The milestones will be accompanied by a status report meeting and additional documentation ensuring all points of the project are on track.

Scope-of-work documentation is approved and monitored throughout the project development cycle to ensure that each and every component of the agreed-upon program is performed. Precise detailing of the scope-of-work document prevents cost overruns from miscommunications at the outset.

E-CRM Database

Bureau options for implementing an electronic customer relationship management (e-CRM) database include outsourcing the software and management of the program or buying off-the-shelf and implementing it in-house. When considering whether to outsource the software management, bureaus should know that they do not have to start from scratch programming customized new software; off-the-shelf software is available. The key is in the utilization and implementation. For the management, consider choosing a third party who is also the software provider. That way, tracking and reporting are more likely to be accurately calculated, and site visitor paths and behaviors can be tracked and used for further marketing and research. In addition, conversions should improve with a highly intelligent e-CRM program and product. An experienced provider who takes responsibility of this process can lead the program and use the CVB's tactical staff for support.

The risks of outsourcing are: (1) hiring a company without experience in destination e-CRM; (2) buying an overly complex product that will not be used or needs heavy staff involvement to fuel the program; (3) buying a simple "cookie-cutter" program that does not adequately benefit your CVB and the site visitors specifically; and (4) failure to have a plan.

Choosing to buy off-the-shelf and implementing in-house require both heavy planning prior to purchase and bureau staff to identify the tracking and implementation needed. In-house staff may have to devote a significant portion of their job duties to this function, and they would need experience in CRM design on large Internet sites and the integration of the data to registration profiles. The benefits of this choice are complete in-house control and less lead time needed for changes and tracking. The risks are faulty subjective evaluation of metrics, possible guesswork associated with the program, and staff cost overruns.

The bureau could also hire a staff person who understands the software and marketing behind the program, but allow a third party to evaluate software against the CVB's needs and be ultimately responsible for goals in this arena, or allow a third party to evaluate the tracking and make suggestions for refining the program.

Back-End Database (for Data-Driven Site) and Content Management

Options for implementation are building in-house or purchasing software and outsourcing content management. The bureau should evaluate the flexibility needed and the usability of the site carefully. This means identifying parameters such as permission levels for multiple users, site portions to be edited, detail listings and data, and multiple category identifiers. Ease of use and data sorting are critical.

The platform is also important for scalability and usage by high site traffic. The platform defines a standard around which a system will be developed. Once the platform has been defined, software developers can produce appropriate software and managers can purchase appropriate hardware and applications (for databases, word processing, spreadsheets, etc.). A platform should be compatible with all of the foreseeable hardware, software, and applications. Scalability refers to how well a system can adapt or expand to increased demands. As traffic to the Web site, and its databases, increases from a few hundred visitors daily to tens of thousands, the ability to expand all existing system components is critical.

Purchasing software is cost-effective and can be obtained with scalability. The risks associated with this are hard-to-use content manager programs and/or a database that will not support growing traffic and trends. These can be managed with experience, forethought, and planning, or by outsourcing to a qualified third party.

The Strategic Internet Marketing Plan

A strategic Internet marketing plan outlines the various strategies and tactics to be deployed online to optimize a destination's Web presence, boost awareness of the DMO's target markets, drive traffic to the Web site, maximize CRM opportunities (for the DMO and its travel partners), provide information digitally, entice and motivate target audiences' interest and response, encourage online transactions, and deliver performance tracking and reporting.

Often, in conjunction with a Web site redesign and launch, the marketing plan will have two phases. The first involves directing all efforts to the CRM program and driving traffic to the site. The second entails creating and implementing consumer-friendly promotions and programs to keep people coming back to the Web site.

There are numerous components of the strategic marketing plan:

- Web target market audiences by segment, geography, interests, and preferences

- Goals, objectives, and agreed-upon metrics for performance measurement

- Annual search-engine marketing plan

- Annual online public relations and communications plan for target audiences

- Affinity-linking strategies and tactics (for how the marketer will get links to CVB or DMO Web pages from other Web sites that share similar content)

- Annual online media schedule (to create awareness of the Web site and direct response)

- Annual online e-mail campaigns (for outbound e-newsletters)

- Online branding and public relations campaigns

- Developing and distributing online press releases

- Incentive and loyalty programs (that encourage and reward Web site visitors or travelers to the destination)

The plan can also include:

- Niche promotions and tactics (for attracting important subsets of visitors, such as golfers, conventioneers, and holiday shoppers).

- Online co-op marketing promotions.

- New packaging strategies (dynamic destination packaging).

- Registration incentive programs.

- Competitive landscape and response programs.

Writing the Internet Marketing Plan

Two options for implementation include outsourcing the writing of the plan to an Internet marketing company or outsourcing to an advertising agency.

When considering an Internet marketing company, look for one with experience in both destination/tourism marketing and in obtaining successful results through *several* Internet marketing strategies. It is preferred that the company understand the entire program—from technology capabilities to tourism branding initiatives, from e-CRM to online direct response marketing, from search-engine marketing to traditional offline marketing.

The benefit of hiring the right Internet marketing company is that it will alleviate the process of research to identify what Internet programs best fit the CVB's goals and objectives.

The risk of not having a qualified partner in this phase is a plan that does not fully meet needs or produce expected results. Choosing an Internet marketing company that focuses solely on online media, or a firm that charges for search-engine rankings or "click-thru" traffic to the Web site does not take full advantage of how the Web works. Relying only on search-engine optimization companies that use tricks or gimmicks such as spyware, cloaking, or doorway pages can provide junk traffic and skewed results and result in possible banning of the site from a search engine.

When considering whether to outsource the writing of the Internet marketing plan to an advertising agency, make sure the agency can demonstrate an understanding of and ability to use the Internet for multi-channel marketing (listing and linking, Web-page optimization, search-engine marketing, direct response e-mail marketing, online community building, etc.) rather than simply as another media buy for ads it creates.

The benefit of having the bureau's advertising agency write the Internet marketing plan should be that its familiarity with the account, brand, and markets will mean a shorter education process and better cross-media marketing of the brand.

The risks here are that the ad agency's Internet marketing or tourism marketing is only a sideline or niche, and that it relies too much on branding impressions, design work, and banner ads—to the exclusion of monthly online marketing services, search-engine optimization, and direct-response e-mail. While the ad agency's role is that of keeper of the brand, its responsibility is to ensure this brand is integrated adequately and appropriately across all channels. What media strategies and tactics have worked in the traditional media such as newspapers, magazine, radio, and television do not necessarily apply in the online world. An advertising agency must be skilled in the technology and consumer usage issues that affect online marketing.

The best bet is to use an Internet marketing company with strong travel marketing experience. Advertising agencies are very good for and extremely important to a destination's overall branding, advertising, and marketing, but most agencies do not routinely provide ongoing online marketing activities such as optimizing Web pages and continually resubmitting them to search engines for better natural ranking, a standing that results from the Web page's programming and contents being in compliance rather than from being paid for. This is just one of dozens of tactics a good Internet marketing company should know and recommend in an Internet marketing plan.

Ongoing Online Marketing, Communications, and Research

The regular application of specific online tactics that follow a guided Internet marketing plan can deliver significant and measurable results. Specific, tactical knowledge of how to maximize all Internet and e-CRM marketing options is the key. Most often, an Internet marketing company specializes in these types of activities, charges a monthly retainer based on service hours, and can provide excellent references.

Ongoing online marketing activities should include continuously reviewing the CVB's search-engine position and ranking relative to those of other search results of popular search terms used by consumers. These terms are determined by search-engine-supplied online tools, competitive travel and destination Web sites, or specific search topics such as festivals, hotels, and events. It also means continuously implementing proven optimizing strategies for the Web site, such as keyword placement and key content throughout the site. Because search engines periodically modify their rating systems (algorithms) and because the rating systems vary from engine to engine, these tactics of reviewing and optimizing Web pages will be ongoing.

These activities also consist of strategic listing and linking strategies and placements for the Web site. A CVB could identify and contact Web sites serving the same target markets as defined by the marketing plan for placing a link to its Web site. Search engines use the number of Web sites linked to that Web site as one of their rating measurements. Also, having these links on targeted Web sites gains additional qualified traffic referred from those linked sites to the CVB's site from their visitors clicking on the CVB's link.

Another element entails direct e-mail promotions to drive year-round business. As part of having an e-CRM module implemented, e-mail addresses will be data-based and e-mails will be sent periodically as the contract states.

Then there are affinity and co-marketing campaigns. An incentive program is a cross-promotional program designed to obtain exposure on Web sites with similar target markets though a retainer instead of media dollars. The purpose is to increase exposure to the CVB's Web site as well as the number of registered users in its database.

Online public relations should include regular delivery of the CVB's news releases to journalists and Web masters via online channels such as e-mail.

Proactive research encompasses implementation of online visitor and non-visitor perception surveys and tracking of Web site traffic, as well as an annual economic impact survey and report.

The benefit of ongoing Internet marketing activities is that they greatly increase results. Choosing an Internet marketing partner—for example, an ad agency or marketing specialist—who does not understand or cannot show results on the best-practices mix of online marketing activities listed here can mean loss of branding exposure, search-engine rankings, Web-site traffic, registrations for e-CRM, online bookings, and other e-commerce revenues, as well as visitors to the destination.

It's recommended that CVBs hire an experienced Internet marketing company on regular retainer to work within specific parameters and deliver expected results. Thoroughly evaluate the experience of the company and its true understanding of Internet marketing programs. If possible, the company writing the bureau's Internet marketing plan should also be in charge of implementing that plan.

E-Team and Staffing (Strategy and Tactical Teams)

CVBs conducting the online activities described here should consider having strategic and tactical "e-teams." Various bureau staff might participate.

The strategic team should be invited to and involved in monthly e-team strategy and reporting meetings. Ultimately accountable in-house, the vice president of marketing is responsible for online vision, goals, brand protection, and identifying duties of other team members. The executive sponsor (bureau CEO) supports vision and leads on program importance. Each one of the strategy e-team executive team members on this level (V.P. of sales, V.P. of communications, V.P. of tourism, V.P. of information technology) is responsible, in his or her own department, for target market goals.

One possible future staffing position to consider is an i-team director responsible for aligning bureau goals to the Internet program goals and setting goals and objectives of the IT (information technology) department. This position may require a bachelor's degree and at least three years of experience in the field. The candidate selected will monitor and maintain the Internet work product, internal bureau technical issues, and the Internet marketing programs and budgets for the bureau. He or she must have a high-level knowledge of the Internet and Internet marketing as it pertains to destination marketing and bureau functionality. The individual must be able to work in conjunction with high-level paid consultants and outside technology providers to strategically plan and implement the bureau's Internet program and must be able to review and report on Internet program performance. The job requires the highest degree of planning, decision-making, and creative thinking. The i-team director should report to senior management or the CEO.

Another position is an i-marketing manager who is responsible for all online marketing, advertising, direct response, and public relations programs. The position should require a bachelor's degree and at least three years of relevant experience. The successful candidate: (1) sets goals and projections and tracks performance of each program for effectiveness; (2) works with outside consulting or development groups to strategically plan and implement online marketing programs and align online efforts with overall bureau marketing initiatives and target audiences; and (3) reviews and reports on online program performance. The job requires the highest level of online knowledge in the i-marketing team and the ability to creatively strategize and plan programs for maximum effect. This person should report to the i-team director.

A tactical e-team comprises at least two staff. One is the content specialist who assists in developing and implementing Web-site content by coordinating with other departments and the bureau's Web copyeditor. This position may require a bachelor's degree with one to two years of experience writing and publishing on the Web. The individual may be experienced in HTML and DHTML programming languages used to create Web pages and forms; DOT-com and other domain registrations; and Web editor programs for creating Web sites with images and sound. He or she relies on the instructions and pre-established guidelines to perform the job, and works under immediate supervision. The primary job functions do not require independent judgment.

The other is the Web manager who follows written goals and objectives for site development and upkeep, with specific tactics and job description identified. He or she coordinates internally and with third-party vendors for development upgrades; troubleshoots issues with existing systems/vendors; and works with appropriate third-party resources to resolve problems; performs backups and ensures user accessibility to the site; and monitors site traffic and helps scale site capacity to meet traffic demands performance. This position may require a bachelor's degree with two to four years of experience. The successful candidate must be familiar with standards, concepts, practices, and procedures for CVB internal communications and needs. He or she relies on limited experience and judgment to plan and accomplish goals, performs a variety of tasks, works under general supervision, and reports to the i-marketing manager or i-team director. A certain degree of latitude in decision-making is required.

Another possibility for the tactical team is a Web graphic designer to develop and maintain the CVB 's portal, improve the bureau's efficiency, and design the look and feel of the site. This position may require a bachelor's degree and two to four years of experience. The successful candidate must have a working knowledge of HTML, JavaScript, and SQL; rely on experience and judgment to plan and accomplish goals; perform diverse tasks; work under general supervision; be creative; and typically report to a manager.

Chapter 8 Outline

The Role of Human Resources Management
Performance Management
    Step One: Planning
    Step Two: Setting Cascading
      Performance Objectives
    Step Three: Performance Reporting
      and Accountability
    Step Four: The 3P Performance Report
    Step Five: The Performance Evaluation
    Step Six: Performance Coaching
    Step Seven: Personal and Professional
      Development
    Step Eight: Continuous and Never-
      Ending Improvement
Best-Practice Organizations

Competencies

1. Describe the role of human resources management, and explain what a human resources department can do for a CVB. (pp. 147–149)

2. Describe the steps in the performance management process. (pp. 149–158)

3. Explain why planning is important in performance management. (pp. 149–151)

4. Describe the process of setting objectives. (pp. 151–153)

5. Describe the process of performance evaluation, and explain how it relates to professional development. (pp. 154–157)

6. Explain the idea of CANI. (pp. 157–158)

8

Human Resources

By *David Camner* and *Wilfred B. Brewer*

David Camner is CEO and senior partner of Performance Management, Inc., which he founded in 1985, and has worked with more than 250 companies since beginning his consulting career in 1981. Also, he has held human relations positions at Xerox and Olin Corporation, and was chief operating officer at ReCon Systems Corporation. A lecturer at the University of Connecticut, the Society for Human Resource Management, and other professional forums, he graduated from the City University of New York and has completed post-graduate studies at the University of Oklahoma and New York University.

Wilfred B. Brewer is COO and a senior partner of Performance Management, Inc., where he has spent the past fourteen years, before which he was with Deloitte & Touche. He consults in management practices, performance management, pay-for-performance compensation and organizational issues, facilitates strategic planning, and coaches senior executives. He is a chartered accountant and an MBA with a graduate economics degree. He has lectured in compensation at the Stern School of Business and facilitated workshops in productivity measurement for SIOP, SHRM, and Fortune 500s. He works with corporations, not-for-profits, CVBs, and convention centers. He is Treasurer and a Board member of the Southern Connecticut Chapter of SHRM and has served on committees of ASTD.

THE ROLE OF HUMAN RESOURCES MANAGEMENT in convention and visitors bureaus (CVBs) is to foster success of the organization by facilitating the creation of the right work environment where the right people can thrive. The key word here is "right." The "right work environment" means that everyone has the tools and resources to do the job, and the organization's structure promotes effective and efficient communications, problem-solving, and decision-making. Working relationships throughout the organization are well-defined and all work is performed with an understanding of the obligations all staff have to one another, the organization, and the stakeholders. The pay practices in place are fair, consistent, logical, and based on contributions to the enterprise rather than personal and/or political considerations.

The right work environment offers freedom to think and grow personally and professionally, as well as freedom from sexual or other forms of harassment. Also, staff members are empowered to make decisions within defined parameters.

Does this sound like just a lot of the "right" words? Wrong. If management does not get it right, it cheats the CVB and its stakeholders out of an environment that fertilizes ideas, encourages top performance, and produces the best results for all stakeholders, including the staff.

147

The right work environment also includes the facilitation and development of the right performance management processes, which are designed to effectively accomplish the CVB's mission. Performance management consists of a systematic cycle of events that, when correctly tied together, produces powerful results. The cycle is based on the best practices of the most effective companies in the country with the most consistent record of exceeding benchmark performance practices measured in terms of return on investment.

This chapter examines the creation, refinement, and implementation of a performance management process using one of the basic principles of effective and positive leadership—continuous and never-ending improvement *(CANI)*, because no matter where a bureau is located, its management can do better.

The "right people" includes people with the right skills, knowledge, experience, attitudes, and values—the right cultural fit to synchronize the parts. In a typical organization, about ninety percent are right, which means that ten percent of the people in an average organization are the *wrong* people. As a matter of fact, based on survey responses from the last twenty years, most CEOs believe that about ten percent of the people in their organizations should be working somewhere else, and another ten percent—the top contributors—should have much more support than they currently receive. Why is that? The same CEOs say it is because they and their organizations do not know how to change the situation. They do not know how to plan; establish and communicate effective or realistic performance objectives; report, track, and evaluate performance; provide effective feedback and coaching; or develop effective programs of continuous and never-ending improvement.

The Role of Human Resources Management

How does human resources (HR) management contribute to getting it right? By playing the role of internal consultant, and by stepping outside of the organization's culture to see beyond politics, functional priorities, and culturally created bottlenecks. An organization's HR department should work with the leadership team to refine or develop all aspects of the performance management process. When CVBs do not have this level of HR management skill available, this role of "stepping outside" must be played by another entity—for example, the leadership team itself—to produce a solid performance management plan. Other responsibilities of HR management are more traditional. From a *strategic* perspective, they include organizational design and succession planning; recruiting plan design; design and implementation of compensation and benefit plans and programs; employee relations programs that include employees' obligations to each other and the organization and, conversely, of the organization to its employees; and training and development of the staff in terms of personal and professional growth. From an *operational* perspective, the role of HR management includes recruiting; employee relations; administration of compensation and benefits; training and development that includes new job training, retraining staff for new positions, and assisting in developing new programs or projects; and compliance.

HR's role extends to communication and motivation to raise the level of productivity and performance. Human resource management also functions as a facilitator, catalyst, resource, and subject matter expert in developing leadership and management programs for the organization and departmental line managers to deliver the tools necessary to accomplish the above. All of this is directed at adding meaning to three critical leadership words: communication, motivation, and performance.

HR also provides research and information to the rest of the leadership team to create a work environment that is most efficient and effective in achieving the CVB's mission, while balancing this with the interests of the staff.

In essence, HR management has three distinct missions: facilitating the achievement of the business purpose of the enterprise; overseeing and linking the "human side of enterprise" to the enterprise's objectives; and acting as an auditor, ensuring all is legal and in compliance. This management function ensures that government regulations including affirmative action, family leave, and many others are followed to the letter.

This chapter focuses on the first mission—the design, creation, and implementation of a performance management process intended to increase the organization's effectiveness and efficiency in achieving its mission.

Performance Management

Performance management is the process of managing people in a manner that allows the organization to execute the vision and mission statements through planning and goal-setting, performance reporting and evaluation, feedback and coaching, and CANI components for business results and the personal and professional development of people throughout the organization. Management ties the elements of success into a seamless, never-ending upward spiral of higher performance and productivity. The performance management process determines what the organization and the people that give it life do, how well it is done, and how to do it better. It includes much more science than art, although both are important. This is the system that drives *alignment* and *focus* and ensures that all human and capital resources are headed in the same direction toward the same performance objectives.

According to management expert Peter Drucker, many people (about thirty-five percent in most organizations) spend much of their time *doing the wrong thing very well.* Performance management focuses on doing the right things well. It starts with long- and short-term planning and ends with continuous and never-ending improvement.

Step One: Planning

In today's world, a strategic plan typically covers a three-year period. The conventional five-year plan is out of the question given the current rate of change in industrial and organizational missions, markets, people, technologies, structures, systems, and processes. In the high-technology industry, long term can be six months! In other words, it is planning within a time frame in which your DMO is capable of growing while giving consideration to industry and consumer trends, broad economic and global trends, regional and local economic issues, and competitor activities. The planning process is also a time for benchmarking best practices and determining the steps needed to approach, emulate, or surpass the best. Another issue is the impact of technology, with its dramatic rate of change and its continuing and profound impact on the way DMOs do business.

Planning will address the most fundamental question: What is the organization meant to look like at the end of the strategic plan, or what is the organization meant to achieve and how will it do that? The planning process starts with revisiting the CVB's vision and mission statements. The mission is its reason for being in business, and the vision is what it aspires to achieve. Easy, right? Wrong. Get it wrong at the beginning and management will get it wrong everywhere else because the mission is the foundation of all other planning processes.

Equally important, to achieve this level of business, one must make changes to the infrastructure support, including CANI in business practices. This relates to systems, processes, and procedures that support a higher scale of operations more efficiently and effectively. It also relates to facilities and space, information technology and reporting, the organization's structure, and the human talent needed to provide the inputs to make the plan happen. More important, the CVB must address the question of how all these exciting plans to grow will be funded. The chief financial officer plays a crucial role in projecting the financial impact of all the potential operating decisions and providing valuable input based on sound financial and cost/benefit analysis.

Short-term planning is where day-to-day operations meet the long-term planning process. The span of the short-term or operating plan is usually one year. It starts where the long-term plan leaves off and focuses on the two to five most important performance objectives necessary to accomplish the CVB's mission. Each objective contains the performance criteria, standards, and measures stated as objectively as possible. The short-term plan also is integrated into the budget, but remember that the budget is the dollar input while the performance objectives are output. Relating one to the other is the basic measure of productivity—the rate of return used by the most progressive DMOs. To be more specific, the ratio of the incremental economic output of visitors to the destination in relation to the CVB's operating budget is the single most important indicator of success and productivity, measured against prior years and other DMOs as benchmarks.

This means that CVB leadership has some fundamental questions to answer, and it will take more than a one- or two-day retreat. Sound, informed, creative thinking requires preparation and homework. All the items listed above must be researched not at the last moment, but continually over time so that decisions are based on facts, not just on hunches and whims. Once the range of issues is addressed and parameters and guidelines are developed, the leadership team is then in a position to develop the strategic plan, starting with the annual business plan for year one, followed by intended outcomes in years two and three, with many of the required action plans identified.

How well do DMOs do as an industry? A few have a crisp, on-target mission statement, but most do not. And what is the final test of an effective mission statement, according to the pros in best-practice companies? It expresses succinctly the reason for being in business and what the organization is meant to accomplish on behalf of its stakeholders. Mission statements vary among CVBs, but most seek to strengthen the local economy by marketing the destination for meetings, conventions, trade shows, and leisure travel.

The stakeholders are the members of the community who have a direct interest in the outputs or impact of the organization.

What do these stakeholders want from the DMO? They want visitors to fuel the local economy, and as a result they want high-quality jobs, an increase in the quality of life for local residents (because visitors support the infrastructure amenities and attractions that locals get to enjoy), and lower taxes (because visitors contribute to tax revenues).

How does the DMO contribute to meeting visitor requirements? Most industry insiders agree that it is by marketing and selling the destination as effectively and efficiently as possible using the bureau's limited human and capital resources, with success measured in terms of economic impact. Room nights multiplied by daily spending equals economic impact, which in turn creates jobs, improves quality of life, and lowers taxes.

The CVB industry's mission might be described as the efficient and effective generation of incremental economic impact directly attributable to the DMO's efforts in bringing visitors to the destination. Conventions and groups are the easiest to measure. They are gauged in terms of the bureau's direct and indirect influence on creating room nights, when factored by the average daily spending rate. This gives some notion of the incremental impact. However, measuring the incremental impact of leisure business cannot be approached in the same way, and therefore presents a very real challenge. The answer is to measure the quality of the CVB's programs that in the normal course of events will lead to the desired result of people visiting the destination and spending money.

Step Two: Setting Cascading Performance Objectives

This most critical aspect of the process means that every function, team, and individual has identified and communicated the mission statements of their jobs as well as the two to five most important priorities needed to accomplish the mission to management. Examples of actual performance objectives at the CEO (organization) level are:

- Room night targets.

- Convention and group bookings.

- Incremental economic impact of visitors to the destination.

- Incremental economic impact of tourism and leisure, or SMERF (social, military, educational, religious, and family) business.

- Leveraging resources through community-based coalitions, partnerships, and alliances.

Exhibit 1   Components of Performance Objectives

What	Who	Performance Measures
Mission	Board	Incremental economic impact
Long-term plan	CEO	What needs to be done over the next three years
Operating plan	CEO	What needs to be done this year; the annual business plan
Performance objectives	CEO	Two to five highest priority performance objectives
Performance objectives	Vice Presidents/Directors (department heads)	Two to five highest priority performance objectives by function
Performance objectives	All employees	Two to five highest priority performance objectives by person

- Refining the infrastructure (the support functions such as finance, administration, information technology, and human resources) so that the line organizations (sales and marketing) have the tools and resources to do the job.

- Developing a formal planning process including a strategic plan, current-year operating plan, performance-based compensation plan, marketing and sales plan, manpower plan, and others.

The intent of this step is to define five or so of the most important ways to achieve the mission and to list them in priority order. These are the performance objectives for the organization, and therefore, the CEO. The CEO's performance objectives outline what the organization owes the board, and through the board, the stakeholders. Each CVB employee then creates two to five of his or her own performance objectives based on and supportive of the more senior performance objectives. The end result is a series of cascading performance objectives that are integrated and mutually supportive—fully aligned with the mission statement and with each other.

One easy way to picture this is to create an organization chart, not of people, but of performance objectives, starting with the mission, moving on to the strategic plan, then the current annual operating plan and budget at the organization level, then the team level, and so on until one hundred percent of the people in the organization have the outputs or deliverables of their jobs explicitly defined in terms of their highest priorities, all integrated, all mutually supportive. Exhibit 1 lists the components of performance objectives at various levels of an organization.

Each function, team, and individual has now identified and communicated the mission statement for its job as well as the two to five most important priorities to accomplish it. The job's mission statement is its summary, which includes its reason for being and its contribution to the organization. Its contribution to the organization can best be expressed by explicitly stating how the job will support the next level of management—an employee's supervisor—and through this process, it moves up to the organization's mission.

Japanese human resource managers use a process called a what/how continuum. The "what" is the organization's mission, and the "how" is the way it is accomplished. Asking what and how starts with a broad abstraction—the vision or mission—and ends with an explicit understanding of what each functional area and employee in the organization is meant to achieve.

In summary, the CVB's mission is to get every type of visitor possible to the destination, have them spend time and money, go home happy, send their friends, and come back. The question is how do CVBs make it happen?

The answer goes back to the basics. The simple fact is that many people spend a lot of time doing the wrong things very well. All organizations have limited human capital, a fixed number of people multiplied by a fixed number of hours, doing the right or wrong things well or not very well. Generally, if an organization is fortunate, sixty-five percent of the hours worked are highly productive. Imagine the impact on an organization if the number of highly productive hours was increased by ten percent—a startling thought!

The performance management process is designed to ensure the maximum effectiveness and efficiency of the human resources of an organization by concentrating on both sides of productivity—the *input* measured in terms of people multiplied by hours, and the *output,* or the deliverables produced to accomplish the business plan's goals and, ultimately, the mission of the organization.

The Specifics of Setting Objectives. As indicated above, the process starts at the leadership team level, where the CVB's performance objectives are identified based on the mission statement, value proposition, annual business plan, and budget. Functional managers determine their departmental requirements to accomplish the organization's objectives. Employees then determine their personal performance objectives to support the functional or department objectives, illustrating the concept of cascading objectives.

Objectives are statements of outcomes and require statements of how success will be measured using direct, quantitative measures, such as room night bookings or event attendance (excluding locals). Just as important is how the action plans will be executed to achieve the objectives and meet the criteria for success. Take, for example, the following implementation or action plan:

> Each sales executive will sell fifteen new clients per month within projected timelines, with one hundred percent data validation and smooth turnover to the client services group for ongoing client management.

This clearly identifies the outcome as selling new clients and defines success as fifteen new client implementations each month within projected timetables, with one hundred percent data accuracy and the ability to hand the client off to another part of the business function without delays or problems.

Step Three: Performance Reporting and Accountability

Performance reporting is a formal process, which in most cases includes reporting the progress, problems, and plans (in that order), related to each of the CVB's performance objectives on a periodic and formal basis. Reports may be made quarterly, monthly, or even weekly, but not just annually. The reason? Performance reports are intended to increase the communication between a staff member and his or her supervisor so that refinements, and adjustments, and responses to circumstances can be ongoing. Reporting after the fact is obviously too late.

Performance reporting is meant to reflect high levels of accountability, transparency, and integrity. *Accountability* refers to results. *Transparency* means what you see is what you get, in clear, concise language with no intent to mislead. *Integrity* is a reflection of the ethical standards of the organization as well as integrity of the process. Members of the CVB staff should fully understand that their signatures mean that they have honestly presented the facts as an accurate and true reflection of performance.

Managers must regularly and systematically monitor and track performance and hold their employees accountable. Staff members need to report to their managers on performance progress; share their problems, obstacles, or shortfalls; and recommend future plans so that adjustments to existing plans can be made along the way to ensure success. A manager's responsibility is to talk to his or her staff to ensure they share problems and issues so timely decisions can be made in the event of poor judgment in implementing action plans or handling situations.

A manager's dream is open and honest communication from employees demonstrated by a willingness to share problems, thereby enabling managers to provide the guidance and direction appropriate to sound actions. Hence the need for systematic, frequent, and timely reporting. This also becomes the forum for ongoing coaching, which is integral to the performance management process and a cornerstone of effective management. CVB experience, sadly, is that too little time is spent on coaching and far too much on dealing with the crisis of the day.

Step Four: The 3P Performance Report

The 3P report details problems, progress, and plans. It is generally a one- to three-page document that should take less than two hours to compose. It facilitates the transfer of information and the performance management processes of reporting and accountability, communication, coaching, and performance improvement. It also becomes the basis for the annual performance evaluation and should eliminate the problem of evaluation surprises because it forces ongoing communication and feedback. The feedback process starts with performance objectives and the related action plans. It continues with the development of the periodic 3P reports. A 3P report may include a recommendation to modify or refine objectives, targets, measures, or due dates because of changed priorities, new technology, competition, or other internal or external events.

A 3P report can provide:

- Shared priorities and consistent effort toward achieving them.

- Clear and explicit communication between managers and staff.

- A forum for line manager follow-up, where employees are responsible for reporting back, and the manager is not required to nag (the previous 3P report becomes the agenda for the next 3P reporting session).

- A basis from which to change direction, solve problems, make decisions, and reallocate resources.

- Factual and objective input for evaluation when determining performance for purposes of salary raises or incentives.

Step Five: The Performance Evaluation

Performance evaluation is the logical follow-up to performance reporting. It is an ongoing process that gauges the performance of each person and unit in the organization. As the major communication and feedback mechanism between levels of the organization, it should occur weekly, monthly, or quarterly, not only semiannually or annually. The annual review is then merely a summary of all the reviews that have come before.

In a best-practice environment, each employee periodically writes a performance report based on performance objectives created and refined with his or her supervisor, and each supervisor writes an evaluation that is shared with the staffer on the same schedule.

Managers should take this process seriously and review 3P reports, consult with individuals who have worked with the employee during the review period, and invite the employee to participate in the process. Employee participation could take the form of an invitation to list five or so major accomplishments over the past year in achieving performance objectives. An invitation to list areas in need of improvement and suggested action plans to address the issues can mitigate potentially threatening aspects of the evaluation by shifting the emphasis to improvement and away from defending implications of incompetence.

The evaluation focuses on two main components: performance related to agreed-upon objectives and an evaluation of the core competencies relevant to the particular job family. For example, the competencies required by individual contributors or subject-matter experts differ significantly from the skills required by line managers or administrative assistants. In most best-practice organizations, performance objectives (the outputs) are weighted much more heavily than core competencies (the inputs). The evaluation's intent is to identify areas needing improvement and to ensure mutual accountability for improvement. The manager is accountable for coaching or ensuring appropriate training, and the employee is accountable for taking all steps required to improve. This becomes the basis for the seventh component in the performance management process: the employee's personal and professional development.

Typically, the rating of performance objectives determines the incentive payout, and the combination of performance objectives and core competencies determines the merit increase. Evaluations must be made on a common review date to ensure uniformity in the evaluation process, and compensation decisions must be consistent and equitable. The use of an internal compensation committee of managers creates mutual accountability to ensure fairness and consistency in approving recommended compensation decisions based on performance evaluations.

Step Six: Performance Coaching

Coaching is a simple concept: the coach stands on the sidelines, thinking, strategizing, and watching the action while team members play. When the players come off the field, the coach critiques, reviews progress and problems, and develops new plans and tactics designed for winning. The players go back onto the field and into the game.

This is the ideal coaching situation. The reality is that the extent to which the manager/coach can place responsibility in the hands of the players—his or her employees—to go ahead and play is a function of experience, skills, judgment, maturity, and complexity of the issues. Some employees are high maintenance, while others are professional, competent, independent, and know when to seek help.

Managers have critical decisions to make as coaches such as how much time to invest in nurturing the personal and professional development of someone who is failing. The deciding factor is simply return on investment. When does the return become insufficient in relation to the investment of time? Investment costs also include the neglect of other competent performers who will lack the extra touch from a good manager and the less tangible negative message to coworkers that it is acceptable not to perform up to required standards.

The focus of performance coaching often goes back to basics in terms of improving the inputs of the job to enhance the outputs. This means concentrating on improving the quality of the tasks being performed and the competencies, skills, and behaviors required to do the job. It moves managers into the realm of personal and professional development, drawing on the substance of previous 3P reports and concentrating on the areas for improvement identified in the evaluation of core competencies from the last performance evaluation.

Coaching is not a casual process with the manager simply telling a staffer what is on his or her mind. It requires subtlety, finesse, a great deal of empathy, and far more thought than is typically given to the impact of one's words on feelings and sensitivities. The two most important coaching skills are asking instead of telling and using the open-ended question to lead employees to the desired answer or outcome. The process then becomes a learning experience, with emphasis on impact of behavior or action as opposed to vague references to an activity or action.

Coaching calls for a balanced response in delivering bad news or confronting an issue. Human nature insidiously induces us to stay away from unpleasantness. Start with genuine positives—phony feedback is disingenuous and diminishes a manager's credibility—and move toward the negatives. When dealing with the negatives, use open-ended questions, active listening skills, and emotional intelligence. Be empathetic and understand the impact of a manager's actions and words on an employee. Always remember to maintain a person's self-esteem. Demeaning or humiliating comments do not motivate.

It is also important to take notes, agree on action plans, and ensure a common understanding by requesting feedback and confirmation of the lessons and learning points from the discussion.

High-performing staff members need the ongoing attention of enlightened and competent managers just as much as those with performance or behavior issues. These employees are ambitious top performers, intent on career growth and striving for excellence. Best-practice companies give their best people the best opportunities with the highest payoffs. According to Jim Collins, author of *Good to Great,* managers are equally responsible for giving attention to the right people who are on the bus and in the right seats, while they work with the wrong people to get them off the bus.

Step Seven: Personal and Professional Development

Personal and professional development is a systematic approach to developing the competencies, skills, talents, knowledge, and related attributes of all employees to enable them to grow and develop. There are two reasons for doing this. The first is that best-practice organizations believe they owe it to employees. The second reason is that they know they owe it to stakeholders and the organization. The fullest development of the human capital of an organization will provide the optimal return on investment.

The process involves first determining which core competencies are necessary to get the job done, generally by job or job family. The second step is to relate the employee's core competencies to the resulting benchmarks. The third step is to close the gap.

Many organizations lack a systematic approach to training and development programs. Programs can apply universally (for example, diversity training), to a selected group (all managers, members of the leadership team, or administrative assistants for "managing up" skills), or to individuals who need to focus on specific skills or competencies (for example, speaking and presentation skills). "Managing up" means that there is effective communication between managers and staff who are mutually supportive, sharing information and goals.

With the support of the human resources department, managers should collaborate with their staff in crafting their individual development plans. It is important for managers to recognize their accountability for the personal and professional development of their staff while recognizing their own deficiencies as coaches. Not all managers are good at everything. A manager may be a poor coach or weak in an area where someone needs development. Mentors or personal coaches may be useful options in these situations. A human resources department should provide a menu of training programs, geared to the CVB's needs and frequently determined from careful analysis of diagnostic surveys that highlight management deficiencies, such as the 360-degree review. Each individual development plan requires a needs analysis and a systematic, phased approach to acquiring the necessary skills and competencies. Ensure that there are clear action plans and timelines for follow-up on progress in the periodic 3P reporting process. Remember to ask staffers what they learned from the training and what can be shared with coworkers.

158 *Chapter 8*

Step Eight: Continuous and Never-Ending Improvement

CANI is an approach to business, part of the ethos or fundamental value system of an organization. It dates back to W. Edwards Deming's original concepts of quality circles (small groups of six to twelve employees doing similar work who voluntarily meet on a regular basis to identify potential improvements in their respective work areas) and total quality management (a management style based upon producing quality service as defined by the customer), which on the surface appear to be passé and superseded by the glitzier notion of Six Sigma (a management system adapted from industry that uses data and statistical analysis to identify "defects" in a product or process, then strives to achieve as close to zero defects as possible). Nevertheless, the fundamentals remain intact. A CVB should know and understand its customers, give the highest quality of customer service, keep error rates and waste at a minimum, and strive for continuous improvement. Continuous improvement was replaced by reengineering in the early 1990s, meaning that radical and dramatic change was the order of the day because insufficient progress was made by the relatively slow pace of continuous improvement. It was undertaken by leading corporations until business leaders began to notice that it was not working. Research shows that it had failed in perhaps eighty to ninety percent of the corporations that had taken the leap.[1] CANI is back and it works.

CANI is an approach that always questions. Why are we doing this? How can we do this better? How do we serve our customers better? How do we do better than our competition? CANI is integral to an organization that fosters creativity and information and encourages its employees to learn, grow, and continually come up with new ideas. It creates an environment where it is safe to innovate and essential if one chooses to be a leader, whether it is the tourism industry, manufacturing, agricultural, retail, or health care. One way it does this is by zero-based planning. This type of planning starts with the mission and objectives rather than reheating the previous year's plan, and includes positive change and prudent risk-taking in performance planning, reporting, evaluation, feedback, and coaching.

Best-Practice Organizations

The success of a performance management program can be measured in terms of achieving the organization's mission and goals, the personal and professional development of the staff, and the organization's productivity. Best-practice organizations, including CVBs, are aligned so all resources, business plans, communications, and values are pointed in the same direction with goals and performance objectives flowing from the top, and performance reporting rolling up from the bottom in a systematic and disciplined way. They pay for performance in an expected and systematic way, so that there is a significant and recognizable difference in the earnings of the best and worst contributors. They do not lay off employees in bad times, because that creates insecurity, sends a message to others that they are expendable, and creates a rift between managers and the rest of the staff. It also creates a morale problem and has staff members worried about their own tenure rather than hunkering down to do the job. In addition, best-practice organizations have an ongoing program of paying close attention to the best and worst contributors and managing each group differently. They use an "up or out" plan for the worst contributors, and a plan of concentrated personal and professional development for the best. An up or out plan means that employment is terminated for chronic underperformance.

They source, screen, and select employees with uncommon rigor, using more science and less art or anecdotal information in making hiring decisions. Their value system is built into the fabric of the company—into policies, plans and practices, meetings, communications, and culture. The values are actually practiced, instead of only preached. Everyone knows it, and deviations are not acceptable.

Best-practice organizations also:

- Exemplify work ethic, management practices, and values.
- Empower staff to make decisions.
- Encourage and reward prudent risk-taking.
- Are egalitarian.
- Use diverse inputs to solve problems and conduct research rather than rely on instinct.

Finally, CVBs would do well to borrow from Ralph Waldo Emerson, who wrote, "Enthusiasm is one of the most powerful engines of success. When you do a thing, do it with all your might. Put your whole soul into it. Stamp it with your own personality. Be active, be energetic, be enthusiastic and faithful, and you will accomplish your objective. Nothing great was ever achieved without enthusiasm."[2]

Endnotes

1. Michael Hammer and James Champy, *Reengineering the Corporation* (New York: Harper-Collins, 1993).

2. Ralph Waldo Emerson, "Circles," *Essays: First Series* (New York: AMS Press, 1968).

Chapter 9 Outline

What Is a CVB Member?
Development
Retention
Dismissal
Dues Calculations
Policies
Publications
Communications
Benefits of Membership

Competencies

1. Describe reasons why businesses would want to become members of a CVB. (pp. 162–163)

2. Identify steps for attracting, retaining, and dismissing CVB members. (pp. 163–165)

3. Describe variables to be considered when establishing a member dues structure. (pp. 165–166)

4. Outline CVB policies related to member care, including refunds, patronage of member businesses, and denial of membership. (pp. 166–168)

5. Identify three types of publications used by CVBs and describe their relevance for CVB members. (pp. 168–169)

9

Member Care

By *Jesse Walters*

Jesse Walters has served as executive director of the Chester County (Pennsylvania) Conference and Visitors Bureau, located in Philadelphia's western suburbs, since 1998. Previously, he was director of membership with the Philadelphia CVB for eight years. He has had a long career in hotel management, working for Hilton, Howard Johnson, Marriott, and several independent hotels in Scranton (Pennsylvania), Niagara Falls (New York), Philadelphia, Allentown (Pennsylvania), and Providence (Rhode Island). He attended Saint Joseph's University, majoring in politics.

EVER SINCE the nation's first convention and visitors bureau (CVB) was formed in Detroit back in the early twentieth century, hotels and other tourism-oriented businesses have seen the need to hire an advocate for their interests, someone who might collectively market for them.

As the story goes, back in 1914 several hotels in Detroit hired a salesman to go out and try to interest groups in holding their meetings in that city and using its hotels. This is believed to be the first joint effort to sell a destination and a group of hotels. Obviously, hotels saw an economy of scale. Paying one person, they could split the salary perhaps six ways, and they would save on entertainment and travel expenses, too. One can guess that they not only sought a person with good sales abilities (and maybe a few contacts as well), but someone with a bit of civic pride and a thorough knowledge of their city and properties. They probably didn't envision it at that time, but they were fashioning the model for the first CVB.

In the lobby of the Philadelphia CVB, there is a large, framed document dating back to the 1940s that is the incorporation paper of that bureau. Typed at the bottom are the names of about twenty-five corporations that signed on as the charter members, or organizers, of that CVB. They were the usual assortment of civic leaders of the day—the electric utility, the phone company, a couple of large banks, and a good dozen hotels.

An examination of the rolls of businesses that are currently members of the Philadelphia CVB reveals many of these same hotels, banks, and corporations, albeit with new names. An organization that comprised about twenty-five founding hotels and companies in Philadelphia has grown to 1,300 member businesses there. They might not have thought of themselves as "members" of the CVB back in the 1940s, but that is what they are now, and at nearly every other membership-based CVB in North America and across the globe.

This chapter will examine member care including membership development, retention, and dismissal; dues calculation; policies; publications; benefits; and communications.

What Is a CVB Member?

These days, some CVBs are calling their members industry partners, but this discussion will stick with the much more common term of members. Not only has the number of members grown exponentially over the years at most bureaus, but memberships have become increasingly varied. Where once the members were mostly hotels, most CVBs now count restaurants and retail establishments as members, as well as most of their city's tourist attractions and museums. In short, any business that feels it might be attractive to individual leisure travelers or convention attendees might join a bureau.

Another category of member businesses that has seen explosive growth in most cities comprises convention services members. These companies do not cater to the average tourist or conventioneer, but rather offer a product or service to the professional planner of a convention. Companies offering shuttle bus service, conference speakers, audiovisual equipment, name badge and registration services, signage, and other types of planning assistance now form generally half of the memberships of most large CVBs located in convention destinations.

Most companies, whether they cater to individual visitors or to convention planners, may not initially be familiar with the concept of joining a CVB. Sometimes explaining why a business should become a member to receive leads or be listed in a visitors guide is difficult because many enterprises think that should be available free, somehow, to anyone who desires such services. Typically, they do understand the concept that a chamber of commerce has member businesses, so equating it to that idea can be helpful. Also, they probably anticipate that they might have to "pay to play," so the idea of paying membership dues to a bureau is usually understood.

Generally, bureaus that are part of city or county government do not have members, and they fund themselves through either hotel tax proceeds or municipal government stipends. But most CVBs still have membership programs, and in the days before hotel taxes, membership dues and fees were usually all that bureaus had with which to fund themselves.

In addition, these trade associations that became known over the years as CVBs generally operated as non-profit, independent agencies, much like chambers of commerce, and had bylaws specifying that they existed for the benefit and promotion of their members. Usually, only members of a bureau may attend its events, receive the benefits of its marketing efforts, and sit on a bureau's board of directors and elect people to it.

Someone once said, "Every business should belong to a chamber of commerce, but not every business should belong to a convention and visitors bureau." This observation is generally true. Banks, chiropractors, plumbers, gas stations, computer sales businesses, grocery stores, and many other businesses with no connection to tourism and conventions have little, if anything, to gain from affiliating with a CVB, unlike a chamber of commerce. However, any hotel, attraction, or convention service provider who does not belong to the local CVB is really missing out. A bureau will never replace a company's own sales efforts, but it can considerably augment those efforts by, for example, identifying a hotel to individuals who have contacted the CVB.

Development

Although some membership department employees at CVBs may have ambitious sales targets and goals, most bureaus realize this is no longer a major portion of their revenue stream given that the budgets of most North American bureaus come from hotel taxes. In fact, dues and fees from members typically constitute just 10 percent of a bureau's budget. In addition, most CVB executives understand that unless their destination is experiencing tremendous growth, particularly in the tourism industry, they may well have "maxed out" on potential members, or at least in members who make sense. There are only so many hotels, B&Bs, and tourist attractions in a given destination. Of course, most CVBs don't want members unless they can help the member to secure business. No one wants to damage the CVB's reputation in the community by signing on companies that will not be helped by bureau membership and that might disparage the bureau at renewal time if they thought they did not received services promised.

Veteran CVB membership salespeople say that most of their prospects come to them, calling or e-mailing because they think they might want to become a member. Perhaps they own a restaurant, have seen the city's visitors guide and want to be listed, or want to be on the bureau's Web site. Perhaps they rent decorative plants and want to see if convention planners might need their services for podiums and backgrounds. Many of the best prospects come to a bureau's membership salesperson rather than through solicitation by the CVB.

However, when the incoming calls are light, successful membership salespeople will peruse privately-operated publications and Web sites, such as the well-known in-room magazine *Guest Informant*, looking for businesses that advertise with other tourism-oriented guides. They might also watch for new enterprises that are opening or even call former members and try to interest them in renewing membership.

Getting an appointment to see a prospective member is a bit easier for a CVB salesperson than it is for salespeople in other industries, because a bureau is usually perceived as somewhat "official." Making face-to-face contact with a prospect can often mean a quicker close of the membership sales pitch. However, a surprising number of prospects will come to the bureau; apparently, seeing the CVB's offices and meeting staff holds some allure for prospective members. Most often, CVBs send prospective members a kit. With the increasing use of the Internet, many CVBs post their membership benefits, as well as membership applications and dues schedules, on their Web sites.

A CVB will be most successful, and not set itself up for disappointment, if it sticks to the core of area businesses that really should be members, as opposed to the entire business community. A great temptation, and a sure way to experience failure, is to try to sign up local corporations. Many a bureau envisions these large, non-tourism-related corporations gladly contributing $1,000, $5,000, or even $25,000. Some major bureaus have even developed special marketing pieces aimed at soliciting these types of corporations, the most appealing being Chicago's in the mid-1990s. The CVB there printed a very professional, high-quality piece that addressed, as well as anyone had been able to do, what it did and why a local corporation might want to financially support those efforts; but it was not all that successful. Although the potential for synergy may exist, a bureau is best served by dedicating the task of working with corporations to one individual, if financially feasible, and involving the bureau's CEO in these meetings. Non-tourism corporations do not view (perhaps rightly) CVBs as charities, but they are willing to sign on as corporate sponsors for events such as an annual dinner, or a summer festival, or to support a meeting planner's familiarization tour.

Although it may be difficult for the membership salesperson to watch funds come in for such sponsorships and not be classified as "dues," there just is no other way. However, if a carefully orchestrated effort is undertaken to involve corporations in such sponsorships, a CVB will obtain the involvement and financial assistance of banks, utility companies, and other corporate entities in its programming and bring those dollars into the bureau, if not necessarily through the membership department.

Other potential members that may prove difficult are chain restaurants and retailers, the latter being particularly hard to harvest. Local store managers seldom have authority to write checks, or even make such basic decisions as joining a bureau or a chamber. Decisions with chain operations rest with an often-elusive regional manager. Some chain restaurants give their managers a small monthly discretionary cash allowance, almost like petty cash, and sometimes a CVB can manage to squeeze the dues, depending on its dues structure, through this system. If a local affiliate of a national chain restaurant sits on top of the convention center, and remains aloof, consult the visitors guides or membership rolls of CVBs in other cities to see if the chain's operation there is a member. Often, the "We don't join bureaus" statement can be politely rebutted by pointing out that restaurants in that chain in Salt Lake City, Boston, and Denver belong to the CVBs there.

Retention

If a bureau's staff and budget are of sufficient size, a CVB may have one or more people take over the role of membership services after the sale is complete. This person should coordinate and be present at member events, such as mixers, orientations, and marketing meetings. New members should be called and thanked for joining, invited to a monthly new-member orientation, and called again about three months after joining.

Meticulous effort should be put into maintaining accurate mail and electronic databases, accessible to all staff, and ensuring that members receive the bureau's communications. A bureau should communicate with members after they join and throughout their association. CVB staff should ask them if they are realizing any business from their association with the bureau, suggest ways to do so, and inquire if they are pursuing bureau leads, and whether they are following up with potential customers, particularly if the member is interested in convention or group tour business.

A membership services person should make six to ten calls a day, especially to members who do not seem to be participating. This person should ask questions such as whether they are getting the CVB's mail and leads, whether their brochures are at the local visitor center, and whether they plan to attend an upcoming mixer or other event.

At renewal time, CVBs should send a letter with the invoice, stress that renewal is optional, and offer to meet with the contact person if they have any doubts about renewing. This is especially important if the contact person has changed and the new person receiving the mail is not sure what the bureau is or why the firm is even a member.

Dismissal

Members should be invoiced for renewal on the anniversary month of having initially joined. This spreads out the invoicing work over all twelve months and ensures a good, even cash flow for the department. It also eliminates having to prorate initial dues.

Bureaus should send invoice renewals with a letter and bill fifteen days before the first day of the member's anniversary month. If the member has not paid by the end of the anniversary month, send a friendly reminder note. If there is still no response fifteen days later, the bureau should make up to two courteous calls to the contact person. The caller should be friendly, reminding the member that renewal is optional, and inviting feedback if voice mail is encountered. The bureau should never come across as a bill collection agency. Finally, members should be asked the reason for their lack of response, even if they do not wish to renew.

Above all, a CVB should always try to establish a date by which payment will be sent, and stick to it. If it is sensed that a contact person must go to a superior for a decision on renewal, or if the member claims he/she never got the invoice and wants a copy faxed, it is still highly desirable to set a deadline date for some action.

When all else is exhausted, usually sixty days after initial invoicing, send a very friendly "drop letter." This letter should stress the disappointment the bureau feels in losing an industry partner, the optional nature of renewal, and the willingness to discuss any dissatisfaction in order to keep the member in the fold. This letter works especially well if sent from the bureau's CEO. It should be sent to as many people as possible at the member business, and especially to the member's decision maker, if known.

If a dropped member should rejoin several months or even a year later, treat the organization as a new member to alleviate confusion and to call attention to its status as a member who is back on board. However, when a member is dropped, be sure all staff knows about it. At that time, the member is removed from all databases and receives no further leads, benefits, or mail.

Dues Calculations

The hotels in Detroit a century ago probably did not initially refer to their contributions to the jointly hired salesman as dues, but today that is what most bureaus term the fee they ask members to pay to avail themselves of the CVB's services and opportunities. There are some contemporary euphemisms for the word dues, such as partner investments, but the idea is the same. At some point, the contributions to pay CVB staff became dues, and the contributors became members.

Hotel dues will prove to be a major source of membership revenue, if one is allowed to collect them. Because most CVBs have room tax revenue, some hotels will often manage to have their dues eliminated. Hotels usually have had their dues calculated on the number of rooms. In convention-oriented cities, dues are usually higher for hotels the closer they are to the convention center. Many bureaus lower dues for hotels the farther afield they are from downtown. Some use circles, others utilize neighborhoods. If a CVB is concerned about sharing leads with hotels that are outside its municipality or room taxing area, the bureau should consider charging a commission to hotels if they land one of its leads, assuming that having such hotels as members is part of bureau policy.

It is generally easier to avoid surcharging or assessing dues for hotels based upon meeting facility square footage. Likewise, avoid calculating restaurant dues on this basis. A good rule of thumb for CVBs is to keep member categories simple. Bureaus should consider a lower dues amount for smaller restaurants, and a higher number for bigger, more popular establishments.

Although shopping or retail members benefit greatly from tourism and conventions, they often do not see it that way. A bureau should keep the dues level for retailers modest. Better to have their participation than to try to maximize the dues budget within this group and drive them away.

Bureaus should remember that attractions are much more accustomed to the concept of dues. Keep in mind the limitations of smaller museums and non-profit attractions, and consider agreed-on higher levels for the handful of big, major attractions. Attendance levels are often used to set dues levels for this category of members, but take into account the possibility that people may consider fudging these numbers to keep their dues lower. It is better to have a buy-in on the whole membership concept than have to deal with verifying such counts.

Finally, regarding convention services members, remember that just one chance to work with a convention planner can pay for such an entity's dues for ten years, but that anything over $500 annually will be difficult to swallow for this group. A bureau should consider identifying ten to twenty members here who truly benefit from its meetings business. Companies like Freeman Decorating, for example, can be powerhouses in a community, and a direct approach asking them to pay much more than a florist or audiovisual company is not only reasonable and fair, but is generally well received.

Policies

Although each bureau will establish its own policies that are appropriate for the type of destination it is and the pulse of its members and potential members, several philosophical policies should be contemplated for most CVBs.

First, strongly consider a money-back policy for all members. Very few businesses will avail themselves of this (in Philadelphia, it amounted to about $2,000 a year in refunded dues out of an overall dues collected of $800,000). It goes a long way to show that the bureau feels confident that it provides value and will make a good-faith attempt to expose a member to business and to provide it with leads. Point to the renewal rate (generally over 90 percent) as proof of member satisfaction. Even if a bureau knows a business has not tracked its customers or worked its leads, processing a refund request guarantees that its reputation will be preserved.

Also, consider payment installments for members whose dues are high, such as hotels and attractions. Many hotels like to be billed quarterly or semiannually.

Establish clear policies that all understand, including the membership and accounting departments. Make sure the members know of them, too, and that they are uniformly enforced. Also ensure that all bureau staff receive a monthly report concerning who has been dropped and who has joined. This is especially important for visitors center staff, phone operators, and any salespeople who send out leads. Bureaus should not let anyone on staff think that a dismissal is only a temporary "hold" on membership, which the company will eventually pay. If the membership department says that a member is dropped, that's it—no leads, no business, no gray area. Tell staff that if and when such members ever pay, they will be informed of the reinstatement and the classification of new member.

Everyone who works for a member business is a "member" in their own minds, but make sure membership databases are always up-to-date. Within financial reason, "the more the merrier" is appropriate when it comes to your mailing list; however, always designate a primary contact person as well as the person who should get the renewal invoice. They may be different, and at payment time it may be helpful to distinguish the primary contact (who may be in public relations or sales) from the person who got the bill (for example, in accounting).

Document complaints against members. Have a subcommittee of the CVB board or another group be responsible for reviewing problem members and have a clear policy for dismissal and refund of dues.

Although this is an internal matter, make sure that all employees are aware that the bureau patronizes only members. Staff should entertain only at member restaurants, use only member printers for publications, and so forth. When visitors or customers inquire about a hotel or restaurant that is not a member, a polite and professional response should be (whether at your visitors center or your administrative office) that the business is not a member of the bureau, so no information is available. Do not denigrate the business; but responding in this way conveys the sense that the non-member does not have the CVB's seal of approval.

From time to time, a bureau may find itself grappling with the issue of whether to accept a membership application from a business. It could be that the business is known to be less than reputable, or it may be an adult-oriented business, or it could just be a motel that has seen better days. Some bureaus have tried to ignore such applicants, but generally these kinds of potential members do not just go away.

Bureaus must balance their reputations, and the kind of businesses they expose their customers (visitors) to, against the possibility of being accused of restraint of trade. Some bureaus have made the dues for adult-oriented establishments prohibitively expensive, but that exposes a bureau to the charge of an uneven playing field. One alternative is to establish a "Code of Ethics" in a membership application that says that the bureau, being a membership organization, reserves the right to reject an application, or to end an association with a member, if complaints are lodged about the business by visitors. General standards can be mentioned regarding cleanliness, customer service, fair pricing, and the like that would warrant dropping a member if that ever becomes necessary.

Bureaus would be well advised to have their legal counsel review such language before it is placed in an application and to consult with legal counsel when contemplating dropping a business from membership due to unsavory or unsatisfactory business practices.

Publications

There was a time when almost all bureaus had three main publications—a visitors guide, a meeting planner's guide, and a group tour manual. Only member businesses were listed in them, which was always a key selling point for a membership salesperson. In many cases, where display advertising was available, only members could advertise, and sometimes this was more important than any other member benefit for certain members, such as restaurants.

Bureaus have also done specialty publications, such as a brochure listing all area wineries, or featuring an antique district, or perhaps a small guide showcasing multicultural members. These specialty brochures are generally done for justifiable marketing reasons or sometimes simply in response to pressure from certain constituencies, such as local bed-and-breakfasts or a particular neighborhood.

With the advent of the Internet, several things changed. Many CVBs now have their meeting planners guide strictly online. The thinking is that meeting planning professionals are too busy and sophisticated to store meeting guides from sixty different destinations on their desk. Many destinations are now doing the same with their group tour manuals.

Of course, this saves a bureau a lot in printing and design costs, with some of the money being diverted to the continual enhancements of a CVB's Web site. But it also has several equally practical reasons that make the member's experience better. Taking publications onto a Web site allows bureau staff to quickly update these lists for customers. As members joined, dropped, or changed their name or address, the old printed guides, which were generally produced annually, were almost immediately outdated in a few months. A bureau also cannot discount the ability to immediately correct a mistake in a listing. Whether the member supplies an incorrect phone number, or a data entry error is made, an electronic guide can be corrected at once and less expensively than a print publication.

More and more meeting planners and group tour planners are consulting destination and other Web sites to make their decisions. Where once money was invested in and pride generated by a glossy four-color cover and guide, funds are being spent instead on a great and functional Web site, with such bells and whistles as requests for proposals, hotel charts, and Flash images of convention facilities or attractions.

Lagging behind this trend a bit are visitors guides. True, this basic visitor information was the first content that bureaus put on their Web sites in the early

1990s, and it remains critical for most destination sites. But for various reasons, consumers still like to have a visitors guide mailed to them or have it to carry around and consult in a car or hotel room. Members enjoy handing them out in their lobbies. Destinations ship them to interstate highway information desks, as well as visitors centers in other cities. The value of a visitors guide for a CVB and its membership program cannot be underestimated. Although there may not be printed visitors guides (or at least significantly fewer copies printed) in another ten years, this may be the last publication to succumb to the electronic world of destination marketing.

Bureaus need another word to define the places (or publications) in which they list CVB members because, although the Internet may have rendered obsolete the traditional printed brochure or guide, Web sites are the new "publications" and are just as important to the customer and therefore to CVB members.

Communications

A bureau's publications and electronic marketing (via a Web site) are administered by its communications department. As such, the membership staff will have as much interaction with these staff members as they do with accounting, the visitor center, and convention sales and services. However, most good communications departments perform a public relations function as well for the destination, and membership staff should be attuned to opportunities there that could benefit the membership.

When stories are suggested to writers, members are often mentioned. When travel writers visit an area for a familiarization tour, members are often asked to provide complimentary accommodations, meals, and admissions. Members should be educated on the value of providing these things. For example, one Philadelphia B&B received seventy-eight reservations from California after a writer who stayed there mentioned the B&B in a *Los Angeles Times* travel section article.

Editorial copy has much more credibility to customers than does paid advertising, and a free dinner or hotel room costs a lot less. There should be more competition among members to supply such freebies than there is, and savvy members benefit more than those who don't understand the concept or consider it an instance of the bureau asking for another handout.

Benefits of Membership

It is often said that CVB membership is like a buffet. Members must pick and choose those benefits that are right for their type of business. Not all of the benefits that a bureau offers work for every member.

Listed below are various benefits offered by most CVBs to their members. Assuming for a moment that one can group CVB members into one of four sets (attractions, lodging, dining/shopping, and convention services), try to decide which of the four groups would appreciate and use a particular benefit as shown below.

1. Member events (mixers, annual dinner, marketing updates)

2. Convention and meeting planner sales leads

3. Group tour or motor coach sales leads

4. Convention services sales leads (after a meeting is booked, the planner may be looking for caterers, audiovisual services, speakers, etc.)

5. Listings in publications and on a bureau's Web site

6. Ability to place brochures in a visitors center

7. Referrals from a visitors center

8. Discounts on health insurance, shipping, or long-distance calling

9. Ability to advertise in the CVB's publications or on its Web site

10. Ability to participate in bureau-sponsored co-op ads

11. Ability to participate in bureau-led sales missions or trade shows

12. Chance to host news media and travel writers

13. Ability to participate in bureau familiarization shows and events

14. Chance to expose one's business to other bureau members

15. Membership plaque or window decal showing membership status

16. Bureau publications in quantity, usually at no charge

17. Complimentary links from a bureau's Web site

18. Subscription to the bureau's newsletter and other insider information

19. Benefit from the bureau's lobbying efforts or access to elected officials

20. Access to and ability to influence the bureau's marketing plan

Chapter 10 Outline

Four Critical Areas in CVB Financial
  Management
    Nondistribution of Earnings
    Primary IRS Classifications of CVBs
    Disclosure of Information Issues
    IRS Filing Requirements and Forms
Cost Allocation Procedures
    Natural versus Functional Reporting
    Direct versus Indirect Reporting
CVB Financial Statements
    Internal Financial Statements
    Chart of Accounts
    Audited Financial Statements
Appendix A: Fiduciary Responsibility and
  CVB Liability
Appendix B: The Importance of
  Implementing Policies and Procedures
  for CVBs

Competencies

1. Explain the difference between the two
    classifications of not-for-profit
    organizations, and describe the
    advantages and disadvantages to each.
    (pp. 174–175)

2. Explain the requirements for CVB
    disclosure of information.
    (pp. 175–176)

3. Explain the requirements for filing
    information and tax returns with the
    IRS. (pp. 176–179)

4. Explain the difference between direct
    and indirect costs for a CVB.
    (pp. 179–180)

5. Describe the elements and preparation
    of internal and audited financial
    documents. (pp. 180–185)

10

Financial Management

By Ed McMillan

Ed McMillan, CPA, has spent his entire career in not-for-profit financial management. He served as controller of the national office of Associated Builders and Contractors and as financial and membership director of the American Correctional Association. A frequent speaker for professional organizations, he has authored several books, including Model Policies and Procedures for Not-for-Profit Organizations, Not-for-Profit Budgeting and Financial Management, *and* Not-for-Profit Accounting, Tax and Reporting Requirements. *He holds a B.S. in accounting from the University of Baltimore.*

THE DEFINITION OF ACCOUNTING is "a system that provides quantitative information about finances and serves as the basis for business decisions." Most convention and visitors bureau (CVB) executives and members of the board of directors are well-schooled in matters involving carrying out their CVB's mission, but often are inexperienced and have very little formal education in accounting and financial management. However, all board members, particularly the treasurer, have fiduciary responsibility for financial management oversight, and staff executives have direct supervisory responsibility regarding the bureau's financial operations.

This chapter will address the basics of CVB financial management in critical areas that *must* be understood by both board members and key staff. It deals exclusively with United States federal regulations. The organization also must meet additional state disclosure of information requirements. This information usually can be found in the state not-for-profit-organization law handbook.

The reader will find guidelines for fiduciary policy from the Phoenix (Arizona) Convention and Visitors Bureau in the chapter appendix. These guidelines should be taken into account by board members when they make decisions regarding the finances of their organization.

Four Critical Areas in CVB Financial Management

Most CVBs are organized as not-for-profit, tax-exempt organizations, and it is important for members of the board of directors and key staff to thoroughly understand the laws that govern the nonprofit operating environment in four areas: nondistribution of earnings, primary IRS classifications of CVBs, disclosure of information issues, and IRS filing requirements (Form 990 and Form 990-T).

Nondistribution of Earnings

A commercial organization that operates for profit typically will distribute after-tax profits to owners, partners, shareholders, and other investors in the form of dividends, draws, and so forth. A CVB can and should operate profitably and plan to increase its unrestricted net assets balance (reserves) to improve solvency and important financial ratios. It is prohibited, however, from distributing earnings to board members and other influential individuals, such as committee members. If the IRS has determined that a CVB has distributed earnings to members, or if individuals realize or receive benefits as a result of their membership, the IRS may revoke the CVB's tax-exempt status, and the bureau could lose all related advantages.

Finally, although board members are prohibited from receiving distributed earnings, it is perfectly acceptable to offer the *staff* attractive compensation packages, performance bonuses, and the like as long as these incentives are reasonable under the circumstances.

Primary IRS Classifications of CVBs

Board members and key staff should understand the various IRS not-for-profit classifications and the basics of what they are allowed to do and not do under the law, as well as advantages and disadvantages of the primary classifications.

CVBs qualifying for exemption from federal income tax are granted exemption under Internal Revenue Code (IRC) section 501(a). Most CVBs are organized under Section 501(c)(6) of the IRC. To qualify for this classification, the CVB must complete Form 1024, "Application for Recognition of Exemption." The primary advantages of this classification are that there are no restrictions on engaging in lobbying or political activities, and contributions made by the CVB may be deductible as business expenses. The main disadvantages are that donors cannot deduct charitable contributions, and postal rates are less favorable than for 501(c)(3) organizations. There typically are fewer state advantages like sales tax exemption, and 501(c)(6) organizations are often ineligible for grants.

It is also very common for CVBs to have an affiliated foundation to take advantage of 501(c)(3) status. To qualify for this classification, the CVB must complete Form 1023, "Application for Recognition of Exemption under Section 501(c)(3) of the IRS Code."

The primary advantages of this classification are:

- Donor tax deductions

- Favorable postal rates

- Exemption from the Federal Unemployment Tax Act

- Exemption from state sales tax and other local taxes, if allowable under state law

- Increased eligibility for grants

The chief disadvantages pertain to lobbying. Only insubstantial amounts can be spent on lobbying to influence legislation, and lobbying in election campaigns is absolutely prohibited.

Disclosure of Information Issues

Due to tax-exempt status, CVBs organized under IRC Section 501(c)(6) (as well as their 501(c)(3) foundations) are *required* to make certain records available for inspection by the general public and by their members. It is crucial for board members and key staff to have a thorough understanding of this requirement and to establish board policies addressing this issue.

For most CVBs that are required to disclose information, the law addresses such things as who has the right to inspect records, what records must be made available for inspection, and what records are exempt from inspection. It also deals with the place and time of inspection, penalties for noncompliance, reimbursement of expenses, inspection of records through the IRS, requests made in writing, exemptions, and state requirements.

Anyone requesting to review applicable documents must be provided access, and individuals need not reveal why they are making the request. Records in question include:

- Forms 990 and 990-EZ, "Return of Organization Exempt from Tax," including all schedules for the three preceding years.

- Form 1023, "Application for Recognition of Exemption under Section 501(c)(3)" or Form 1024, "Application for Recognition of Exemption under Section 501(a)."

- All correspondence submitted by the not-for-profit organization and issued by the IRS that supports the above documents.

Not-for-profit organizations are *not* required to provide public access to the following:

- Form 990-T, "Exempt Organization Income Tax Return."

- Form 1120-POL, "U.S. Income Tax Return for Certain Political Organizations."

- Names and addresses of contributors.

If names and addresses of contributors have been included in schedules submitted with the Forms 990 and 990-EZ, this information can be deleted from the package of information provided to the inspector.

The place of inspection can be the CVB office and satellite locations. If an organization has more than one location, a copy of the applicable documents must be made available for inspection at the other locations. Documents required to be disclosed must be provided on the day of request, or the next business day if unusual circumstances exist. The time taken to provide requested documents cannot exceed five days.

Responsible persons of a tax-exempt organization who do not provide the required informative returns may be subject to a penalty of $20 per day for as long as the failure continues, for a maximum of $10,000. There is no maximum penalty for failure to provide a copy of an exemption application. An individual denied access to applicable records can alert the IRS and request enforcement action through the director of the exempt organizations division.

A not-for-profit organization can charge the inspector for photocopying and postage expenses. Reimbursable expenses include $1 for the first page and $.15 for subsequent pages of photocopying and actual costs for postage.

Copies of Forms 990, 990-EZ, and 990-PF, and applications for exemption, are available for public inspection and copying on request directly through the IRS. A request for inspection must be in writing and must include the name and address of the organization that filed the return. A request to inspect a return also should indicate the number of the return and the years involved. The request should be sent to the disclosure officer of the district where the requester desires to inspect the return or application. If an inspection at the IRS national office is desired, the request should be sent to the IRS Freedom of Information Reading Room at 1111 Constitution Ave. N.W., Washington, D.C., 20024. An inspector can request a copy of the documents by using Form 4506-A. There is a fee for photocopying.

Written requests for documents must be fulfilled within thirty days of the request or within thirty days of receiving payment for expenses. Organizations may be exempt from the requirement of providing copies if they have already made the copies widely available on the Internet (the organization must make available its URL) or the Secretary of the Treasury determines, on application by the tax-exempt organization, that the organization is the object of a harassment campaign.

The discussion here concerns information and documents that must be disclosed by law. If a not-for-profit organization elects to allow access to other records, an applicable policy on who may inspect what records should be included in the organization's board-approved manual on accounting and financial policies and procedures.

IRS Filing Requirements and Forms

CVBs organized under IRC 501(c)(6) and their affiliated 501(c)(3) foundations must report the results of their operations and other important matters to the IRS annually.

As a practical matter, board members and key staff should be provided copies of these documents and have a basic understanding of their contents. Most CVBs are required to report their activities to the IRS on Forms 990, "Return of Organization Exempt From Income Tax," 990-EZ, "Short Form Return of Organization Exempt From Income Tax," and 990-T, "Exempt Organization Business Income Tax Return."

Form 990. Form 990 is an *information* return because the organization filing it is not required to pay taxes, and this document, as stated earlier, is open for public inspection. It may be surprising or unsettling to note that part five of Form 990 includes the compensation of officers, directors, trustees, and key employees of the

CVB. This information is required and cannot be removed or crossed out when providing this document to individuals requesting it.

Qualifying not-for-profit organizations must file Form 990 or Form 990-EZ if their gross receipts are normally more than $25,000. Not-for-profit organizations with gross receipts of $25,000 or less are not required to file.

Forms 990 and 990-EZ are due on the fifteenth day of the fifth month following the close of the calendar or fiscal year. An extension of time to file is granted by completing Form 2758, "Application for Extension of Time to File Certain Excise, Income, Information, and Other Returns." Form 2758 must be filed by the original due date for Form 990 or 990-EZ. A penalty of $10 per day is assessed to organizations filing late. The penalty will not exceed the smaller of $5,000 or five percent of the organization's gross receipts. The penalty is assessed from the due date of the return. Also, there are severe penalties, including other fines and imprisonment, for willfully filing fraudulent returns or not filing returns. Finally, both forms must be made available for public inspection.

Form 990-T. Form 990-T is a *tax* return and, as such, is a proprietary document, which means there is no requirement that it be open for public inspection like Form 990. Generally, CVBs with *gross* income of $1,000 or more for the year from an unrelated trade or business must file Form 990-T. CVBs can request an automatic extension of six months to file a return by submitting Form 7004, "Application for Automatic Extension of Time to File Corporation Income Tax Return."

CVBs subject to the tax on unrelated business income are taxed at prevailing corporate tax rates. Bureaus must make quarterly payments of estimated tax on unrelated business income under the same rules as corporations. Generally, if a CVB expects its tax to be $40 or more, estimated tax payments are required. Estimated tax payments, computed by using form 1120-W, are due on the fifteenth day of the fourth, sixth, ninth, and tenth months of the tax year.

CVBs should deposit all estimated tax payments with Form 8109, the "Federal Tax Deposit Coupon." These deposits must be made with an authorized financial institution or a Federal Reserve Bank in accordance with the instructions on the coupon

The organization is required to pay ninety percent of the final tax liability to avoid an estimated tax penalty. An interest penalty effective from the due date of the tax is assessed for underpayment of estimated taxes. This interest rate is adjusted quarterly by the IRS. Keep in mind that the penalty for filing Form 990-T late is five percent of the tax due per month, to a maximum of five months, or twenty-five percent of the tax due.

In this discussion, unrelated business income consists of revenue generated by a tax-exempt organization that possesses *all three* of the following characteristics:

- The income must be from a *trade or business.*

- It must be from a trade or business that is not substantially related to carrying out the exempt purpose for which the organization exists.

- The trade or business must be *regularly carried on.*

The term *trade or business* generally includes any activity undertaken for the production of income from selling goods or performing services.

Trade or business is related to exempt purposes, in the statutory sense, only when conducting the business activities has a substantial causal relationship to the achievement of exempt purposes (other than through the production of income). The activities that generate the income, to be substantially related, must contribute importantly to the accomplishment of the organization's exempt purpose. To determine whether activities contribute importantly to the accomplishment of an exempt purpose, the size and extent of the activities involved must be considered in relation to the nature and extent of the exempt function they intend to serve.

For example, for income from activities that are in part related to the performance of an organization's exempt function, but are conducted on a larger scale than is reasonably necessary for the performance of the function, the gross income attributable to the portion of the activities in excess of the needs of the exempt function is income from an unrelated trade or business. This income is not from the production or distribution of goods or the performance of services that contribute importantly to the accomplishment of any exempt purpose of the organization.

Business activities of an exempt organization ordinarily will be considered to be "regularly carried on" if they show a frequency and continuity and are pursued in a manner similar to comparable commercial activities of nonexempt organizations.

The following revenue sources are specifically excluded from tax on unrelated business income:

- Dues (excluding associate member dues)
- Dividends and interest
- Annuities
- Royalties
- Gains from the disposition of property
- Contributions
- Proceeds from the sale of goods or services produced in the course of the organization's exempt function
- Income from any trade or business in which a substantial amount of the work is performed by volunteer labor
- Income from any trade or business carried on for the convenience of members
- Income from the sale of donated merchandise or gifts
- Income from the rental of mailing lists by two 501(c)(3) organizations

The following revenue sources are specifically included in the computation of unrelated business income and are the most common:

- Advertising fees
- Rental income from debt-financed property
- Income from controlled organizations

Advertising income is revenue generated by an exempt organization from the sale of any paid commercial advertising in its publications, on its Web site, and so forth.

The term *debt-financed property* means any property that is held to produce income and for which there is an organizational indebtedness at any time during the tax year, including real estate and personal property. Tax-exempt organizations that acquire or improve income-producing property with borrowed funds or with existing debt have acquisition indebtedness on the property.

For each debt-financed property, the unrelated debt-financed income is a percentage of the gross income derived during the tax year from the property. The percentage is the debt/basis percentage. The formula for deriving unrelated debt-financed income is:

$$\frac{\text{Average Acquisition Indebtedness}}{\text{Average Adjusted Basis}} = \text{Gross Income from Debt-Financed Property}$$

The exclusion of interest, annuities, royalties, rents, and so forth does not apply when an exempt organization receives them from an organization it controls. If the controlled organization is a stock corporation, control generally means stock ownership of at least eighty percent of all shares with voting power and at least eighty percent of the total number of shares of all other classes of stock in the corporation.

This tax is computed on *net* revenues, not gross. Net income is that derived from any unrelated trade or business, less deductions directly connected with carrying on the trade or business.

CVBs that engage in lobbying must either pass on a statement to their members indicating what percentage of dues are not tax-deductible due to lobbying activities, or pay a proxy tax. If an organization elects to pay the optional proxy tax on lobbying expenditures, it is noted on Form 990-T.

Cost Allocation Procedures

Natural versus Functional Reporting

The recommended chart of accounts will enable financial reporting to be easily performed on a natural or functional line-item basis depending on how accounts are sorted. Natural reporting allows CVBs to present revenues and expenses as consolidated figures on their statements of activity. Functional reporting allows CVBs to monitor both profit and cost centers by breaking the statements down by departments, such as administration, membership, conferences, or publications.

It is recommended that the natural account for personnel costs be converted to a functional basis by allocating the appropriate percentage of time spent for each job title to a corresponding organizational/functional activity.

Direct versus Indirect Reporting

The primary purpose of a bureau is to promote the destination that it represents. Specifically, bureau funding is typically used for convention and/or tourism sales and marketing related activities. Thus, these sales and marketing activities are considered direct costs, while all other costs would be considered support (indirect) activities. Recommended functional classifications for DMAI reporting purposes are, for direct costs, convention sales and marketing, and tourism sales and marketing. For indirect costs, they are convention services and housing, visitor services, communications and publications, and membership administration.

CVB Financial Statements

Although CVB board members and key staff are not expected to be experienced accountants, they should have a basic knowledge of financial statements, know how to look for danger signs, and be prepared to take corrective action to protect the bureau's assets. CVBs may design internal financial statements in any format that meets their needs. Audited financial statements prepared by CPAs, however, must adhere to Generally Accepted Accounting Principles according to standards declared by the Financial Accounting Standards Board, an arm of the American Institute of CPAs.

The DMAI has developed a standardized method of financial reporting and encourages CVBs worldwide to adopt these standards for consistency. Once consistent reporting behaviors are established, comparative analysis tools can allow bureaus to identify operational strengths and weaknesses, as well as to improve organizational efficiency and effectiveness. The DMAI's recommended uniform system of accounts (which can be found online at DMAI's Web site) comprises internal financial statement formats, a chart of accounts, and cost allocation procedures.

Internal Financial Statements

Internal financial statements are those prepared by the CVB's staff accountant or outsourced accounting service. Once again, these statements can be prepared in any format that meets the bureau's needs. At a minimum, the CVB board of directors and key management employees should review the statement of financial position (or balance sheet) and the statement of activities (or income statement), showing actual versus projected budget data for both the current month and year to date. Sample internal statements are shown in Exhibits 1 and 2.

The internal financial statements form the basis for a bureau's chart of accounts. Although internal financial statements can be designed to meet the needs of a particular bureau, the statements should utilize industry terminology and standards, where possible, to accurately portray financial operations for comparative reporting purposes. The internal statement format should be similar (and easily converted) to audited financial statements.

Only currently licensed CPAs are authorized to audit a CVB. After the audited statements have been prepared, they should be presented to the board by the CPA firm for discussion, questions, and answers. In addition, if a management letter outlining deficiencies and suggesting improved operating procedures was issued by the CPA firm, the conditions noted should also be addressed.

Once the audited financial statements have been prepared, each member of the board and key staff should receive a copy. The board is free to distribute other copies to anyone it deems appropriate. The management letter, however, is a

Exhibit 1   Sample Statement of Financial Position as of December 31, 20XX

CURRENT ASSETS		
Cash & Cash Equivalents		2,752,641
Investments		321,344
Accounts Receivable	1,218,684	
Allowance for Doubtful Accounts	(25,000)	1,193,684
Prepaid Expenses		278,903
Inventory		78,820
TOTAL CURRENT ASSETS		**4,625,392**
FIXED ASSETS		
Furniture & Fixtures	1,061,044	
Accumulated Depreciation	(591,638)	469,406
Equipment & Leasehold Improvements	1,212,621	
Accumulated Depreciation	(678,219)	534,402
Land & Buildings	303,155	
Accumulated Depreciation, Building	(173,163)	129,992
TOTAL FIXED ASSETS		**1,133,800**
OTHER		266,776
TOTAL ASSETS		**6,025,968**

CURRENT LIABILITIES		
Accounts Payable, Vendors		1,139,864
Accounts Payable, Personnel		230,398
Accounts Payable, Current Portion Debt		109,135
Deferred Revenue		551,742
TOTAL CURRENT LIABILITIES		**2,031,139**
LONG TERM LIABILITIES		
Notes Payable		
Equipment	400,165	
Mortgage		
Total Notes Payable		400,165
TOTAL LONG TERM LIABILITIES		**400,165**
NET ASSETS		
Unrestricted		1,191,429
Temporarily Restricted		1,186,409
Permanently Restricted		1,216,826
TOTAL NET ASSETS		**3,594,664**
TOTAL LIABILITIES & NET ASSETS		**6,025,968**

Source: Destination Marketing Association International.

Exhibit 2   Sample Statement of Activities

REVENUE		
Public Sources		
Room Tax		3,547,485
Restaurant Tax		55,052
General City Tax		—
Other Primary City/County Tax		61,789
Secondary City Funding		81,933
General Sales Tax		—
General County Tax		6,350
General State/Province Tax Funds		28,515
Donated Products & Services		4,496
Other		—
Total Public Sources		**3,785,620**
Private Sources		
Membership Dues		231,306
Advertising:		
Print	116,003	
Web site	11,162	
Cooperative	109,943	237,108
Promotional Participation		91,135
Event Hosting		48,847
Publication Sales		2,992
Merchandise Sales:		
On-Site	24,414	
E-Commerce	2,022	26,436
Ticket Sales		35,134
Convention Service Fees:		
Housing	45,342	
Registration	27,320	
Registrar Assistance	31,178	
Other	—	103,840
Chamber of Commerce		1,315
Building Revenue		—
Donated Products & Services		113,155
Investment Income		126,879
Other		—
Total Private Sources		**1,018,148**
TOTAL REVENUE		**4,803,768**
EXPENSE		
Personnel		**1,767,370**
Marketing/Promotion		
Travel & Entertainment		151,096
Trade Show Participation		137,360
FAM Tours/Site Visits		41,208

Exhibit 2 *(continued)*

Event Hosting:		
Industry	119,045	
Local/Community	73,258	192,303
Advertising/Marketing:		
Media	746,325	
Website	36,629	
Print	288,456	1,071,410
Merchandise:		
Giveaway	41,208	
Resale	18,314	59,522
Tickets for Resale		13,736
Research		36,629
Fulfillment		73,258
Donated Products & Services		117,651
Other		173,989
Total Marketing/Promotion		**2,068,162**
Administrative/General Operations		
Audit & Legal		82,416
Dues & Subscriptions		36,629
Bad Debt		4,578
Depreciation		73,259
Amortization		24,395
Insurance		22,893
Data Processing/Computer Expense		32,050
Rent		155,675
Bank Fees		16,789
Interest		13,736
Telecommunications		68,680
Postage		64,101
Photocopying		45,876
Maintenance Contracts		32,459
Other Equipment Rental/Contracts		36,629
Office Supplies		50,365
Repairs & Improvements		22,893
Miscellaneous		164,832
Total Administrative/General Operations		**948,255**
TOTAL EXPENSE		**4,783,787**
EXCESS REVENUE OVER EXPENSE		**19,981**
BEGIN NET ASSETS UNRESTRICTED BALANCE		**1,171,449**
END NET ASSETS UNRESTRICTED BALANCE		**1,191,430**

Source: Destination Marketing Association International.

proprietary document, and discussion or distribution outside of the board members and key staff should be on an as-needed basis.

Chart of Accounts

The chart of accounts should be constructed to provide a trained accountant with an immediate understanding of the logic of the account numbering system. It should include a brief description of the use of each account. Generally, a chart-of-account number is composed of a series of digits that identify the account's purpose. For example:

Number	=	Class–Natural Account–Department–Project			
# of Digits	=	x	xxxx	xx	xxx

Class—Represents type of account where:

1	=	Assets
2	=	Liabilities
3	=	Net Assets
4	=	Revenue
5	=	Expense

Natural Account—Represents actual account number. Examples include:

Checking	=	1000
Accounts Receivable	=	1100
Accounts Payable	=	2000
Deferred Revenue	=	2020
Unrestricted Net Assets	=	3000
Room Tax	=	4000
Membership Dues	=	4030
Personnel Cost	=	5000
Rent	=	5320

Department—Represents function/department. Examples include:

Convention Sales & Marketing	=	10
Tourism Sales & Marketing	=	20
Administration	=	80

Audited Financial Statements

As previously stated, when independent CPAs issue audited financial statements, they are required to adhere to the provisions of auditing standards set by the Financial Accounting Standards Board. Currently, there are four standards that must be taken into consideration:

- Statement of Financial Accounting Standards #116: "Accounting for Contributions Received and Contributions Made"

- Statement of Financial Accounting Standards #117: "Financial Statements of Not-for-Profit Organizations"

- Statement of Financial Accounting Standards #124: "Accounting for Certain Investments Held by Not-for-Profit Organizations"

- Statement of Financial Accounting Standards #136: "Transfer of Assets to a Not-for-Profit Organization or Charitable Trust that Raises or Holds Contributions for Others"

These standards are very complex, and questions concerning how they affect individual CVBs should be directed to the CVB's independent CPA.

Board members and key staff should, however, have working knowledge of the basic concepts outlined in this chapter to help them ensure that the organization is run smoothly. Their jobs will be easier if they understand the financial aspects of managing a CVB and the regulations and tax requirements governing nonprofit organizations.

Appendix A

FIDUCIARY RESPONSIBILITY AND CVB LIABILITY

Basic Principles:
Generally, while the board of directors is responsible for policymaking and key staff are responsible for carrying out the day-to-day management of the organization, both volunteer members of the board of directors and key staff with positions of responsibility have the following duties:

- DUTY OF CARE

  A broad concept requiring these individuals to exercise ordinary and reasonable care when making decisions, and all decisions should be made in the best interests of the organization. There is also an obligation to protect confidential information.

- DUTY OF LOYALTY

  A concept requiring officers and key staff to give undivided allegiance to the organization and as such avoid real, perceived, or potential conflicts of interest.

- DUTY OF OBEDIENCE

  Requires officers, directors, and key staff to follow prevailing federal and state laws, as well as the corporate governing documents such as articles of incorporation and bylaws.

Also, inherent within these duties, these individuals are expected to:

1. Act reasonably and prudently.

2. Avoid negligence and fraud.

3. Avoid conflicts of interest.

Potential Personal Liabilities:
As long as members of the board of directors and key staff adhere to the principles noted above, they are usually not held personally responsible for actions of the organization. There are, however, exceptions to this protection if these individuals:

1. Engage in willful ignorance and/or intentional wrongdoing.

2. Make decisions with the intention of causing injury or damage.

3. Make decisions or take action outside their authority.

REDUCING RISKS:

While certain responsibilities are obvious, such as attendance and active participation at meetings, individuals serving on the board of directors and key staff can take steps to avoid potential personal liabilities, as well as organization liability, if they document and review the following:

1. Indemnification of individuals by the organization.

2. Proper insurance policies have been contracted for officers and directors, errors and omissions, liability policies, etc.

3. Understanding state volunteer protection laws.

4. Review internal financial statements routinely.

5. Meet with the organization's independent CPA firm's representatives to discuss the annual audited financial statements and management letter and taking action accordingly.

6. Meet with the organization's general counsel when necessary to become aware of not-for-profit laws, and consideration of a legal audit on occasion.

7. Ensure the board of directors has implemented and approved policies and procedures in the following areas:

   - Internal control policies

   - Investment policies

   - Budget approval policies

   - Financial and accounting policies (crucial in the event of an IRS audit)

   - Office administration policies

   - Personnel management policies

   - Risk reduction policies

8. Ensure minutes are current and accurate.

9. Exercise due diligence in all matters.

In summary, this is a very basic guideline on fiduciary responsibilities and liabilities, and is not intended to be considered legal advice. It is the responsibility of the organization to secure professional legal advice on all organization matters with legal ramifications.

Source: Phoenix (Arizona) Convention and Visitors Bureau.

Appendix B

THE IMPORTANCE OF IMPLEMENTING POLICIES AND PROCEDURES FOR CVBs

Another crucial area is the importance of well-considered policies and procedures in the following areas:

- Financial and accounting
- Internal controls
- Office administration
- Personnel
- Risk reduction

Financial and Accounting

These policies and procedures are important for two very practical reasons:

1. They are invaluable in the event of an IRS audit.
2. They eliminate any misunderstanding concerning financial management.

Internal Controls

The importance of effective internal controls is, of course, to reduce the possibility of embezzlement or fraud and should be reviewed by the independent CPA.

Office Administration

These policies are designed primarily to ensure the CVB is operating in accordance with prevailing laws such as the Americans with Disabilities Act.

Personnel

These policies should be in the CVB's employee handbook and address such matters as compliance with the federal Fair Labor Standards Act.

Risk Reduction

These policies are to ensure the CVB has taken into consideration the element of risk and include such items as fidelity bond coverage review.

Source: Phoenix (Arizona) Convention and Visitors Bureau.

Chapter 11 Outline

Competencies

1. Describe the roles and responsibilities of a CVB board of directors. (pp. 191–192)

2. Explain the function of bylaws to the effective operation of a CVB's board of directors. (pp. 192–196)

3. List factors to be considered when forming a CVB board of directors. (pp. 193–196)

4. Describe the purpose of board member orientation. (pp. 196–197)

5. Explain the reasons for board evaluation and outline the areas that should be evaluated. (pp. 197–198)

11

Board Governance

By *Joe Lathrop*

Joe Lathrop is president of OCG, an 18-year-old consulting firm specializing in CVBs and serving a nationwide client base that also includes hotels, attractions, and associations. He specializes in organizational assessment and development, with an emphasis on strategic planning, destination development, and performance measurement. A featured speaker on CVB issues and related tourism topics at the state and national level, he has worked with sixty CVBs of all shapes and sizes across the country. He holds a master's degree from the University of Central Florida.

MOST CVBs are required by federal and state regulations to have a non-compensated board of directors that has governance and fiduciary responsibilities detailed in a set of bylaws. This chapter describes these responsibilities and presents strategies for establishing and maintaining an effective CVB board. This chapter also presents key components of CVB board governance, with examples that can be implemented as is or customized for specific situations.

In general, the CVB board of directors has philosophical, legal, and financial responsibility for the operation of the bureau. Within this broad parameter, the board's specific role and the level of its involvement will vary depending upon the needs and dynamics of the bureau's internal and external constituencies, as determined by the board.

A typical CVB board fulfills the following roles and responsibilities:

- Defines the purpose of the bureau and establishes its governing principles.
- Provides advice and consent with respect to overall bureau policy and goals.
- Approves the annual operating budget and monitors the bureau's finances.
- Approves membership structure and fees.
- Provides direction and oversight for the bureau's operations.
- Monitors the performance of the CEO or president or executive director.
- Represents the bureau's interests among external audiences and serves as advocate for tourism and destination management issues.

The extents to which a CVB's board is directly or indirectly involved in the bureau's planning, operations, and staffing and where the boundaries lie between board and staff responsibilities are issues that must be addressed and clarified for every individual CVB. The bureau's success depends heavily on how board governance is defined, communicated, and executed.

191

Structural and Functional Dimensions of Board Governance

Board governance can be viewed as having two dimensions. The *structural dimension* consists of the tangible aspects that can be seen and touched—the nuts and bolts of board governance. This includes the makeup of the board, job descriptions, meeting schedules, bylaws, code of conduct, and any other documentation that defines the board and its performance criteria.

The *functional dimension* consists of the way in which the structural components are applied. The board may have all the right nuts and bolts, but if they are not used, or if they are used incorrectly, they will not yield good results, much like a strategic plan that is brilliantly conceived but never taken off the shelf.

The structural dimension is relatively easy to address. It is not difficult, for example, to create a set of bylaws or job descriptions. It is much more difficult to turn them into documents the board will actually use to guide and monitor its own performance.

It is up to the board's leadership to ensure a self-governing process that includes regular board evaluations to determine (1) how well the board is functioning (both individual members and the board as a whole) and (2) if the overall structure of the board remains optimal in light of changing conditions.

In this regard, discussion of the *functional dimension* of board governance centers on board evaluation, using a simple evaluation tool. But again, the tool, which is itself a *structural component*, must be applied.

Bylaws

The responsibilities of the CVB board are detailed in a set of bylaws, as mandated by the CVB's articles of incorporation. Bylaws provide strict guidelines to which the organization *must* adhere, thereby establishing certain legal protections as well as providing a clear definition of board and staff roles. Bylaws are the framework within which all decisions are made and governance is executed.

Even if the CVB's legal structure does not specifically mandate bylaws, detailed policies and procedures must be formalized and documented in some form to establish the framework for operations and to provide the legal protections that derive from instituting and following a clear set of guiding principles.

The importance of bylaws must be clearly understood. An organization that does not adhere to its bylaws is vulnerable to a wide range of potential problems, from lawsuits to Internal Revenue Service complications. Because bylaws detail how the organization is *supposed* to function, failure to follow them invariably results in reduced effectiveness.

Once established, bylaws must remain constant and be followed consistently. However, they are not forever carved in stone. Bylaws are subject to periodic review and modification as needed to accommodate changing internal and external conditions. Such review and modification should be undertaken through a formal process spelled out in the bylaws, and that includes input and communication mechanisms designed to protect the integrity of the bylaws document.

Bylaws may vary somewhat depending on the bureau's structure. However, most of the basic ingredients for success will be consistent for all bureaus, as discussed below and as illustrated in the example of bylaws provided by the Niagara (New York) Tourism & Convention Corporation at the end of the chapter (see Appendix A).

Board Structure and Makeup

Defining the makeup of the board is a function of the bylaws, and it is one of the most critical decisions the bureau will make. It may also be a politically-charged decision, as constituents who seek to exert influence on the organization lobby for representation. Among the issues to consider when structuring (or restructuring) the board are the following.

What specifically does the bureau need from board members? Obviously, the board needs people who can get things done, but that often requires influence in the community more than time or talent. Depending on the dynamics that exist among the bureau's key constituents, visibility and influence may be paramount to success; and they are sometimes the more difficult commodities to come by. However, without the contribution of time and talent, the work of the board does not get done. The key is to ensure the right mix of individuals by recognizing what the needs are and filling available positions on the board with individuals who can satisfy those needs.

Does the board membership represent a blend of tourism industry and other businesses? CVB boards are typically composed predominately, if not exclusively, of representatives from the tourism industry, based on the idea that overseeing the bureau's work requires an understanding of, and direct interest in, destination marketing and other industry-specific issues. However, in addition to oversight responsibility for bureau operations, the work of the board involves funding issues, political negotiations, developing community relationships, and other high-level destination management priorities. In this regard, individuals representing banking, retail, manufacturing, health care, and so forth are less likely to be viewed as self-serving when lobbying for the tourism industry's best interests. Also, they have important connections throughout the community that the industry may lack. Collectively, they can yield greater influence in accomplishing the bureau's strategic goals. In addition, all business sectors and the community as a whole have a vested interest in destination management, and having those interests represented on the CVB board can make it easier to get things done and help to ensure they are done right. The most successful CVB boards have a blend of representatives from different sectors of the tourism industry and the wider business community.

Is geographic representation critical? Geographic representation offers little or no benefit for a destination that is basically homogenous in terms of visitor offerings, marketing requirements, political/financial districting, and other considerations that may affect the allocation of bureau funds and marketing focus, particularly if the destination is small. However, if the bureau is responsible for a large destination that includes multiple municipalities, different taxing structures, and/or a variety of visitor attractions, the board needs to reflect the diverse interests of its

Exhibit 1   Board Representation Checklist

Name	Years in Community	Industry Knowledge/ Influence	Political Influence	Availability	Membership on other Boards	Other

constituency. Without appropriate geographic representation in this case, the bureau is more vulnerable to criticism from and conflict among different factions of the destination.

What is the optimal number of board members? Generally speaking, a smaller board is better from a purely practical standpoint. Actions and decisions tend to get bogged down when many diverse individuals try to reach consensus, particularly when addressing complex issues. A smaller board is likely to be more flexible, more efficient, and easier to manage. Therefore, the number of members should be limited to that which is required to satisfy the need for political, geographic, and business/industry representation.

Ensuring the appropriate representation on the board involves identifying the relative strengths of each member and reviewing these strengths (and, therefore, what deficiencies may exist) when filling vacant positions. A simple checklist is helpful in this regard (see Exhibit 1). The checklist indicates the qualities that are needed on the board, along with a rating for each director (or nominee) as to which need(s) they fill. This checklist provides a visual reference to quickly identify what areas the board may be lacking.

Standing Committees

Standing committees of the board are established within the bylaws. These committees enable the board to accomplish certain functions more efficiently and effectively than would be possible by involving the full board. Standing committees act on behalf of the full board, with the bylaws defining the committees' composition, level of authority, specific duties, and other details of how they are to carry out their mandate. The use of standing committees should be limited to those ongoing functions that are appropriately carried out by a few selected members of the board. These typically include:

- Executive Committee—Has specific responsibilities detailed in the bylaws. Typically composed of the officers and one or two other board members.

- Strategic Marketing—Serves as a conduit for constituent inclusion in the marketing strategy.

- Resource Development—Serves to secure the resources necessary for success.

The executive staff member should be included on all board committees, and, unless his or her compensation is being discussed, should attend all meetings. For other, time-limited functions, the board can create temporary task forces, with clear parameters defined with regard to outcomes, deadlines, and reporting and approval requirements.

Board Powers, Roles, and Responsibilities

The bylaws provide a mechanism to formalize the powers of the board with respect to its authority over the CVB's operation. Specific areas of board responsibility are also itemized. Through this mechanism, critical boundaries are established and maintained between the board and the staff. Without these boundaries, there invariably will occur confusion, conflict, duplication of effort, inefficiency, and unfulfilled expectations.

Board Members: Selection, Officers, and Job Descriptions

The bylaws should specify the qualifications for board membership, the term of office, the process by which new board members are nominated and selected, and how vacancies are to be filled. Any ambiguity here has the potential for significant political fallout. For example, a board member with an agenda for change might be dismayed to find his or her term will expire before these objectives can be accomplished.

Officers. The officers of the board typically include a chair, vice-chair, secretary, and treasurer. As with board membership criteria, the bylaws should detail the process and timing by which officers are elected or appointed, their terms of office, and succession procedures. The duties and responsibilities of each officer should also be clearly described in detail.

Job Descriptions. Job descriptions have historically had limited application among boards of directors. As with any organization, however, job descriptions offer an invaluable tool for clarifying roles and responsibilities, establishing boundaries, and holding individuals accountable.

It is often assumed that board members understand their roles, but the most dysfunctional boards are those that try to micromanage the staff rather than focusing on broader strategic issues or are not adequately engaged around key roles and responsibilities. When board members do not understand their role and its relevance to the organization, they tend to focus on staff responsibilities, or simply sit on the sidelines and accomplish little.

For a CVB to be successful, the board must be actively engaged in removing obstacles that inhibit the organization from achieving its mission. This role is critical, but if it is not understood, it will likely go unfulfilled.

Separate job descriptions should be created for each of the officer positions, as well as one for all board members. Each job description should include a statement of purpose, requirements for the position, and a detailed listing of attendant responsibilities. Examples of job descriptions created by the Providence/Warwick (Rhode Island) CVB are provided at the end of this chapter (Appendixes B and C).

Meeting Parameters

What is the process by which meetings are scheduled, and who is authorized to schedule them? What constitutes a quorum? What is required to constitute an "act of the board"? These are questions that should be answered clearly in the bylaws. Again, any ambiguity will invariably lead to confusion and potential conflict.

Other Structural Components of Board Governance

Orientation

The more informed the board members are about the bureau and about the details of their board responsibilities, the more effective they will be. Therefore, all existing and new board members should be given a thorough orientation that equips them to do their jobs. Orientation materials can be compiled into a board handbook for ongoing reference by board members. The orientation should include, at a minimum, the following components:

- Overview of the bureau organization
- Articles of incorporation and bylaws
- Strategic plan
- Board of directors position descriptions
- Code of conduct and confidentiality statement
- Contact information for board members, committees, executive management team
- Current calendar
- Meeting minutes

Properly conducted, the orientation will require a significant commitment of time by participating board members, whose busy schedules often make that difficult. However, the orientation process should not be compromised to accommodate a participant's time constraints. Individuals who are unable or unwilling to attend the orientation likely will not be prepared to devote the time and energy needed to serve effectively on the board.

Whenever possible or practicable, several board members can undergo the orientation together. Group orientations offer an efficient alternative to the one-on-one approach, and more important, they provide opportunities for cross-pollination of ideas and questions that will invariably enrich the overall experience.

Code of Conduct

The effectiveness of the board as a whole depends on the way in which individual board members conduct themselves. This can be reflected in attendance at board meetings, willingness to participate in board activities, openness and honesty in interacting with fellow board members, demonstrated loyalty and commitment to the bureau, and how board members represent the bureau to external audiences.

Although certain ethical standards, values, and behaviors are naturally expected of board members, these qualities are not always adhered to. A formal code of conduct adopted by the full board and agreed to by all of its members decreases the likelihood that interpersonal issues and individual performance deficits will interfere with the board's productivity and ability to succeed.

In addition, by pledging to abide by the code of conduct, board members give each other permission to bring to their attention any behavior that is not consistent with the code. Thus, it reduces the need for confrontation and provides a relatively safe framework within which to discuss individual board member performance.

The code of conduct created and used by the Pittsburgh (Pennsylvania) CVB is included at the end of the chapter (Appendix D).

Board Objectives

Any annual marketing/business plan should include objectives and performance measures for the board. These objectives generally center on the board's leadership roles; that is, improving resources, political influence, or product development. They set the board agenda for the year and provide a clear road map of where the board is headed. Objectives also provide the basis for establishing performance measures and assessing how well the board is doing.

Board Evaluation

A board, by its nature, must be largely self-governing. It is up to the board members themselves to ensure that they are effectively fulfilling their roles and achieving their goals, both individually and collectively, and that they remain effective throughout changing conditions, shifting priorities, and turnover of directors and officers. The code of conduct provides a mechanism for regularly addressing the performance of individual board members. Procedures and evaluation tools must also be in place for determining how well the board is functioning as a whole.

A board self-evaluation should be conducted periodically. It should include a structure inventory (that is, have changing conditions created different requirements for board makeup, bylaws) along with a performance review. Examples of relevant forms are included at the end of this chapter (Appendixes E and F).

Ideally, the board self-evaluation forms are completed by each of the directors, anonymously and confidentially, with results compiled by an independent, non-biased resource from outside the bureau. In this way, directors will more likely be open and honest in their appraisal, and thus the results will have greater credibility and usefulness. An outside facilitator may also be useful in helping the board develop and implement strategies for improvement.

Board Governance: A Case Study

Townsville was a third-tier destination in the geographic heart of the United States with an inventory of 2,000 hotel rooms. Industry indicators were at a fairly comfortable 65 percent occupancy and an average daily rate of $120. The market mix was distributed about evenly among business, group, and leisure travelers. The CVB received 60 percent of a 4 percent bed tax collected countywide. According to self-imposed performance standards, the CVB was performing well.

However, the entire hotel community was frustrated regarding its limited input to and its deliberate exclusion from the decision-making processes. The CVB's board of directors had sixty members, with only five seats for the accommodations industry. These five seats were occupied by hoteliers who represented downtown convention-related properties, hoteliers who were generally satisfied with the CVB's performance. The remaining fifty-five seats were held primarily by non-tourism-industry business and political leaders.

Because there were no term limits, several board members had served more than ten years. In electing new members, the board had long been successful in excluding the more critical hoteliers, portraying them as counterproductive to the success of the CVB and the destination.

This strategy appears to have been quite effective in limiting negative discussion and allowing the staff to manage the board (or at least giving the staff the *illusion* of managing the board). The CVB executive believed he was protected by key board members and that his actions were shrouded from scrutiny; thus, he became complacent.

Eventually, an aggressive and frustrated hotelier was admitted to the board. At the same time, the CVB executive made a mistake in judgment—not a particularly grievous mistake, but it provided the opening the hotel community had been waiting for. The pent-up frustration was evident and organized, and the news media were used effectively. The CVB executive resigned under pressure with a limited severance package.

What are the lessons to be learned from this case study?

- The bylaws must clearly define the role, responsibility, and code of conduct for the board and staff. The importance of effective bylaws cannot be overstated.

- Do not exclude key community constituents simply because they might not agree, or because it is easier not to deal with them. The old adage—"Keep your friends close and your enemies closer"—holds true in the case of board composition.

- Limit the size of the board. Because of the sheer size of the board in this case study, it was virtually impossible for the chair or the executive to manage it effectively.

- Board turnover is a good thing and should be a key aspect of the bylaws. As long as there is a nucleus of experienced board members and an effective orientation process, the regular introduction of new members should not be a problem.

- Embrace board governance as an effective management and leadership tool.

If the CVB executive had not made his fateful mistake in judgment, would he still be employed there? Perhaps. But all executives make mistakes. The key issue in this case was the pent-up frustration that was inevitably going to find an opening. Relying on specific board members for protection put this executive in a highly vulnerable and volatile position. The structure and function of the bylaws offer the best protection.

Appendix A

BYLAWS OF
Niagara Tourism and Convention Corporation
Adopted 2002

Article I
Organization

Section 101.   Name

The name of the Corporation is Niagara Tourism and Convention Corporation, which will be referred to as "NTCC" in this document with offices located in the City of Niagara Falls.

Section 102.   Mission

The mission of NTCC is to enhance the economic prosperity of Niagara County by promoting, selling and marketing the county as a premier destination for meetings, conventions and leisure tourism.

Section 103.   Fiscal Responsibility

The fiscal year of the NTCC is from January 1st to December 31st.

The Board of Directors will make lawful and adequate provisions for sound fiscal policies and practices of the NTCC, including the preparation of an annual audit by a certified public accountant, the preparation of an annual budget, and ample fidelity bonding of officers and employees entrusted with the handling of funds or property of the NTCC in accordance with state laws.

Section 104.   New York State Law

The NTCC is a not-for-profit corporation and is governed by the applicable provisions of the New York State Not-For-Profit Corporation Law and it will be a 501.C6 tax status ("N-PCL").

Section 105.   Liability/Indemnification

Nothing in these Bylaws will constitute Directors, or officers of the NTCC as partners for any purpose. No Director, officer, agent, or employees of the NTCC will be liable for the acts (or failure to act) on the part of any officer, Director, agent, or employees. All Directors, officers, and employees shall be entitled to and have such immunity from and limitations upon their liability as such, and such indemnification from and against same, as is and shall be provided by law or by action of the Board of Directors.

Article II
Directors

Section 201.   Structure and Make-Up of the Board

1 seat – City of Niagara Falls (Mayor or Mayor Designee)
1 seat – City of Lockport (Mayor or Mayor Designee)
1 seat – Niagara County (Chair of the Legislature or Designee)
4 seats – General Business (non-tourism)
5 seats – Accommodations
7 seats – Tourism Industry
President serves as ex-officio member of the board.

Section 202.   Qualifications

Each elected Director must be an owner, operator, or officer (or at a management level) in the respective organization represented of the NTCC at the time of his nomination and throughout his or her term as Director.

Section 203.   Nominations/Selections

A nominating taskforce appointed by the Chair of the Board would nominate potential new Board members that are consistent with the Board of Director structure and criteria. The full Board, including outgoing members, will by written vote elect new Board members within 30 days of the beginning of the fiscal year.

Section 204.   Term of Office

Subject to the provisions of the preceding and following sections:

a.) The term of each Director is for two years and until his or her successor has been elected and qualified. Directors may be reelected to serve a second term, but not more than two consecutive terms except as hereinafter provided. A Director who has served two consecutive terms is eligible for reelection one year after the expiration of his or her second term. A Director elected to fill an unexpired term of less than one (1) year shall be eligible for reelection to two consecutive two-year terms.

b.) Whenever there is a vacancy on the Board of Directors (except for a vacancy caused by the normal expiration of a Director's term), the Chair can appoint an eligible person to fill the vacancy. The appointed person will serve until the next election at which time an individual will be elected by the Board to serve the remainder of the unexpired term of office.

Section 205.   Regular Meetings

The Board of Directors will schedule and announce the dates, times, and places of its regular meetings for the coming year at the NTCC's Annual Meeting which shall be held pursuant to New York State Law within the first quarter following the completion of the fiscal year. Regular meetings shall occur at a bi-monthly minimum.

Section 206.   Special Meetings

The Chair of the NTCC may call a special meeting of the Board of Directors at any time, and must do so whenever asked by any one-third of the total number of Directors. In the second case, the request must be made in writing and the meeting must be set for no sooner than seven days and no later than fourteen days from the date the request is made.

Section 207.   Quorum

A majority of the entire number of Directors is a quorum for the transaction of any business. If, at any point during a meeting, a quorum is no longer present, then the meeting must be adjourned.

Section 208.   Voting

All Board action shall be taken only upon formal vote of the Directors at a duly constituted meeting of the Board. A majority vote of the Directors present at a duly constituted meeting, as long as they have a quorum, will constitute an act of the Board.

Section 209.   Powers of the Board

The Board of Directors will manage the NTCC. All of the corporate powers (except as otherwise provided in the Certificate of Incorporation or in these Bylaws) are vested in, and will be exercised by, the Board of Directors.

Section 210.   Board Roles and Responsibilities

(a) Create policy and overall direction for NTCC
(b) After a decision has been reached, speak publicly as one voice
(c) Perform appropriate fiduciary responsibilities
(d) Act in the best interest of the NTCC and Niagara County as a whole, not on the basis of individual interests
(e) Retain a President to manage NTCC operations, monitor the President performance against policy, strategic objectives and ROI
(f) Review the results of the NTCC efforts and hold the NTCC accountable for achieving objectives
(g) Serve on committees and task forces as requested by the chair
(h) Be advocates for the industry and the NTCC in the community

Article III
Executive Committee

Section 301.   Composition

The Executive Committee will consist of the Chair of the Board, Vice Chair, Secretary, Treasurer and such other Directors as the Board may in its discretion elect at the first regularly scheduled Board of Directors meeting following the Annual Meeting. The term of an Executive Committee member will be one (1) year. The Executive Committee will not exceed five (5) members. The President will serve as an ex-officio member of the Executive Committee.

Section 302.   Authority

The Executive Committee will be an advisory body serving the Board of Directors. It will advise the Board of Directors on agenda and matters of policy, including but not limited to performance review of President and oversight of budgetary and fiscal matters. All of its actions will be subject to the approval of the Board of Directors.

Section 303.   Regular Meetings

The Chair of the NTCC will schedule and announce the dates, times, and places of Executive Committee meetings for the coming year at the NTCC's Annual Meeting.

Section 304.   Special Meetings

Special meetings of the Executive Committee may be called by the Chair of the NTCC or, in his absence by the Vice-Chair. A special meeting must be called upon the written request of two members of the Executive Committee. Executive Committee members must be notified of each special Executive Committee meeting at least three days in advance.

Section 305.   Vacancies

Whenever there is a vacancy on the Executive Committee (except for a vacancy caused by the normal expiration of an Executive Committee member's term), the Chair of the NTCC can appoint an eligible person to fill the vacancy. The appointed person will serve until the vacancy has been filled by vote of the Board of Directors at their first regularly scheduled meeting after the Annual Meeting.

Section 306.   Quorum

At all meeting of the Executive Committee a majority of the full Executive Committee will constitute a quorum.

Section 307.   Voting

A majority vote of the Executive Committee members present at a duly constituted meeting, as long as they have a quorum, will constitute an act of the Executive Committee.

Section 308.   Chair

The Chair or Vice-Chair of the NTCC, or in their absence a chairperson chosen by the members present, will preside at all meetings of the Executive Committee.

Section 309.   Performance Review

The Executive Committee, in conjunction with the President, will develop performance targets. The President's performance will be evaluated annually based on accomplishment of said targets.

Section 310.   Removal

Executive Committee members may be removed for cause or not for cause by vote of two thirds of the total number of the Board of Directors. The removal of an Executive Committee Member will be without prejudice to contract rights, if any.

Article IV
Officers

Section 401.   Qualifications

Every officer must be a natural person over twenty-one years of age and a member of the Board of Directors. No officer will hold more than one office at a time.

Section 402.   Classification

The officers of the NTCC will be:

- Chair
- Vice-Chair
- Secretary
- Treasurer

Section 403.   Appointments

a.) The Board of Directors will elect officers of the NTCC at the first regularly scheduled Board meeting following the annual election of the Board and no later than January 31.

b.) Whenever an officer's position becomes vacant (except for a vacancy caused by the normal expiration of an officer's term), the Chair of the NTCC can appoint an eligible person to fill the vacancy, subject to the approval of the Board of Directors. The appointed person will serve until the vacancy has been filled by vote of the Board of Directors at the first regularly scheduled Board meeting following the Annual Meeting.

Section 404.   Removal

Officers may be removed for cause or not for cause by vote of two thirds of the total number of the Board of Directors. The removal of an officer without cause will be without prejudice to his contract rights, if any. The appointment of an officer will not of itself create contract rights

Section 405.   Term of Office

Subject to the provisions of the preceding section, officers will serve as such for one year and until their successors have been elected and qualified. An officer may serve in the same capacity for a maximum of two consecutive years.

Section 406.   Powers and Duties of the Chair

The Chair will preside at all meetings of the membership, the Board of Directors, and the Executive Committee. He or she will have and exercise general charge and supervision of affairs of the NTCC, subject to the direction of the Board. The Chair will appoint persons to chair all standing and ad hoc committees established by these Bylaws or the Board of Directors.

Section 407.   Powers and Duties of the Vice-Chair

At the request of the Chair, or in the event of the Chair's absence or disability, the NTCC will perform the duties and possess and exercise the powers of the Chair.

Section 408.   Powers and Duties of the Secretary

The Secretary will ensure that the documents and papers of the NTCC and the Corporate Seal are properly kept. The Secretary will ensure that minutes of all meetings of the Board of Directors and the Executive Committee of the NTCC are taken.

Section 409.   Powers and Duties of the Treasurer

a.)   The Treasurer will ensure that all funds, property, and securities of the NTCC are properly kept, subject to any regulations imposed by the Board of Directors.

b.)   The Treasurer will ensure that checks, notes, and other obligations to the NTCC are collected, and then properly deposited at whatever banks or depository the Board of Directors may designate.

c.)   The Treasurer and whatever other officers or employees are designated by the Board of Directors are empowered to sign NTCC checks and bills of exchange and promissory notes issued by the NTCC.

d.)   The Treasurer will ensure that necessary and proper payments from funds of the NTCC are made. He or she will ensure that the books of the NTCC are kept and that full and accurate accounts of all monies and obligations received, paid, or incurred by the NTCC are entered in them on a regular basis.

e.)   The Treasurer, or, in his or her absence, a Director or employee designated by the Treasurer, will make regular reports on the state of NTCC finances at all regular Board of Directors meetings.

Section 410.   President

Duties. The Board of Directors shall employ a President whose duties, performance review and compensation will be outlined in an employment contract between NTCC and the President. The President shall be the principal executive officer of the NTCC. The President shall be administratively responsible to the Executive Committee.

Hiring Employees and Delegation of Duties. The President shall have the right to hire, within the approved budget, such staff as may be needed to delegate the duties the President may desire. The President shall have the right to discharge employees for good cause, set the hours, establish salaries and duties of the employees.

Reporting. The President will ensure that all marketing activities are aligned with the strategic plan as approved by the Board. The President shall prepare and administer an annual budget approved by the Board.

Article V
Standing Committees

Section 501.   Standing Committees

All standing and ad hoc committees will report to the Board of Directors. They will submit all recommendations to the Board for approval. All recommendations that constitute a change in NTCC policy will be submitted to the Board for review prior to submission to the full Board of Directors.

The following committees will be considered standing committees of the NTCC:

- Executive
- Strategic Marketing
- Resource Development

Article VI
Amendment of Bylaws

Section 601.   By Directors

The Board of Directors will have the power to make, amend, and repeal the bylaws of the NTCC. They may do this by a two-thirds vote cast by persons legally entitled to vote, excluding blanks or abstentions, at a regular or properly called meeting at which a quorum is present. Notice of the Proposed changes shall be mailed to the Board of Directors at least ten (10) days prior to the meeting at which the changes will receive a vote.

Appendix B

PROVIDENCE WARWICK CONVENTION & VISITORS BUREAU
Requirements and Responsibilities of the Board of Directors

I. *PURPOSE OF POSITION:*

Collectively, the Board of Directors assumes philosophical, legal and financial responsibility for all Bureau activities. The Board of Directors shall advise and consent on all Bureau policy, approve the annual budget, approve membership policy and fees and approve the overall goals of the Bureau.

II. *EACH BOARD MEMBER SHOULD HAVE:*

- A particular interest in, and basic understanding of, the Bureau's purpose and objectives.

- Experience and/or knowledge in one of the following areas: business administration, finance, advertising/marketing/public relations, tourism, economic development or other area of expertise in general business and industry which allows contribution to the overall objectives of the Bureau.

- A commitment of 2 – 4 hours per month to prepare for and attend Board meetings, committee meetings and to participate in other appropriate Bureau activities.

- The commitment to make decisions based on the best interests of the destination.

III. *JOINT RESPONSIBILITIES:*

Board members are jointly responsible for:

Administration:

- Adopting policies which determine the purpose, governing principles, functions and activities, internal operations and courses of action for the Bureau;

- Together with the President, developing an annual work plan of goals, objectives and activities for the Bureau;

- Administering the Bureau activities in accordance with the Bylaws and other policies adopted by the Board of Directors;

- Working to insure that the Bureau fulfills all legal requirements in the conduct of its business and affairs.

Finance:

- Approving the annual operating budget and monitoring the finances of the Bureau;

- Advising and consenting to levels of fees charged for Bureau membership and the fees for subscription services offered to members and non-members;
- Insuring that sufficient funds are available for the Bureau to meet its objectives;
- Authorizing an annual audit;
- Insuring that the Bureau is operating in compliance with the fiscal policy developed and approved by the Board;
- Reviewing and assuming responsibility for all expenditures necessary for the operation of the Bureau outside the scope of the annual budget, which shall be administered by the President.

Public Relations:

- Overseeing and participating in the Bureau's mission, purpose, objectives and activities to the community;
- Giving sponsorship and prestige to the Bureau and inspiring confidence in its activities;
- Advising and consenting to the utilization of outsource services in the public relations arena;
- Serving as advocates for the Bureau, tourism and related economic development.

Evaluation:

- Regularly reviewing and evaluating the Bureau's operations and maintaining generally accepted standards of performance;
- Monitoring the Bureau's activities;
- Advising and consenting to the utilization of outside consultation services on an as-needed basis;
- Counseling and providing good judgment on plans of committees to the President.

Personnel:

- Making recommendations to the Chairman of the Board on the selection, hiring and evaluation of the President;
- Advising and consenting to policies governing personnel administration;
- Advising and consenting to proposed salary levels and fringe benefits for all Bureau employees.

IV. INDIVIDUAL RESPONSIBILITIES:

A responsible Bureau Board member should:

- Support Board decisions even when he or she may differ personally with the majority decision;

- Understand the mission of the Bureau and promote the goals and activities of the Bureau to his or her own constituent groups, other members and the community as a whole;

- Become familiar with all materials, information issues and documents relating to the Bureau and its operation, especially those relating to financial matters and member services;

- Prepare for and attend Board meetings as scheduled and at other times when called. Absence from more than three meetings in a year without compelling reason shall constitute just and proper cause for removal from the Board;

- Attend the annual planning retreat for the Board of Directors;

- Serve as an active member or chairman of at least one standing Board committee and attend the committee's meetings as scheduled;

- Attend activities, programs and workshops sponsored by the Bureau for its members and the general public as frequently as is reasonably possible;

- Contribute knowledge and/or time to the Bureau when needed and appropriate;

- Be willing to assume a leadership role with the Bureau as an officer, committee chairperson or other position when requested;

- Not become involved with the day-to-day administration of the Bureau, respecting the need for the President to be the Bureau's chief executive officer—reporting only to the Board Chairman;

- Offer opinions and insights honestly and with an open mind, without reservation and in a constructive way, with a desire to accomplish the best for the Bureau;

- Not commit more time to the Bureau than can be realistically afforded or fulfilled;

- Promote unity within the Bureau and seek to resolve any conflicts of the Board;

- Encourage other Board members to express their opinions openly in all Board meetings;

- Support membership recruitment and retention.

Name: _____ Date: _____

Representing: _____

Appendix C

PROVIDENCE WARWICK CONVENTION & VISITORS BUREAU
Requirements and Responsibilities of the Officers of the
Board of Directors

Chairman of the Board

Presides at all meetings of the Board of Directors and Executive Committee, if present. Provides leadership to the Board in reviewing and deciding upon matters that exert major influence on the Bureau's business. Acts in a general advisory capacity to the President & CEO of the PWCVB. Respects the confidentiality of Board discussions and publicly supports actions take by the Board.

Responsibilities:

- Advises and gives counsel to the President/CEO and other officers and chairpersons of the PWCVB. Reviews major activities and plans with the President/CEO to ensure conformity with the Board's view on corporate policy.

- Approves the agenda for the meetings of the Board of Directors and the Executive Committee.

- Participates as signatory on PWCVB bank accounts.

- Assumes liaison responsibilities with Committees assigned.

- Participates on a minimum one Committee and a maximum of two Committees during the term.

- Participates in outside activities, which will enhance the PWCVB's visibility and fulfills the PWCVB's public obligations as a member of the community.

- Networks with community leaders regarding the conditions of the industry.

- Directs the Board of Directors in formulating policies that will further the goals and objectives of the Bureau.

- Carries out special assignments in collaboration with the President/CEO, other officers and members of the Board.

- Strives to govern and develop long-range plans for the PWCVB.

- Acts for the Board when appropriate on Committee matters.

- Attends PWCVB activities, including membership functions, special events, etc.

- Reveals any potential conflicts of interest and removes oneself from votes on those issues.

Vice Chairman

Assumes the responsibility of the Chairman in his or her absence. Assists the President & CEO in carrying out the functions of that office and performs specific duties delegated by the Chairman. Ensures that the mission, goals and strategic plan of the Bureau are fulfilled by participating, deliberating and making good decisions that are in the best interests of the Bureau, the industry and the common good of the community. Respects the confidentiality of Board discussions and publicly supports actions taken by the Board.

Responsibilities:

- Assumes the duties of the Chairman in his/her absence.
- Reports to the Board/Executive Committee at each meeting on the progress of the Strategic Plan.
- Serves as a member of the Board of Directors and Executive Committee.
- Performs duties assigned by the Board Chair, which may include serving on one or more Bureau Committees.
- Assists the Board Chair in the performance of his/her duties whenever requested to do so.
- Attends special meetings as directed by the Board Chair.
- Represents the PWCVB with other organizations as requested by the Board Chair.
- Attends PWCVB activities including membership functions, special events, etc.
- Reveals any potential conflicts of interest and removes oneself from votes on those issues.

Treasurer

Ensures the integrity of the fiscal affairs of the Bureau. Ensures that records are maintained of all PWCVB, Board and Executive Committee meetings. Serves on the Board of Directors and the Executive Committee. Ensures that the mission and goals of the PWCVB are fulfilled by participating, deliberating and making decisions that are in the best interests of the PWCVB, the industry and the common good of the community. Respects the confidentiality of Board discussions and publicly supports actions taken by the Board.

Responsibilities:

- Serves as a member of the Board of Directors and Executive Committee.
- Ensures that the Bureau maintains accurate financial records, and presents these to the Board at each meeting, maintaining comprehensive knowledge of the financial analysis and reporting processes.
- Ensures that the records are maintained for all meetings of the Board of Directors and the Executive Committee.
- Participates as signatory on Bureau bank accounts.

- Ensures that provisions are made for an independent annual audit of Bureau finances.

- Performs other duties as assigned by the Board Chairman, including serving as Chair of the Finance Committee.

- Represents the PWCVB with other organizations as assigned by the Chairman of the Board.

- Promotes active participation in the PWCVB on the part of membership.

- Attends PWCVB activities including membership functions, special events, etc.

- Reveals any potential conflicts of interest and removes oneself from votes on those issues.

Secretary

Ensures that the mission and goals of the PWCVB are fulfilled by participating, deliberating and making decisions that are in the best interests of the PWCVB, the industry and the common good of the community. Respects the confidentiality of Board discussions and publicly supports actions taken by the Board.

- Serves as a member of the Board of Directors and Executive Committee.

- Ensures that the records are maintained for all meetings of the PWCVB for the Board of Directors and the Executive Committee.

- Performs duties as assigned by the Board Chair, which may include serving on one or more Committees.

- Keep a record of all the proceedings decisions, directives and resolutions of the Board of Directors and its Committees.

- Responsible for certifying and keeping at the principal office of the PWCVB the original, or a copy of the Bylaws as amended or otherwise altered to date.

- The Secretary shall also cause notices to be sent for each meeting of the Board of Directors and its Committees and shall preside over the Board of Directors in the absence of the Chairperson and Vice-Chairperson.

- Serves as a member of the Executive Committee.

- Represents the PWCVB with other organizations as assigned by the Board Chair.

- Promotes active participation in the PWCVB on the part of the membership.

- Attends PWCVB activities including membership functions, special events, etc.

- Reveals any potential conflicts of interest and removes oneself from votes on those issues.

Appendix D

Greater Pittsburgh Convention and Visitors Bureau Code of Conduct

The purpose of this policy is to provide employees with a Greater Pittsburgh Convention and Visitors Bureau Code of Conduct consisting of standards of ethical conduct and behavior, as well as core values most important to achieving the Bureau's mission, goals and objectives.

Bureau values and policies require each of us to observe high standards of ethics and integrity. We are expected to practice honesty and integrity in dealing with each other, industry partners, the business and hospitality community, internal and external stakeholders, suppliers, vendors, elected officials, government authorities and the public.

SCOPE

This policy applies to all employees, regardless of employment status.

ETHICS define what is acceptable and not acceptable in the business and social environment. Ethics are principles of conduct and moral obligations governing our actions, and our professional and personal standards of conduct. Ethics is a system of moral principles and values that the Bureau, its stakeholders, and the public have every right to expect from each other.

INTEGRITY is defined in this context as demonstrating high moral character, and adhering to the Bureau's CVB Code of Conduct standards without hedging, quibbling or evasive statements that are technically correct, but are meant to mislead.

CVB CODE OF CONDUCT STANDARDS

1. Courage to act with truth and conviction.
2. Value and respect the dignity and diversity of Bureau staff, clients, customers, stakeholders and constituents, building goodwill and better relationships.
3. Behavior and decisions should be committed to excellence. Decisions must be fair and beneficial to all concerned, and must pass public scrutiny.

The Bureau's Code of Conduct standards work closely and in conjunction with the Bureau's Business Ethics Policy.

Primary areas covered by the Bureau's Code of Conduct:

Financial Reporting: The same set of books, reported in the same fashion to internal and external stakeholders, for decision-making and action using GAAP and FASB standards.

Performance Reporting: Internal progress reports that focus on major performance objectives of every position, function and organizational structure of the Bureau team.

Interpersonal Relationships: includes interaction with staff, stakeholders, business partners, clients and constituents, as well as other obligations the Bureau shoulders beyond the written terms of an agreement for service.

1. It is the personal responsibility of each Bureau employee to adhere to the CVB Code of Conduct and to conduct him or herself accordingly, whether imposed by law or by Bureau business ethics policy or similar standard. Employees who do not adhere to the CVB Code of Conduct and business ethic standards are acting outside the employment scope. For clarification of activities that are in violation of our Code of Conduct, cross-reference GPCVB Policy #1013, Conduct/Job Performance. Employees engaging in prohibited activities risk disciplinary action and/or discharge.

2. It is the personal responsibility of each Bureau employee to maintain loyalty to the Bureau and to discharge his or her assigned duties and responsibilities with dedication to achieving the Bureau's mission, goals and objectives.

3. All Bureau employees, beyond legal and ethical compliance, are expected to observe the CVB Code of Conduct, demonstrating business and personal ethical behavior in the discharge of their assigned duties and responsibilities. This requires the practice of integrity and honesty in each aspect of Bureau activity, including interaction with fellow staff members, the Board, public, partners, stakeholders, the business and hospitality community, vendors and governmental/regulatory authorities.

4. All Bureau employees are expected to refuse to engage in or sanction any activities for personal gain at the Bureau's expense.

5. All Bureau employees are expected to impartially serve all Bureau constituents, to provide no special privilege to any individual constituent, nor to accept special personal compensation from an individual constituent, except with the approval of governing stakeholders.

6. All Bureau employees are expected to comply with all levels of governmental regulations concerning lobbying and political activities and to utilize only legal, ethical and moral means and methods when attempting to influence legislation or regulations affecting the Bureau and/or the CVB industry.

7. It is expected that Bureau employees will not issue false or deliberately misleading statements or advertisements concerning the GPCVB workplace or community, or any other CVB, community or related industry to the media, the public, or any other industry either affiliated with or unrelated to the convention and visitor bureau industry.

8. The Bureau actively encourages a multi-cultural and diversified workplace through the inclusion of qualified individuals of diverse backgrounds. The Bureau refuses to engage in or allow discrimination or harassment, according to Bureau-stated sexual harassment and other employment-related policies and procedures, and in compliance with government regulations.

9. Reasonable steps will be taken by the Bureau's management team to communicate CVB Code of Conduct standards and ethical policies and procedures. The Bureau's business ethics policy and Code of Conduct is built into our business plans, performance objectives, and organizational mission, goals and objectives.

10. Ethics training will be provided periodically to Bureau management and staff.

11. The Bureau will document compliance efforts and results of evidence of its Code of Conduct commitment to comply with stated ethics policies, standards and procedures.

ADMINISTRATION

The Code of Conduct is to be periodically reviewed by Bureau management and Board members to ensure compliance with the spirit and intent of Bureau policies and practices.

It is the obligation of staff to make recommendations and refinements to the Code of Conduct to ensure its continued applicability and conformance with established principles of integrity and ethical conduct. Such recommendations and refinements will help ensure the Code of Conduct meets or exceeds industry standards, weaknesses are reported, and monitoring, auditing, and reporting systems are updated and/or corrected.

Every staff member has an ethical obligation to report breaches of this Code of Conduct to their supervisor, Human Resources Director, or the President/CEO.

An investigation of a reported breach will be conducted, report of the inquiry will be prepared, recommendations will be made as to the disposition of the ethics issue, and changes in the Code of Conduct recommended, if necessary. The Bureau may disclose the results of an investigation to law enforcement agencies, depending on the nature of the violation.

Disciplinary measures will be taken against any employee who violated the spirit of the Code or other business ethics standard, up to and including termination of employment.

It is a violation of this policy to intimidate or impose any form of retribution to an employee who utilizes such reporting system in good faith to report violations (except that appropriate action may be taken against any Bureau employee(s) if the individual is one of the wrongdoers.)

INTERPRETATION AND CONTROL

The Bureau's President and CEO, along with outside legal counsel, HR Director, Department Directors, and supervisors, will be responsible for interpretation and administration of this policy.

Appendix E

CVB Board Structure Inventory

Please check either yes, no, or don't know to indicate which of the following structural components the Bureau has in place.	Yes	No	Don't Know
1. Does the board have appropriate representation in terms of:			
a. Business/Industry Blend			
b. Geographic considerations			
c. Diversity of talents			
d. Board experience			
e. Visibility/Influence			
f. Overall Board size			
2. Does the Board periodically review its structure and bylaws to determine if any changes need to be made?			
3. Does the board have a written code of conduct?			
4. Do all board committees have a written statement of purpose?			
5. Do all officers and board members have job descriptions that explain their respective roles and responsibilities?			
6. Does the board have a succession plan for itself in terms of how board members are identified, reviewed and selected?			
7. When identifying a potential new board member, does the board have a mechanism for determining what specific qualities are needed?			
8. Are all board members are given a comprehensive orientation to the Bureau and the Board?			
9. Does the board have a clear set of goals and objectives?			
10. Does the board have an effective problem-solving process?			
11. Does the board have a policy and procedure for removing non-contributing members?			
12. Does the board have a written procedure for evaluating the President's performance?			

Appendix F

CVB Board Self-Evaluation

Please indicate your level of agreement with each statement.	Strongly Disagree	Disagree	Agree	Strongly Agree
1. Roles and responsibilities of Board members are clear.				
2. Individual board members actively participate in board decisions and activities.				
3. Most board members devote adequate time to their board responsibilities.				
4. The board uses effective procedures for getting things done.				
5. Board members can discuss their ideas and concerns openly with each other.				
6. The information board members receive in advance of board meetings is useful.				
7. The board recognizes and utilizes the strengths of each of its individual members.				
8. Individual board members are held accountable for adhering to the Board's Code of Conduct.				
9. The leadership of the board runs effective meetings.				
10. The board regularly refers to approved goals and objectives to guide its actions and decisions.				
11. Board members look beyond their own individual priorities to focus on the board's overall agenda.				
12. The board understands and honors the boundaries between board and staff.				
13. A high level of trust exists among members of the board.				
14. A high level of trust exists between the board and the Bureau President.				
15. Board members work well together.				
16. Morale within the board is high.				
17. The board welcomes ideas for improving its effectiveness.				
18. As a whole, the board responds well to change.				
19. Overall, I would rate the effectiveness of the board as very high.				

Chapter 12 Outline

The Importance of Strategic Alliances
Stakeholders
Potential Alliance Partners
    Government Stakeholders
    Park Districts
    School Districts
    Colleges and Universities
    Business Alliances and Service
      Organizations
    Community Members and Local
      Citizens
    Corporate Community
    Hospitality Industry Associations
    CVB Associations
Making Alliances and Partnerships Work

Competencies

1. Explain why alliances and partnerships can be beneficial to CVBs. (pp. 219–220)

2. Explain the importance of stakeholder relationships to CVBs. (pp. 220–221)

3. List the alliance partners for CVBs and describe programs they might put into place. (pp. 221–226)

4. Describe an example of a CVB and a corporation forming a mutually beneficial relationship. (pp. 224–225)

5. Explain the importance of industry associations to CVBs. (pp. 225–226)

12

Alliances

By *Fran Bolson*

Fran Bolson, CDME, began her work with CVBs in 1996, and in October 2001 was appointed president and CEO of the Lisle (Illinois) Convention and Visitors Bureau. Before joining the bureau, she spent several years as a retail executive for Sears Roebuck headquarters in Chicago and as an adjunct faculty member of the College of DuPage where she taught business and information technology courses. She holds a master's degree in education and human resource development from University of Illinois and earned her undergraduate degree at DePaul University.

CONVENTION AND VISITORS BUREAUS (CVBs) are, for the most part, networking organizations and can be considered models for public-private partnerships. CVBs serve as a hub for an area's hospitality, travel, and tourism organizations. Therefore, forming partnerships and alliances is a basic part of a bureau's day-to-day activities.

This chapter will examine strategic alliances and partnerships and why they are critically important to bureaus in extending their reach and scope to achieve maximum economic impact in the markets they serve. The key word here is strategic, and it is becoming more and more important for destination management organizations like CVBs to be part of and perhaps at the center of strategic alliances.

The terms partnership and alliance are used interchangeably in this chapter. It is possible to differentiate the two because alliances are more formal by nature and have a broader scope. But in general, partnerships and alliances are cooperative efforts by two or more organizations that seek common goals and have a synergistic effect. When the parties bring their resources together, the benefits are greater than when they attempt the same effort alone.

When referring to strategic partnerships and alliances, various terms come to mind, such as funding, stakeholders, associations, public awareness, and the corporate community. This chapter will examine the strategic alliances and partnerships with stakeholders in and around a CVB's area, and primarily within the public and nonprofit sectors.

The Importance of Strategic Alliances

Strategic alliances are essential for communicating that investment in tourism brings great economic return to the community in terms of additional revenue. Bureaus are not large organizations, and key stakeholders can be invaluable in communicating the economic benefit the bureau brings to the market. Often, having government officials on the bureau's board of directors, and even participating in marketing projects, drives home the value of the destination marketing efforts.

By far, the leading source of public funding in North America is the hotel room tax. Lodging rooms are taxed to generate revenue on the state, provincial, county, and local levels. Governmental bodies mandate this room tax and, in many cases, stipulate its use for convention and visitor promotion. In municipalities where the hotel tax dollars are not restricted to tourism, the industry must make the case to earmark the proceeds for continuing or developing the tourism industry. With public-funding dollars comes the need for community awareness of the CVB.

Fiscally challenging times bring additional demands on already stretched public monies. Budget deficits often lead to tourism budget cuts. Knowledgeable partners—either local government officials or owners of major businesses like hotels—can be extremely effective in communicating the need for continued tourism promotion to build revenue.

According to the World Tourism Organization, tourism is one of the world's largest employers. However, CVBs, even in large markets, are small organizations that employ a small number of people in the local community. Therefore, public understanding of what a CVB does is often unclear. CVBs also spend most of their marketing dollars outside the market they serve; therefore, their efforts can go unnoticed by the local community. Strong public, private, and third-sector partnerships and alliances within the community can help spread the word and articulate the value, purpose, and economic impact of the tourism industry to the community.

Measuring the economic impact of the tourism industry is challenging because it takes research that can be expensive, although this cost can be reduced by partnering with local universities and altruistic consultants. Partnerships and alliances can facilitate knowledge sharing, which can be a cost-effective way to obtain the information a CVB needs for economic impact measurement, as well as a management tool for marketing efforts.

Effective alliances and partnerships produce better marketing and eventually stronger returns on those efforts. By pulling resources together, organizations increase their offerings, thus increasing their ability to attract visitors. In strategic alliances, the whole can truly be greater than the sum of its parts.

Stakeholders

The tourism industry comprises many elements, such as transportation, lodging, attractions and tours, food and beverage enterprises, entertainment and arts, convention centers, retail shopping, sporting venues, and meeting and convention services. Some of these are primarily targeted to hospitality and travel, but other areas, such as restaurants and retail, cater to the local community as well as to travelers.

Identifying the various public and nonprofit entities with which a bureau works helps determine potential partners for a CVB. Stakeholders are the stockholders of the nonprofit world—the various individuals, organizations, and communities that benefit from the destination's CVB and local tourism industry. A CVB's board of directors might consist of representatives from various stakeholder segments within the CVB's market area. For example, a typical CVB board may comprise representatives from local government, the hospitality/hotel industry, attractions, restaurants, and local non-tourism businesses. Community stakeholders can be partners or competitors for local tax revenues. Frequently, community stakeholders are also the trustees of the venues and attractions that the CVB markets or uses to host events. Convention centers, sports stadiums, arts facilities, and museums are just a few examples of publicly-owned venues that are both local community amenities and visitor attractions.

Potential Alliance Partners

Government Stakeholders

Many bureaus' service areas can include several cities, both large and small. Other bureau service areas are defined by county boundaries. Local governments have the authority to impose and collect taxes, and have considerable control over the appropriation of the revenues. Many bureaus have funding agreements with the government entities they serve, and thus have city or county government officials on their board of directors to help keep the lines of communication open and improve the level of awareness for all officials. In recent years, CVBs have also developed improved performance measurements and regular mechanisms for reporting to their local governments, enabling officials to see the return on investment in tourism promotion. It would be unrealistic to say that the understanding is always clear and the relationship between local governments and CVBs is always harmonious. This is not the case, which is why other alliances play such an important role in communicating economic impact.

Communication is not the only link between CVBs and local government. In markets where a convention center, sports complex, or multi-use facility is municipally owned, the bureau and local government are also marketing partners in their joint efforts to promote the facility and ensure its success. The local government depends on the bureau to book events in venues that generate hotel room nights, resulting in strong economic impact for the community.

CVBs can engage in various activities to build strong alliances with government. For example, they might create a public relations piece, possibly in a special newsletter or e-newsletter, highlighting current economic impact data. They also could schedule presentations at trustee and board meetings to outline the bureau's efforts in marketing their venues and attractions. Other avenues include ensuring bureau involvement on key committees and economic development commissions, such as a downtown business development group, and maintaining good working relationships with local government staff. Focus on projects such as community volunteer days and community improvements. Remember to involve government officials in welcoming messages and hospitality events for incoming groups and conventions.

Park Districts

Park boards and districts are also included in this government stakeholder category. They serve as trustee of local resources that bureaus may be marketing, such as museum campuses, water parks, beaches, athletic complexes and fields, and green space. Park districts also have programming that may be of interest to the CVB, as well as events they can bring to the area. A bureau, in turn, can prove valuable to the park district in marketing to travelers and increasing visitation to their facilities. These efforts can also bring additional revenue to the district in the form of rental fees and concession business.

The Rockford (Illinois) Area Convention & Visitors Bureau and the Rockford Park District have worked together to attract and host amateur sports tournaments since the mid-1980s. The park district's sports facilities were originally built to provide soccer and softball fields for local teams and largely sat empty on weekends. Working together, the bureau and the park district have developed one of the nation's premiere amateur sports destinations and annually welcome more than one hundred tournaments to the region.

School Districts

School districts also can be effective partners for local CVBs. Similar to the park district, the school district is rich in resources related to both facilities and programming. Schools can offer opportunities to host a variety of events and academic and athletic competitions that can bring visitors to the area. A CVB can be a valuable resource to the school in helping with the planning, marketing, and implementation of an event. In many cases, an event may not be sponsored or hosted by the school itself, but school facilities may prove to be a valuable venue for the CVB's sports marketing efforts. The school can realize some financial benefits in facility rental, or sometimes in situations where its booster clubs can sell merchandise or run concessions. A CVB can help a school district by participating in a business partnership that can augment the school's curriculum through student programming and activities. Many CVBs offer internships and can provide expertise and resources to the school district. For example, a bureau might help junior high schools students learn about the tourism and hospitality industry through an assignment creating brochures and other promotional materials.

Colleges and Universities

Colleges and universities also can form valuable alliances with local CVBs. In college towns, the university is often the major attraction to out-of-town visitors, and indeed may be *the* industry in town. Like park and school districts, colleges and universities hold the key to resources that benefit the CVB and the local hospitality industry. First, a college draws visitors who may be prospective students, as well as parents of students and participants in academic and athletic events. Second, a college might have facilities that help a CVB market and bid on hosting events in the area. Conversely, the tourism industry can help a college by championing the cultural assets of the community, thus helping the higher education community attract students. As in the case of local schools, a CVB can be a worthwhile partner to a university in hosting events within the community.

The village of Lisle, Illinois, Benedictine University, and Lisle's hospitality community have embarked on a groundbreaking public-private partnership that entails building a new sports complex on the university's campus. As in many communities near major metropolitan areas, the cost of land makes development of publicly funded and operated venues prohibitive. This partnership leverages the strengths and resources of each of the participants to produce a new and exciting venue for the area. The university donates the land, the village of Lisle issues the bond for the funds to build the complex, and debt is repaid using a portion of the hotel taxes generated by Lisle's hotels. The Lisle Convention and Visitors Bureau is working with the university and the municipality to attract events that create additional overnight stays to the area. Without this alliance, the sports complex would not exist.

Activities that can build strong alliances with the educational community include developing and working with interns from local colleges, community colleges, and high schools; developing a school-business partnership with school districts or colleges where the CVB provides a guest lecturer to introduce the hospitality industry to students; and serving as a community and educational liaison between the college hospitality programs and the students in the area. The CVB could contact program coordinators and suggest where the partnership can best benefit both parties.

Business Alliances and Service Organizations

A CVB might interact with various organizations and associations in the course of its day-to-day business. These associations play a role as marketing partners and stakeholders. They can be important partners for the CVB in improving an area's economic health, but they also can compete with the CVB for resources.

The chamber of commerce can serve as a conduit for the CVB by connecting it to businesses that are not related to tourism or part of the daily interactions within the tourism, travel, and hospitality industry. Local chambers and the CVB can partner in programs that appeal to both the local community and to visitors, such as downtown events and festivals. The partnership can extend their marketing dollars, which in turn can expand the efforts. A bureau's marketing materials, such as its Web site, travel guides, and calendar of events, often prove valuable resources for such events.

Downtown business alliances are another source of partnership opportunities for CVBs. In 2004, the Greater Des Moines (Iowa) Convention and Visitors Bureau teamed up with the Des Moines Downtown Community Alliance and created a nonprofit corporation to operate a convention facility that would have been closed by its original board of supervisors. This alliance saved an important venue and will ensure its role in the development of new and larger venues.

Partnerships with service organizations such as the Lions Club, Kiwanis, Rotary, and Knights of Columbus are also a good way for a bureau to build community goodwill. The bureau, in turn, can be a resource to the service organizations for volunteer workers and event organization expertise.

Various activities can build strong alliances with local service organizations. For instance, where appropriate, promote and support projects of those organizations by volunteering time, office resources, and committee or task force involvement. Also, visit and talk with the organizations about the services and responsibilities of the bureau within the community, and offer to write articles about the CVB for their communication vehicles, such as their magazines, newsletters, and Web sites. A bureau may also contribute articles about other topics as a public service.

Community Members and Local Citizens

A CVB has many ways to reach the citizens in its marketing area. Many residents are involved in one or more of the organizations previously described, from a government agency to the Elks Club. Still, there frequently remains a gap in a community's understanding of what a bureau does for its community. This is particularly evident in communities that are not popular leisure tourism destinations. Many CVBs have a strong interaction with the conference and meeting market, which represents high-value travelers, yet this is somewhat unseen or overlooked by the local community.

To tell its story, the bureau can highlight amenities that are sources of local pride, such as the recreational, historic, and cultural venues that enhance the residents' quality of life. Bureaus also create materials and guides that are useful for local residents, such as brochures about local attractions and multi-purpose maps. Some bureaus do special mailings of their materials for the community. This enables the CVB to directly interact with local residents and expand their awareness of the tourism industry's value. Local citizens are voters; therefore, it is a good idea for the industry to have their support.

The Cincinnati (Ohio) Convention and Visitors Bureau formed a strategic alliance after research told it that the top reason people visit Cincinnati was to visit family and friends. In partnership with WKRC Channel 12, the visitors center, and the city, the "Good Morning Cincinnati" show is broadcast live from the bureau's visitors center. This promotes all of the things to see and do in greater Cincinnati, and local residents learn more about what the region has to offer visitors and invite their friends and family to experience the destination. By informing local residents of the amenities and features of the destination, the CVB creates ambassadors for the region.

Corporate Community

The local corporate community is another area where bureaus can form strategic marketing partnerships. Increasingly, CVBs are forming alliances with the corporate community in their market areas. Financial institutions such as banks can partner on projects involving event sponsorship and advertising cooperatives. Many communities have an industry or a particular corporation that forms the foundation of its economic base. These firms can be effective strategic partners for the bureau in attracting and retaining visitors.

As part of their day-to-day marketing efforts, many CVBs have created travel packages as a way to make travel to their area more convenient and, at the same time,give the irprintandInte rne tmarke tinga str onger calltoaction. Mor e and more, though, CVBs are entering into less traditional partnerships as a way to stretch their budgets and reach more markets. For example, the Ohio Division of Travel and Tourism developed a partnership with a grocery chain that gave the industry additional opportunities to connect with consumers across the Midwest.

Many tourism destinations, particularly in larger markets, have developed affinity programs with corporate partners. The San Francisco Convention & Visitors Bureau has developed a preferred travel program with Visa where travelers can use their Visa card and receive special discounts for dining, shopping, and attractions in San Francisco. Tourism Vancouver has a similar program with its hospitality partners called Vancouver Rewards. Vancouver Rewards was developed as part of the Tourism Vancouver Signature Partners program. As a mandate between Tourism Vancouver and leaders in airline, credit card, and other industries that target the travel sector, this program was developed to leverage marketing budgets, augment marketing reach, and increase Vancouver visitation and visitor spending.

Several CVBs list their business partners in many, if not most, of their marketing materials. The Atlanta Convention & Visitors Bureau has a special section on their Web site for business partners and even lists various partners as "the official provider" of Atlanta's hospitality and travel industry.

The list of corporate alliances within destination marketing organizations is endless. CVBs that ar e successful at facilitating and growing alliances are CVBs that will thrive and grow in future years.

Hospitality Industry Associations

Association is another term often used in conjunction with partnerships and alliances. Members of trade associations have a common goal of advancing a cause through education, professional development, or industry awareness. The tourism industry claims several associations, such as the American Hotel & Lodging Association (AH&LA), the Destination Marketing Association International (DMAI), the Travel Industry Association of America (TIA), the Convention Industry Council (CIC), and the National Tour Association (NTA), just to name a few. Many travel associations have counterparts on the state level, too. Alliances with travel and hospitality associations are vital to CVBs for creating industry awareness and advancement, as well as strong marketing partnerships.

Examples of bureaus working with industry associations abound. The Greater Madison (Wisconsin) Convention & Visitors Bureau (GMCVB) has worked with the Madison Area Wisconsin Innkeepers Association to partner on a project that reflects caring for others and exemplifies civic responsibility. "Hospitality with a Heart" is a program that began to help Madison's Salvation Army and New York City hospitality employees and their families who were affected by the terrorist attacks of September 11, 2001. The GMCVB and more than one hundred other hospitality-related organizations donated packages to be auctioned on the bureau's Web site. This successful effort has expanded into an ongoing program since 2001 and has demonstrated how hospitality partners can come together to assist community members in need.

CVB Associations

CVBs sometimes compete, but they also can unite for a common cause. For example, state CVB associations may join together to lobby state governments, where the tourism organizations, both large and small, pool resources to build a stronger position.

This is particularly true in challenging economic times when many state and provincial governments have major budget deficits. In Illinois, for the 2004–05 budget proposal, the governor's office proposed a fifty-four percent cut in tourism funding to help offset the budget deficit. The state CVB association joined together with other tourism-related organizations to launch a very aggressive campaign to show how this drastic cut to tourism funding would continue to reduce revenues to the state. This effort proved to be hugely successful in the way that it mobilized the different sectors of the hospitality industry and forced those involved to get into the public eye and articulate the case for tourism.

State and regional marketing partnerships also help supplement a larger destination's product offering and increase the area's ability to attract visitors. For example, in the Chicago area, sixteen CVBs joined to form ChicagoPLUS. After nine years of operation, it applied for and received official status as one of Illinois' regional tourism development offices. This cooperative was originally formed by Chicago's suburban bureaus to collaborate on leisure marketing efforts to pool funds for advertising in media that otherwise would be financially unfeasible. The Dallas (Texas) Metroplex Cooperative operates in a similar way with partners joining forces for specific marketing projects.

The cooperative called "Rhythms of the South" is a partnership of Atlanta, Nashville, and New Orleans in collaboration with eleven Southern states to produce a regional marketplace for 120 international tour operators and media members. This combination of bureau resources allows participating states to promote these distinct destinations with a common tie. Once again, this is a market where the combined effort of several markets allows them to compete effectively with other major international destinations.

Destination Marketing Association International. It goes without saying that a strong industry association can be an asset to state and local CVBs. The association can play a large part in the industry's advancement by offering professional development for CVBs in educational programming, networking, professional certification, and accreditation.

Sharing knowledge is priceless. The DMAI's "Brand Leadership Campaign" exemplifies how a national or international organization can assist the bureau community in redefining and promoting its value to its stakeholders. DMAI research shows that CVBs suffer low brand awareness and marginal market penetration. Many studies note that the great diversity of CVBs can be an advantage; however, the downside to this is a lack of consistency. The international organization—that is, DMAI—can offer programming that applies consistency where it is needed, and can bring a wide range of professional sources and opportunities to bureaus both large and small.

Making Alliances and Partnerships Work

Strategic alliances and partnerships are a fundamental aspect of the way in which a bureau pursues its mission. Regardless of the industry or type of work, there are some tenets that apply to cooperation. The rewards are considerable. It is not always about the size of budget and the dollars available, for partnerships are about leveraging dollars *and* optimizing participants' strengths for the benefit of all involved.

The following list appeared in Michael Adams's 1994 article entitled "Working in Sync: Partnering is the Trend of the 90's" in *Successful Meetings*.[1] The points serve as a good guideline for making the best of strategic alliances and partnerships.

- Treat collaboration as a personal commitment; people make partnerships work.

- Anticipate the time and budget to be expended.

- Mutual trust and respect are essential.

- Both partners must get something out of the deal; mutual benefit and mutual sacrifice.

- Every alliance needs agreement and early resolution of unpleasant issues.

- During the course of collaboration, circumstances and conditions may shift. Recognize the problems and be flexible.

- Partners should have clear expectations of the arrangement, including a timeline that defines major milestones.

- Get to know your partners.

- Appreciate the different cultures.

- Recognize your partners' interests and independence.

Applied to CVBs, these points can foster solid working relationships among diverse community sectors that will boost tourism's impact, improve civic and business operations, and enhance a community's quality of life.

Endnotes

1. Michael Adams, "Working in Sync: Partnering is the Trend of the 90's," *Successful Meetings,* August 1994, 38–43.

Chapter 13 Outline

National and Provincial Tourism Structure
    Canadian Tourism Commission
    Tourism Industry Association of
       Canada
Provincial Agencies
    Travel Ontario
    Tourism British Columbia
    Travel Alberta
Canadian CVBs
Case Study—Tourism Vancouver
    Initiative-Based Strategic Planning
    From Membership to Customer Focus
    From Destination Marketers to
       Destination Managers
    Creating Conditions to Generate
       Demand
Case Study—BestCities.net

Competencies

1. Describe the role of national agencies such as the Canadian Tourism Commission in developing and marketing Canada as a destination. (pp. 230–233)

2. Identify similarities and differences among various provincial tourism agencies in Canada, and explain how these agencies achieve their goals to enhance tourism within their spheres of influence. (pp. 233–236)

3. Explain the difference between destination marketing and destination management, and describe how some tourism organizations in Canada are moving toward a destination management model of operation. (pp. 233–241)

4. Describe how membership in BestCities.net benefits Tourism Vancouver and other members of the alliance, and identify the goals of the organization as a whole. (pp. 241–242)

13

Destination Management in Canada

By *Paul Vallee*

Paul Vallee, executive vice president of Tourism Vancouver, directs that organization's overall strategic focus. Previously, his professional career included tourism development and planning consulting in Vancouver and Toronto. He also has chaired BestCities.net and Vancouver's successful 2010 Winter Olympics bid tourism committee, and he currently chairs the British Columbia Institute of Technology's tourism committee. He holds a master's degree from the University of Waterloo, where he focused on travel motivations. His undergraduate degree was earned at Carleton University in Ottawa.

CANADA IS A HIGHLY COMPETITIVE DESTINATION on the global stage, ranking seventh overall in visitor arrivals (see Exhibit 1). The importance of the tourism industry in Canada has earned the attention of senior levels of government and the broader business community, which have helped facilitate the industry's growth. Tourism controls its own destiny because most governing bodies that regulate the management, operations, and marketing of destination products and services are in industry's hands.

The tourism industry in Canada has evolved over the years to a point where most public, quasi-public, and private-sector organizations are emphasizing more robust approaches to destination management. National, provincial, regional, and local organizations have stepped up their capacity and capability for delivering a broad range of services beyond the traditional role of promotions. Although marketing remains the primary focus, many of these groups now delve into such matters as infrastructure enhancements and investments, public policy matters, crisis management, and labor issues. However, an integrated approach to destination management involving the country's multiple stakeholders has yet to be developed.

This chapter provides an overview of destination management in Canada. It begins with an overview of the national and provincial tourism structure, with a specific look at the Canadian Tourism Commission and three provincial destination management organizations—Travel Ontario, Tourism British Columbia, and Travel Alberta. The chapter then focuses on Canadian convention and visitors bureaus, followed by an overview of the evolution of Tourism Vancouver, including its global partnership in BestCities.net.

Exhibit 1   2002 International Tourist Arrivals and Share

Rank	Arrivals (Millions)	Share (%)
World	**703**	**100**
1. France	77.0	11.0
2. Spain	51.7	7.4
3. United States	41.9	6.0
4. Italy	39.8	5.7
5. China	36.8	5.2
6. United Kingdom	24.2	3.4
7. Canada	**20.1**	**2.9**
8. Mexico	19.7	2.8
9. Austria	18.6	2.6
10. Germany	18.0	2.6

Source: World Tourism Organization.

National and Provincial Tourism Structure

The regional and sector level of Canada's tourism industry is supported by and works in partnership with provincial and national agencies. Similar to other jurisdictions, the regional and sector groups primarily work through the provincial level, which in turn deals with the national level; however, in some cases they work directly with the national tourism agencies.

All federal, provincial, and territorial governments are involved in tourism. Within the federal government, more than twenty departments and agencies have some type of role in and responsibility for the industry, all of which is coordinated by Industry Canada, a federal department. These departments and agencies are involved in such matters as borders, environment, parks, heritage sites, transportation, business development, First Nations affairs, agriculture, rural development, convention centers, and visitor information centers. Nationally, the marketing of Canada is managed by the Canadian Tourism Commission (CTC), a Crown corporation of the federal government structured as a partnership between the public and private sectors.

At the provincial and territorial level, the departments or agencies responsible for tourism are mostly departments related to economic development or tied into recreation, culture, and/or heritage. The scope of responsibility and nature of funding varies significantly from one province or territory to another. For the most part, the well-developed destinations, such as British Columbia, Ontario, and Quebec, are better funded than other areas in the country.

Exhibit 2   Tourism Investments by Federal, Provincial, and Territorial Governments in 2002–2003

Type of Investment	Total
Infrastructure	$999.40 million
Marketing	$266.20 million
Visitor info services	$174.93 million
Product/business development	$165.59 million
Research and statistics	$19.44 million
Human resources	$9.07 million
Other	$35.38 million
Total	**$1,670.01 million**

Source: Industry Canada, National Tourism Strategy.

According to the National Tourism Strategy (2003) that was coordinated by Industry Canada (similar to the CTC), most provincial and territorial organizations are considered industry-led. British Columbia, Alberta, Ontario, Saskatchewan, the Yukon, and the Northwest Territories have tourism offices that focus on marketing and management with the private sector. They have boards of directors with strong private representation. Manitoba, Newfoundland, Nova Scotia, and Prince Edward Island have created advisory boards that involve private-sector representation.

The National Tourism Strategy estimates that federal, provincial, and territorial governments invested some $1.67 billion in tourism-related initiatives in 2002. "Tourism-related" is a key term here given that much of the investment includes areas that are geared equally or more so to local residents. Investments such as roads, bridges, and parks get rolled into this figure, as outlined in Exhibit 2.

Canadian Tourism Commission

In Canada, the responsibility for marketing the country at the national level rests with the CTC. Created in 1995 as a special operating agency within Industry Canada, then made a Crown corporation in 2001, CTC is intended as a partnership between the federal and provincial/territorial governments and the private sector. CTC operates with an annual budget of approximately $83 million (Canadian).

The mission of CTC is "to increase awareness of and interest in Canada as a premier four-season tourism destination." One of CTC's primary objectives is to work with public and private partners; in fact, leveraged partner resources are a critical measure of CTC's success. CTC's activities go beyond marketing to provide and conduct: (1) macroeconomic, market, and industry research; (2) product and industry development; and (3) advertising and promotional activities in markets across the globe.

The activities of CTC "aim to increase tourism-sector revenues by attracting more and higher-yield tourists from international markets and by encouraging more Canadians to travel at home." In addition to Canada, the Ottawa-headquartered organization is globally represented in Australia, China, France, Germany, Italy, Japan, Mexico, the Netherlands, South Korea, Taiwan, the United Kingdom, and the United States.

CTC's private-sector component is at the core of its operations, from the board of directors to working committees responsible for individual program areas. Seventeen of the twenty-six seats on the board are reserved by law for the private sector, representing all segments of Canadian tourism and all regions of the country. The other seats are held by public-sector officials from provincial and territorial government bodies responsible for tourism. Seats from the provinces, territories, and the private sector are rotated regularly to ensure fair national coverage on the board at any one time.

The board has working committees that help deliver CTC programs. For each working committee, the board allocates resources and selects a chair from the private sector. Each committee develops the strategic plan and tactics for the program that it directs. Seven working committees are responsible for defined areas:

- Canada marketing

- U.S. marketing

- Meetings, conventions, and incentive travel marketing

- Europe and Latin America marketing

- Asia-Pacific marketing

- Research

- Product development

The strategic approach developed for each market varies. For the Canadian market, for example, the approach entails converting business that would otherwise go out of the country to stay within Canada, through inter-provincial campaigns aimed primarily at the consumer. For the U.S. market, the focus is on building awareness and generating sales through trade, media, and consumer campaigns. In overseas markets, such as Europe and Asia, the strategy is primarily geared toward partnering with the travel trade in programs that build capacity where most needed. For example, CTC offers a training program aimed at overseas travel agents with the objective of increasing knowledge of Canadian products and experiences.

CTC places a strong emphasis on activities that lie beyond the core marketing and sales functions of destination marketing organizations. Its strategies and programs have a considerable research component, whether that involves analyzing demand- and supply-side matters or analyzing domestic and international surveys. Canada was the first country in the world to publish a tourism satellite account—a database that processes information from supply-and-demand surveys to provide a composite view of the country's tourism industry. Canada was also the first country to develop and publish national tourism indicators based on the tourism satellite account, which provides relatively current monitoring data.

Another area that attracts significant attention at CTC is product development. Programs are in place to enhance product offerings, as well as identify certain tourism sectors on which to focus attention, such as outdoor tourism. Over the past eight years, CTC has worked with the tourism industry in Canada to establish thirty-four product-based clubs, the objectives of which are to increase the range and quality of tourism products in Canada, build business networks to increase the exchange of information, and encourage cooperative ventures and partnerships. These product clubs are intended to provide industry groups with a cooperative approach to addressing issues of common concern and to building alliances to tackle these issues. For example, product clubs have been formed with organizations focused on garden tours, northern wilderness adventure, and sport tourism.

Tourism Industry Association of Canada

The Tourism Industry Association of Canada (TIAC) is a national lobby group for the tourism industry. It is headquartered in Ottawa, the nation's capital, which provides the group with access to the federal political pulse. Founded in 1931, TIAC works to influence government thinking and action on behalf of Canadian tourism businesses, promoting measures intended to help the industry grow.

TIAC represents the industry as a whole, enabling the association to address a broad range of issues facing Canadian tourism. Its activities focus on legislative and regulatory barriers to the growth of Canadian tourism. TIAC works on a policy approach to advocate on behalf of industry in such matters as financing, sustainable tourism, labor supply, taxation, transportation (including air policy, customs, safety, and security), and public health.

TIAC plays an extremely important role in the interface between the public and private sectors on industry matters that are influenced in some way, either positively or negatively, by the federal government. Its work helps expand the horizon of tourism into destination management matters through efforts geared toward pushing for a government agenda conducive to a growing and sustainable tourism industry.

Provincial Agencies

Although every province and territory in Canada has an agency responsible for tourism, this section will focus on the provincial destination marketing organizations in Ontario, British Columbia, and Alberta. They have been highlighted purely for illustrative purposes.

Travel Ontario (Ontario Tourism Marketing Partnership Corporation)

Ontario has Canada's largest tourism industry, accounting for 34 percent of Canada's tourism revenues and 43 percent of its visitors. It is the largest gateway into Canada, with Lester B. Pearson International Airport the busiest airport in Canada.

The Ontario Tourism Marketing Partnership Corporation (OTMPC) was formally launched as a government agency in 1999. The OTMPC's purpose is to collaborate with the tourism industry and other government agencies to develop and deliver research-driven marketing programs that establish the appeal of Ontario as a destination. The organization is centered on partnering opportunities with the industry, particularly in leisure and business marketing and sales programs in Canada, the United States, and overseas markets. OTMPC also supports events and festival marketing programs.

OTMPC reports to an industry-led board of directors, which in turn is accountable to the Minister of Tourism and Recreation. The board has broad policy powers to approve budgets, as well as business and marketing plans. Industry-nominated product and market committees work with the OTMPC to develop strategies in the following areas:

- Markets: North American, overseas (primarily Asia and Europe)

- Sectors: Meetings, convention and incentive travel, Northern Ontario tourism, outdoor, city

OTMPC's operations encompass strategic planning, marketing research, product development, media advertising, consumer information services, publications, travel trade, and media relations. Through these operations, OTMPC creates demand, builds the brand, and generates awareness of Ontario's tourism opportunities, while its partners close the sales, deliver customer value, and provide industry feedback.

Tourism British Columbia

Tourism British Columbia (Tourism BC) became an independent Crown corporation in the province of British Columbia in June 1997. The corporation is governed by a fifteen-member, industry-led board with full management, financial, and legal authority, and is funded through a percentage of provincial hotel room tax revenue. This dedicated funding source is unique in Canada at the provincial level. The benefits to the corporation and the industry are: (1) Tourism BC does not have to lobby the government every year for an allocation from general revenues, and (2) it brings the organization closer to the industry, in that as the industry's financial performance changes, so does Tourism BC.

The mandate of Tourism BC is to promote development and growth in the tourism industry and to increase economic benefits throughout British Columbia, aiming to build the long-term growth of the province's $9.3 billion industry. Tourism BC works closely with British Columbia's tourism industry, including city-based organizations in Vancouver, Victoria, and Whistler, as well as regional and sectoral groups. Tourism BC also works closely with other provincial agencies, as well as the Canadian Tourism Commission.

Tourism BC markets British Columbia to consumers and the travel industry through various joint marketing and promotional campaigns in countries around the world. Some of the key markets include the United States, Japan, and the United Kingdom. It is responsible for marketing the *Super, Natural British Columbia* brand to the world. Tourism BC also manages a network of visitor information centers throughout the province, and it owns and operates call centers, central reservation services, and servicing training programs. The organization carries out its role by marketing BC as a tourism destination, providing information services for tourists, and encouraging enhancement of standards of tourist accommodations, facilities, services, and amenities. It also enhances professionalism in the tourism industry and encourages and facilitates job creation. Beyond that, it collects, evaluates, and disseminates information on tourism markets, trends, employment, programs, and activities, as well as on availability and sustainability of infrastructure and services that support tourism activities. Last but not least, Tourism BC generates additional funds for tourism programs.

Although some of Tourism BC's efforts are influenced by political pressure and influence, the nature of the organization's structure and funding ensures that its decision-making is primarily rooted in business principles. A major contributor to the business philosophy of the organization is the involvement that the Council of Tourism Associations (COTA) of British Columbia had in the origins of Tourism BC. Prior to 1997, Tourism BC was a government department guided more by public policy matters than business needs. COTA, which is a provincial association similar to the Tourism Industry Association of Canada, organized a strong lobbying group to pressure the provincial government to adopt legislation creating an independent provincial agency with private-sector control. Hence, Tourism BC was born, and it has served as a model from which other jurisdictions can learn.

Travel Alberta

Travel Alberta is the destination marketing organization for the province of Alberta with a mandate to increase the number of visitors to and within Alberta and the subsequent economic impact of tourism spending in the province. The organization is guided by the Strategic Tourism Marketing Council (STMC), comprising members from Alberta's tourism industry and three members representing the provincial government—all appointed by Alberta's Minister of Economic Development. STMC's primary role is to annually establish the three-year strategic marketing plan and to advise the Minister of Economic Development on issues affecting tourism marketing in Alberta. Formed in 1998, the STMC currently has nineteen members representing diverse tourism sectors across Alberta.

Travel Alberta management is accountable for and provides direction to its two marketing contractors, Travel Alberta In-Province and Travel Alberta International. Travel Alberta In-Province is responsible for executing marketing programs aimed at markets within Alberta, British Columbia, and Saskatchewan, while Travel Alberta International has responsibility for the Americas, Europe, and Asia-Pacific markets. Travel Alberta also works with six tourism destination regions— Alberta North, Alberta Central, Alberta South, Edmonton, Calgary, and Canadian Rockies—within the province that provide marketing funding to industry consortia with a goal of increasing tourism for these regions.

Travel Alberta's marketing strategies aim to keep residents traveling within the province, attract other Canadians to visit, and build business from the United States and overseas. The agency gathers and distributes market intelligence, as well as provides an integrated tourism support system through Web sites, tourism databases, visitor information centers, and contact centers. As with other provincial agencies, Travel Alberta develops marketing partnerships with the CTC, the tourism industry, and partners who are not involved in tourism as their core business, such as newspaper and broadcasting companies.

Canadian CVBs

The CVB industry in Canada is well-established in some areas, while fairly new in others. Similar to other jurisdictions, Canadian CVBs have a varied approach to structure, funding, governance, and responsibility. In some respects, all CVBs in the country are to a degree affected and influenced by public and government policy. At the same time, they are mostly governed by private-sector boards, with a fair degree of autonomy and industry-oriented accountability.

The primary role of Canadian CVBs is to market their communities' economic development products to the world. Some CVBs have a relationship with the economic development commissions in their region, either through a reporting relationship or by way of funding. Generally, the smaller communities' CVBs are tied in some way to economic development commissions, while those in mid-size and larger cities are independent agencies.

Most Canadian CVBs are legally registered as societies under the relevant legislative act for the province where they are located. These societies are non-profit and require a duly elected board of directors and bylaws to govern the groups' affairs. The boards report to the members on fiscal, marketing, and membership performance measures.

Canadian CVBs operate mostly under the corporate label of "tourism," which covers a broad spectrum of responsibility. Unlike in the United States where "tourism" tends to be used to describe activities related to leisure travel, in Canada it defines all types of activities, both leisure and business. Lately, a few CVBs have been changing their name to destination, away from tourism, such as Destination Halifax and Destination Winnipeg. The destination label arguably broadens the scope of the organization. Destination Winnipeg, for instance, speaks about a range of issues with respect to industry, economic development, the city's economy, tourism, and related sectors.

CVBs are located across the country. Canada's largest cities—Montreal, Toronto, and Vancouver—are represented by strong, aggressive, and innovative CVBs. Ranging in budgets from $10 million to $25 million (Canadian), these CVBs have a long history in their communities; for example, Tourism Vancouver is more than 100 years old.

Mid-size cities—such as Quebec City, Halifax, Ottawa, Winnipeg, Edmonton, Calgary, and Victoria—are also represented by bureaus with a great degree of expertise and strong success. Smaller places also have CVB representation, such as Kelowna, British Columbia; Lethbridge, Alberta; Saskatoon and Regina in Saskatchewan; Windsor, Ontario; Gatineau and Sherbrooke in Quebec; St. John, New Brunswick; and St. John's, Newfoundland. Resort communities such as Whistler and Banff also have developed innovative and successful destination marketing organizations.

Exhibit 3 provides a brief synopsis of Canadian CVBs and tax-based funding.

Exhibit 3   Examples of Canadian CVBs

	Structure	Budget	Markets	Segments
Large Cities				
Montreal	Nonprofit association	CDN$17 million	N. America, Asia, Europe	Business and leisure
Toronto	Nonprofit association	CDN$25 million	N. America, Asia, Europe	Business and leisure
Vancouver	Nonprofit association	CDN$10 million	N. America, Asia, Europe	Business and leisure
Mid-size Cities				
Victoria	Nonprofit association	CDN$3.9 million	N. America	Business and leisure
Calgary	Nonprofit association	CDN$5.1 million	N. America	Business and leisure
Halifax	Nonprofit association	CDN$2 million	N. America	Business and leisure
Smaller Cities				
Regina	Nonprofit association	CDN$1.4 million	Canada	Leisure
St. John's	Nonprofit association	CDN$1 million	Canada	Leisure
Sherbrooke	Economic development	CDN$660,000	Canada	Business

Although not as pervasive as in the United States, some Canadian CVBs are funded through hotel bed taxes or levies. In British Columbia and Quebec, the use of hotel taxes for funding has been well-established and is enabled through statute. In British Columbia, Vancouver, Victoria, Richmond, Surrey, and Kelowna have put into place a 2 percent hotel tax that is used by their respective CVBs for marketing and sales. In Quebec, Gatineau, Montreal, and Quebec City have a two-dollar-per-room-night charge. Recently, in Toronto, a 3 percent destination marketing fee has been put into place; however, the fee is not legislated by government—it is voluntary as far as which hotels have agreed to pay it.

Case Study—Tourism Vancouver

Tourism Vancouver—the Greater Vancouver Convention and Visitors Bureau—focuses on generating demand from travel influencers, that is, meeting planners and tour operators, and end-users such as individual visitors, convention delegates, and cruise passengers. Its efforts are designed to increase demand for

Greater Vancouver hotel rooms, attraction visits, retail sales, sightseeing tours, airline seats, restaurant meals, event tickets, and more. This private-sector association represents more than 1,000 member businesses in tourism and related fields. The organization's mission states that Tourism Vancouver is committed to creating exceptional experiences and delivering long-term value for customers.

Tourism Vancouver's mandate has been broadened substantially over the past fifteen years. In responding to emerging opportunities by taking a leadership position in the local community, such as bidding on the Winter Olympics, Tourism Vancouver has enhanced its relevancy and credibility as an organization and the industry it represents. In fact, for more than ten years, tourism has been recognized as the most important industry in Greater Vancouver by local residents, far outstripping other industries in a blind, unprompted questionnaire conducted by Synovate that is available to the public through Tourism Vancouver.

The organization has undertaken four important shifts in an evolving mandate:

- In 1993, Tourism Vancouver adopted an "initiative-based" strategic planning model that entrenched long-term planning as the foundation of the organization.

- In 1997, the focus of the association shifted from a "members come first" to a "customers come first" organization.

- In 1998, the organization broadened its strategic mandate from destination marketers to destination managers.

- In 2003, Tourism Vancouver implemented a multi-pronged approach to managing its business, covering a set of eight conditions that had to be addressed to be successful.

Initiative-Based Strategic Planning

In 1993, recognizing that the organization's planning tended to be narrowly applied and somewhat short-term, Tourism Vancouver instituted a business process change to embrace an organization-wide involvement with longer planning horizons. The new planning approach was rooted in the philosophy that strategies drive initiatives, which in turn drive tactics. Initiative-based planning was designed to involve most, if not all, Tourism Vancouver employees in setting the direction of the organization.

The plans developed by Tourism Vancouver over the years have gained recognition among fellow CVBs, as well as customers. Each plan is characterized by five basic principles:

1. *Consultative.* From client advisory boards to membership input sessions to stakeholder consultations, the intention is for many people and organizations to contribute to the plan.

2. *Dynamic.* The annual business plan is focused and directed, but it is not set in stone. The ever-changing nature of business dictates that the plan must be responsive to new opportunities that arise.

3. *Performance-driven.* Monthly tracking of some seventy measures and quarterly reporting to the industry were introduced in 1993, featuring the investment effectiveness index that analyzes the accomplishment of goals against investment made.

4. *Long-term.* The initiatives laid out in the plan have a minimum three-year horizon. Tourism Vancouver's approach was to ensure continuity to both sellers and buyers in the marketplace.

5. *Team-oriented.* Initiative teams develop, deliver, and evaluate their initiatives with support from management and the board of directors. The successful execution of the plan is predicated on the basis of highly-qualified and motivated teams delivering superior service to customers.

From Membership to Customer Focus

Vancouver is known worldwide for its exceptional setting. The impetus for the destination's success has come from satisfying the maxim—"location, location, location." Yet the notion popularized in author W. P. Kinsella's *Field of Dreams*— build it and they will come—is far too simplistic to pass muster in the complex environment of destination management.

In 1997, Tourism Vancouver reoriented itself to focus on the needs of customers, such as meeting planners, tour operators, and independent consumers, instead of the wishes of members. For a member-based association, this shift required a significant amount of persuasion, debate, and strategic thinking.

The notion was that providing exceptional value through customer service would be the strategic difference that would keep moving Vancouver toward the top of the list of international destinations. Speaking to the DMAI at its 1993 conference in Atlanta, marketing consultant Alf Nucifora stated, "The margin will be in the attributes that surround the product, not the physical product itself. The real product value is in the surrounding components...the atmospherics...service, delivery and responsiveness."

In the tourism industry, hospitality has always been at the root of the business. Yet sometimes the customer is taken for granted, or worse, overlooked by local politics and membership demands. The implications for CVBs and the industry are to risk becoming order-takers rather than sellers and service providers, price-driven rather than value-focused, and short-term operators rather than long-term strategists.

The challenge identified by Tourism Vancouver was to ensure the bureau and its members stay one step ahead of not only the competition, but also the customers by anticipating and responding to their needs. The objective was to truly entrench service as an attribute of Vancouver, to change the equation for success from:

$$\text{Setting} + \text{Facilities} + \text{Access} + \text{Service} = \text{Success}$$
$$\text{to}$$
$$\text{Service} \times (\text{Setting} + \text{Facilities} + \text{Access}) = \text{Success}$$

The calculation with the formula results in the notion that without service, success cannot be achieved. As service levels increase, the bureau and the industry will have a far greater impact and success ratio than they did with the old equation.

At the time, Tourism Vancouver unveiled its business plan, *"Tourism. New Rules. New Game,"* using customer research and testimonials to support the approach. The plan reviewed the principles of innovation focused on the end-user. More resources were allocated to building one-to-one relationships with best customers. The objective was to develop strong connections to get a greater share of each customer's long-term business. Through technology, new methods were created for ongoing customer dialogue. In sum, Tourism Vancouver began investing more significantly in key customer partnerships.

From Destination Marketers to Destination Managers

The board of directors of Tourism Vancouver faced two unprecedented opportunities to build the industry in Vancouver. In both these cases, the board decided to take a bold, somewhat unconventional approach for a CVB that had cemented the association's relevancy and importance with the community, stakeholders, and politicians. By doing so, the mandate of Tourism Vancouver has evolved from being destination marketers to destination managers.

The first situation was the 2010 Olympic Winter & Paralympic Games. Tourism Vancouver launched a bid in 1998 to pursue the games by committing cash, resources, and senior management staff. Winning the bid in 2003 ensured that Tourism Vancouver is partially responsible for an event that will fundamentally alter Vancouver and British Columbia's brand, infrastructure, and community aspirations, well beyond tourism.

The second situation was in 1999 when Tourism Vancouver convened key business groups in the city to develop a business plan for expansion of the convention center. Following acceptance of the plan by various levels of government, Tourism Vancouver entered into an agreement with the province of British Columbia that will see the organization receive guaranteed and legislated funding for thirty-five years in return for a $90 million contribution. The significance for Tourism Vancouver is similar to the Olympics in that the organization's mandate has moved beyond marketers to managers of the destination, responsible for initiating much-needed infrastructure for building Vancouver's success.

Creating Conditions to Generate Demand

As the mandate has grown, so has the way in which Tourism Vancouver builds its strategic planning and thinking. Although the bread and butter for the association remain sales, marketing, and servicing, Tourism Vancouver also develops and implements plans for other interrelated core business considerations, such as crisis management. An example of such a crisis would be potential visitor reactions to the SARS epidemic.

In 2003, Tourism Vancouver identified its purpose as *creating a set of conditions that generate demand.* The set of conditions that the organization endeavors to influence moves through phases that lead to a customer purchasing and, ultimately, experiencing Vancouver. These conditions ensure a multi-pronged approach to how business success is planned for, implemented, and evaluated.

The conditions are composed of the following strategic areas:

- *Members*—with an emphasis on promoting a network of engaged member businesses committed to quality customer-oriented products and services.

- *Partners (strategic alliances)*—with an emphasis on leveraging competitive impact in the marketplace through local, national, and global partnerships.

- *Corporate planning*—with an emphasis on the right human resource strategies, relevant technology, effective governance, responsive crisis management, and a solid revenue base to support the organization.

- *Sales, marketing, and servicing*—with an emphasis on strategies that drive the performance of the various sales, marketing, and servicing business units of the organization.

- *Destination development*—with an emphasis on influencing public policy to improve Greater Vancouver's tourism access and infrastructure.

- *Branding*—with an emphasis on delivering a clear and relevant promise that reflects what the destination and CVB stand for.

- *Channels*—with an emphasis on relationship selling, supported by print and electronic communications.

- *Customers*—with an emphasis on establishing and keeping long-term relationships through exceptional service with targeted customers.

This layered approach to planning and executing strategies that enhance the conditions of success places Tourism Vancouver's mandate in the realm of destination managers. Almost every aspect related to the tourism industry in Vancouver has involvement, either directly or indirectly, from Tourism Vancouver. The primary destination management challenge facing Tourism Vancouver is to continuously articulate plans for supporting members' economic activities, today and well into the future, while not losing sight of the destination's overall environmental and social well-being.

Case Study—BestCities.net

In 2000, Tourism Vancouver joined counterparts in Boston, Copenhagen, Edinburgh, and Melbourne to form BestCities.net, the first and only global convention bureau alliance. The alliance set out to address the growing expectations of clients and CVB stakeholders through shared information on best practices and defining a collective set of service standards. The alliance has since expanded to nine members, with the addition of Cape Town, Dubai, San Juan, and Singapore.

The BestCities.net approach runs counter to a common misconception held in the tourism industry that often confuses partners with competitors. Undoubtedly, competition exists among the alliance members, but leveraging knowledge and expertise globally is an innovative step for the industry. Recently, the Georgia Institute of Technology's Economic Development Institute recognized BestCities.net for its best practices in professional development.

BestCities.net operates with a strongly cooperative spirit designed to leverage each partner's participation. The alliance was launched with the notion that CVBs could learn from strategies successfully practiced in other industries. Air carriers, financial institutions, and automobile manufacturers are examples of industries where alliances have become an essential long-term business strategy.

The mission of BestCities.net is to be "an international alliance of convention bureaus leading the way in developing global best practices through innovation, knowledge exchange, professional development, and client servicing in the meetings industry." The alliance has as its primary objectives:

- To access and leverage resources through an exclusive, partner-based network of convention bureaus with a common purpose. These resources include financial, new market, and organizational expertise.

- To facilitate the exchange of best practices, ideas, and knowledge; market intelligence; and foster the development of new convention bureau programs among the partners.

- To share costs for joint activities of collective benefit, particularly in the areas of sales, research, and marketing.

- To gain a competitive advantage by developing an alliance brand that raises the profile and increases the exposure of all partners as key players in the international convention market.

Partnership in BestCities.net is reserved for convention bureaus that have demonstrated their ability to provide superior and consistent services to the meetings industry, as well as dedication to exchange knowledge and identify best practices. On top of that, each city is a highly appealing destination as proven by such factors as strong delegate attendance.

The alliance is a strategic response to international meeting planners who are demanding higher levels of service and quality standards. The lack of standards that exists within the convention bureau environment can frustrate buyers and suppliers. The essence of BestCities.net is a service charter and thirty-five client service standards that outline the commitment made by the partners to deliver exceptional service. The service standards are organized into six main categories: destination expertise; bid assistance; convention planning; attendance building; on-site event servicing; and post-event support. A client advisory board reviews the standards regularly. Each year, the partners conduct a self-assessment on where they stand with their service practices. The evaluations are shared with the group, and areas of improvement are identified and discussed.

The goal of BestCities.net is to become a preferred source for clients seeking potential meeting destinations, so that the BestCities.net brand will be broadly recognized as a standard for trustworthy convention bureaus and desirable destinations. The alliance is planning to establish joint service development programs and joint certification of its members. Each partner would align its own corporate objectives with those of the alliance and establish the necessary processes so that all partners may serve clients in the same way.

Chapter 14 Outline

Historical Development of CVBs and DMOs
  in the United Kingdom
Organization of the Tourism Industry in the
  United Kingdom
The Nature and Role of CVBs
  Structure
  Funding and Budgets
  Staffing
  Activities and Customer Services
Conference Desks and Conference Offices
Opportunities and Challenges for
  U.K. CVBs
Current Changes and the Emergence of
  New Entities
Case Study: U.K. Destination Marketing

Competencies

1. Explain the historical evolution of
   CVBs and DMOs in the U.K.
   (pp. 245–246)

2. Explain the roles of national and local
   tourism organizations in the U.K.
   (pp. 246–248)

3. Describe the ways in which U.K. CVBs
   are funded. (pp. 248–249)

4. Describe a U.K. CVB's marketing
   activities and the services it offers its
   customers. (pp. 249–250)

5. Describe the opportunities and
   challenges that U.K. CVBs face.
   (pp. 251–253)

6. Describe the different types of DMOs
   that can be found in the U.K. today.
   (pp. 253–255)

Destination Management in the United Kingdom

By *Tony Rogers*

Tony Rogers is chief executive of the British Association of Conference Destinations, a post he has held since 1989. Since 2000, he also has filled a similar role for the Association of British Professional Conference Organisers. Previously, he worked as a career advisor; for a world development charity; and most recently in economic development with Birmingham (United Kingdom) City Council. A regular contributor to the conference trade media, he is the author of two books on the international convention industry, including Conferences and Conventions: A Global Industry, *published in 2003. He attended the University of Birmingham, where he earned a degree in modern languages, and the University of Sheffield, where he earned a teaching degree.*

THE CONCEPT OF destination management, as opposed to destination marketing, remains in its infancy in the United Kingdom. The term "DMO" is used to describe both destination marketing organizations and destination management organizations, although it is really only the former that is widely understood and for which many practical examples exist. The structures of destination marketing and management are undergoing considerable change as of spring 2004, with several different models emerging across the different countries and regions of the United Kingdom. A couple of years or more may pass before any clear pattern is defined, and it is not at all certain that this will lead to a consistent and coherent approach for the country as a whole.

This chapter will examine the organization of tourism in the United Kingdom; the historical development of convention and visitors bureaus (CVBs) and DMOs there; the nature and role of CVBs, including structure, funding and budgets, staffing, activities and services, and conference desks and conference offices; opportunities and challenges facing CVBs; a case study of the York Tourism Bureau; and current changes and new entities.

Historical Development of CVBs and DMOs in the United Kingdom

The origins of CVBs and destination marketing organizations in the United Kingdom can be linked directly to the formation of the British Association of Conference Destinations (BACD). BACD began life as the British Association of

245

Conference Towns (BACT) in 1969, the brainchild of a small group of destination marketers who saw the benefit of collaborating to generate and refer conference business between them. The founding members were Bournemouth, Brighton, London, and Scarborough. The primary objectives of BACT at the outset were sales and marketing, information sharing, and education on "how to bring home the bacon," in the words of the first BACT chair.

In the early years, BACT membership comprised primarily seaside resort destinations eager to attract conferences to fill their bedrooms in the "shoulder" seasons of spring and autumn, complementing their leisure tourism business of the summer months.

The first U.K. CVBs were founded in the early 1980s: London in 1980 and Birmingham in 1982. During the same decade, many cities with a previously strong industrial and manufacturing heritage began looking to tourism and its related services to regenerate their economies. Cities such as Bradford, Liverpool, and Newcastle, for example, established offices to promote themselves to the conference and business tourism market, although these offices were more like the conference desk model discussed below than true CVBs. The real push for the establishment of CVBs began in the early to mid-1990s, driven both by the desire to involve the private sector in destination marketing and by the need to generate new funding and revenue streams as public-sector resources diminished.

During the late 1990s, the four constituent countries of the United Kingdom—England, Northern Ireland, Scotland, and Wales—began operating independently of one another, with governmental structures and decision-making shifting away from the central U.K. government, a process called devolution. The term refers to the political process of moving the government structures and decision making to the individual countries and, in the future, regions in the U.K. and away from central government. Tourism development and marketing were among the functions affected by this change. Scotland, for example, has its own national tourism body—VisitScotland—that reports to, and is funded by, the Scottish Executive (and through it the Scottish Parliament, *not* the U.K. government), while Wales has the Wales Tourist Board reporting to the Welsh Assembly. In Northern Ireland, matters are more complex because of the halting peace process designed to end civil strife there and foster coexistence between the Catholic and Protestant communities. These developments, among other things, have created an all-Ireland tourism organization called Tourism Ireland, Ltd. The Northern Ireland Tourist Board finds itself in the somewhat ambiguous position of working both with Tourism Ireland, Ltd. and VisitBritain, the body that promotes the United Kingdom to overseas markets.

Organization of the Tourism Industry in the United Kingdom

VisitBritain was created in April 2003 to replace the former British Tourist Authority and the English Tourism Council. VisitBritain has a dual role: It is responsible for promoting England as a tourist destination and for promoting the United Kingdom internationally. VisitScotland and the Wales Tourist Board are expected to work in partnership with VisitBritain when undertaking overseas activities, but they are free to act independently in terms of domestic marketing.

Below this national level, there are regional or area tourist boards covering all of the United Kingdom and representing substantial geographical regions, such as South West England, North Wales, and the Highlands of Scotland. In some cases, especially in Scotland, a dedicated convention bureau exists as part of the area tourist board, but generally the boards have focused on leisure tourism activities. The structure and role of these regional/area tourist boards is changing, as discussed later.

In cities, towns, and in some cases counties, many local authorities or municipalities have a tourism development and promotion department. However, without exception, such departments are non-statutory organizations, and their level of funding and resources is entirely at the discretion of each local municipality. CVBs exist mainly at the city or county level. Some concentrate purely on the convention and business tourism market; others take responsibility for both business and leisure tourism marketing and development.

The Nature and Role of CVBs

In the United Kingdom, there are about eighty DMOs active within the conference and business tourism sector. Of these, some fifty could be described as CVBs, with the balance operating as "conference desks" or "conference offices." In the U.K., bureau is a generic term that covers a variety of structures in terms of their staffing, funding, and operations, although all share the same fundamental mission, which, in the words of destination marketing expert Richard Gartrell, is to "solicit and service conventions and other related group business and to engage in visitor promotions which generate overnight stays for a destination, thereby enhancing and developing the economic fabric of the community."[1]

Structure

CVBs, also known as tourism bureaus and conference bureaus (but see also the references to conference desks and conference offices below), are usually formed and financed as partnerships between public- and private-sector bodies. In the United Kingdom, this can include local authorities or municipalities, chambers of commerce, local economic development agencies, hotels, tourist venues, and similar businesses. CVBs are set up as not-for-profit organizations, controlled by a management board and representing a specific destination, frequently a city. In most cases, the CVB is established independently of the local authority or authorities it represents, but in others, such as North Wales Conferences and Blackpool Conference Bureau, the bureau remains an integral part of the local authority structure. Marketing Manchester is a public-private sector partnership, while Destination Cambridge falls under the jurisdiction of the local environment and planning department. VisitLondon is a public-private sector partnership with a board of nonexecutive members drawn from different categories of membership, local government representatives, and VisitBritain representatives. The board sets policy and overall strategy for the organization. All of these organizations promote

Exhibit 1   Funding Sources of U.K. CVBs

Source	Bureaus receiving funding from this source
Local authority or municipality	90%
Central government	8%
European Union	25%
Regional government or agency	28%
Membership fees	58%
Commercial activities	63%
Private sector sponsorship	30%
Other	2%

Source: BACD membership survey, 2003.

themselves without using the words "convention and visitors bureau" in their titles, a practice that is quite common in the U.K.

Funding and Budgets

Funding for CVBs is derived from public-sector contributions, often the largest single source; private-sector membership fees from venues like historic sites, theme parks, accommodation/housing providers, professional conference organizers or independent meeting planners, destination management companies, transport operators, audiovisual companies, and other kinds of suppliers; sponsorship; joint commercial activities with members, and, in some cases, commissions that are charged to members on business placed with them.

The United Kingdom does not have a system of bed taxes or hotel transient occupancy taxes as is found in North America. As a consequence, budgets are substantially smaller in the United Kingdom, with staffing budgets for convention and business tourism activity averaging £77,515 (approximately U.S. $140,000) in 2003, according to the 2003 BACD membership survey. However, this figure covers a broad range of staffing budgets, with only eighteen percent of bureaus having a budget of £100,000 or more. Marketing budgets averaged £73,330, but it should be noted that forty-one percent of bureaus had a marketing budget of less than £20,000 for convention and business tourism marketing. Exhibit 1 lists the most common sources of funding for CVBs in the U.K.

Some bureaus prefer to charge a high membership fee that covers a full package of benefits and services to their members, with few, if any, hidden or extra charges. Other bureaus opt for a much lower membership fee that provides core benefits, but invite their members to buy into additional activities and services on a partnership basis.

The high membership fee, which can amount to as much as £5,000 annually for large hotels, enables longer-term planning to be undertaken with greater confidence, provided, of course, that the bureau can also achieve a high retention level among its membership. The bureau knows that it should receive a certain membership income in ensuing years and can plan its activities and expenditures accordingly. This model also means that the CVB does not have to go back to its members periodically to seek their financial support for specific activities, which can be time-consuming for the bureau and irritating to the membership. The weakness, or perhaps more accurately the challenge, of this funding model is the need to guarantee significant returns to the members for their high investment in the bureau.

The lower membership fee typically would be one of several hundred pounds. This can make it easier to sell CVB membership because the initial outlay for them is much smaller. There is greater flexibility for members to buy into CVB activities—such as a stand or booth at a trade exhibition or an entry in a piece of promotional print—that most interest them and that match their budgets. They do not have to buy into a full package of benefits, some of which they may not require. On the downside, there are significantly higher administrative costs with this model. It can also be argued with some justification that those members paying a lower membership fee are likely to be less committed to the bureau than those who have paid a high fee and need to see the CVB succeed to justify their investment.

There is no right or wrong approach. Each organization and its members must agree on what is appropriate for them, then develop and fine-tune the model based on experience. Bureaus are dynamic entities that must continue to evolve in light of local circumstances, changes in market trends, the demands of clients, and many other factors.

Staffing

U.K. CVBs average three staff members (typically a general manager, a sales executive, and an administrative assistant with information technology skills) to handle the conference, meeting, and business tourism market, but the range is from just one staff member up to twenty. Additional staff are employed where the bureau is also responsible for leisure tourism marketing, and in many cases this will include the staff employed to run tourist information centers, of which there may be several in major tourism destinations.

Activities and Customer Services

CVBs provide a range of services, many free of charge, to conference organizers and meeting planners. They aim to offer a "one-stop" inquiry point for their destination, giving impartial advice and assistance. Such services are likely to include some or all of the following:

- *Pre-booking the event:* This involves provision of destination literature and information, venue location and selection advice, availability checks and rate negotiation, provisional booking service, familiarization/inspection visits, preparation of bid documents, assistance with presentations to a selection committee/board, and subsidies and sponsorship.

- *Preparing for the event:* This entails numerous activities, such as block accommodation (housing) booking service for delegates/attendees and coordination of the full range of support services, including transportation, registration, translation, and office support. In some cases, these will be provided in conjunction with a professional conference organizer or destination management company. Other aspects are promotional and public relations support to maximize delegate numbers and increase awareness of the event in the host destination; supply of delegate information packs and undertaking delegate/attendee mailings and confirmations; and planning partner programs, social programs, and pre- and post-conference tours.

- *During the event:* Services here encompass provision of "welcome desks" for delegates/attendees at major points of entry; public relations support; guided tours and contributions to social and partner programs; coordination of destination resources, including transportation and entertainment; civic welcome and recognition; provision of tourist information; handling travel inquiries and ticket sales; and registration.

- *After the event:* Finally, there are aspects such as post-event evaluation and follow-up research, and consulting support to the destination hosting the next conference.

Many of a bureau's marketing activities are implicit or explicit in the list of services it offers to conference organizers and meeting planners. A typical portfolio of activities for a U.K. CVB will include some or all of the following:

- *Direct marketing:* particularly direct mail, but also electronic sales and, occasionally, via a salesperson on the road

- *Print and audiovisual production:* compiling conference destination guides and other promotional print materials, as well as videos, CD-ROMs, and Internet sites

- *Exhibition attendance:* sponsoring stands or booths at trade shows such as International Confex, National Venue Show, Meetings & Incentive Travel Show, EIBTM (Barcelona), and IMEX (Frankfurt)

- *Overseas trade missions:* participation in overseas road shows and workshops, often organized by VisitBritain

- *Familiarization visits:* organizing visits for groups of buyers and press representatives

- *Receptions:* coordinating receptions, lunches, and occasionally, small workshops to which key clients, existing and potential, are invited

- *Advertising:* in local and national media

- *Public relations:* circulating information and releases to the media and often to influential community organizations

- *Ambassador programs:* identifying, recruiting, training, and supporting key individuals in the local community (often university academics, hospital staff, leading industrialists, members of the business community, trade unionists) to be "ambassadors" for the destination, assisting them to bid for and attract the annual conference of the professional institution or trade union to which they belong

Conference Desks and Conference Offices ———————

Conference desks and offices are normally established as part of a local authority's tourism marketing activity if there is no CVB in operation. The staff, typically a conference officer with one or two assistants, is directly employed by the local authority and is usually located in a department involved with economic development or leisure services. In some cases, they can tap into other staff resources such as computer and administrative services, marketing, and destination investment available within the broader municipal or county structure.

Conference desks undertake many of the same marketing activities as CVBs, and offer similar services to conference and event organizers. The main differences between a conference office and CVB relate to structure and funding. A conference office does not have a formal membership, but it may coordinate the activities of a conference or tourism association, bringing together the main conference players to collaborate in marketing activities for which financial or in-kind contributions are required. Conference office staff do not report to a management board but instead to the managers and elected officials of a local government department. However, there is a need to report on the success of the marketing programs where a conference association has been established. The budget for the conference office is determined by the appropriate council or municipal committee, but is often supplemented by private-sector contributions. Frequently, the conference office may also have direct responsibility for promoting one or more civic buildings as conference venues.

Opportunities and Challenges for U.K. CVBs ———————

In 2003, U.K. CVBs were asked by BACD to list the five greatest opportunities and the five greatest challenges/threats facing their destination. Opportunities were described under four headings, and the bullet points below highlight the most important opportunities identified by participating CVB managers.

Infrastructure

- Construction of new transport facilities and services

- Development of new *regional* product/infrastructure

- Building of dedicated conference or convention centers

- Refurbishment of existing conference venues

- Investment in/developments to general destination infrastructure (retail, leisure, regeneration projects)

- Increase in hotel rooms through new hotels and/or refurbishment programs

Marketing and Services

- Development of the destination brand, plus growing awareness and positive perceptions of the destination

- New marketing activity
- New destination management system with online booking facility, and other information technology product developments
- New and/or complementary tourism strategies for city and/or region
- Development of an effective Web site

Economic/Political (National/International)

- Political stability and peace
- Greater awareness and an increase in the volume of business tourism
- Close U.K.–U.S. ties (post–Iraq war)
- Sterling weakening against the euro
- Increased domestic business due to the threat of international terrorism

Funding and Resources

- Increase in dedicated conference staff
- Increased regional development agency financial support
- Development of a regional development agency strategic vision
- Involvement of and partnerships with the private sector
- Increased funding and larger budgets

Challenges and threats were described under the same headings. The bullet points below highlight the most important challenges and threats identified by CVB managers.

Infrastructure

- Difficult access or poor transportation infrastructure
- Cutbacks in air services, lack of affordable or international flights
- Lack of large or dedicated conference centers
- Lack of accommodation (housing), loss of hotel rooms
- Poor quality of hotel rooms
- Limited car parking

Marketing and Services

- Investment and competition from other destinations
- Emergence of new international conference destinations
- Perception as an unsafe destination
- Not meeting market expectations

- Weak destination brand coupled with perception and image problems

Economic/Political (National/International)

- Worldwide factors such as 9/11, SARS, war, economic downturn
- Strength or weakness of the local economy
- Political instability
- Strength of sterling
- Being out of European monetary union
- Need to rationalize the roles and responsibilities of the many public-sector agencies involved in tourism to ensure greater focus, cooperation, and accountability
- Change of local political administration/lack of political support
- Perceived high cost of the United Kingdom and London as destinations
- Staff retention coupled with service and skills development in the industry

Funding and Resources

- Reduction in or inadequate public-sector funding and resources
- Membership retention (losing members to competitors)
- Withdrawal of partnership support
- Lack of local venue staff understanding of or commitment to business tourism
- Complacency and apathy of venues

Current Changes and the Emergence of New Entities ———

Major changes to tourism structures are being experienced across the United Kingdom. Accompanying them is the creation of the first destination *management,* as opposed to destination *marketing,* organizations. The changes are not following any consistent pattern, nor is there standard terminology, so the industry must familiarize itself with a range of new acronyms and abbreviations. Apart from the term DMO, which is still in its relative infancy in the United Kingdom, DMPs, RTPs, RTOs, subregional organizations, and hubs are just some of the most frequently encountered new terms in relation to destination marketing and management.

RTPs, for example, are regional tourism partnerships, of which there are four covering the whole of Wales. RTOs, or regional tourism organizations, are found in Northern Ireland, although not covering the whole of the province. In South East England, the favored terminology is different again, with subregional organizations being in vogue. In Scotland, it is quite possible that CVBs may disappear by 2005 as the existing structure of fourteen area tourist boards (eight of which include a CVB within their operation) is scrapped and replaced by fourteen hubs directly linked to the national tourist board, VisitScotland. DMPs are destination management partnerships between public and private sector organizations.

Northwest England is pioneering the creation of destination *management* organizations. This region stretches from the Scottish border down to the Cheshire plain, and includes such renowned tourism attractions as the Lake District, Blackpool, and Chester, plus the cosmopolitan cities of Manchester and Liverpool. In March 2004, the Northwest Tourist Board and the Cumbria Tourist Board, which had been responsible for promoting the region as a tourism destination and also for supporting and developing the tourism product through quality assurance schemes, accreditation, product development, training, and research, were abolished and replaced by five DMOs to cover the following subregions: Cumbria, Lancashire and Blackpool, Liverpool, Manchester, and Cheshire and Warrington.

The ethos of these DMOs embraces equal partnership between the public, private, and voluntary sectors. The DMOs need the "wholehearted commitment of major players but no single interest or political influence should dominate," according to the 2003 Review of Tourism Destination Services in Cheshire and Warrington. They should be entrepreneurial in outlook, but not lose sight of strategic objectives in the pursuit of income-generating activity. One of the key issues to be resolved is the extent to which the DMOs should take over functions rather than work with existing bodies; that is, finding the right balance between coherence and integration.

Each DMO is to provide leadership for its own subregion and be responsible for the management and marketing of its own tourism product, including quality assurance, accreditation, training, and research, which formerly lay within the purview of the Northwest Tourist Board and the Cumbria Tourist Board. In reality, the breadth of these responsibilities is such that DMOs are expected to specialize in one or two of these fields and procure the specialist expertise for other fields as necessary from other DMOs. Decisions about key regional infrastructure investments, such as the construction of a major convention center envisaged in the region's strategic plan, *The Tourism Vision for England's Northwest,* will be taken under the guidance of a regional tourism forum, with input from the Northwest Development Agency (NWDA). NWDA is one of nine regional development agencies across England established by the U.K. government in 1998 to oversee the economic regeneration and development of their regions.

The emphasis, therefore, in England is on devolution and regionalization, with relatively little being done on a pan-England level, especially in the business tourism sector. In Scotland, a very different scenario is evolving, almost moving in the opposite direction toward a much more centralized, national approach. In March 2004, the Scottish Tourism Minister announced that the fourteen area tourist boards would be replaced by an integrated VisitScotland network. He announced that this Scotland-wide network would consist of local tourism hubs that would be responsible for delivering the national tourism strategy in their area. As noted in *Scottish Tourism—Going for Growth,* they would also be expected to "respond to circumstances in their areas and link with the growing number of private-sector tourism action groups across Scotland." Unlike the area tourist boards, the new VisitScotland network would not be a membership organization, but would charge for all its services to tourism businesses. It is not yet clear what responsibility these hubs will have for the management of their destinations, but it would appear that it will be at a much lower level than that evolving in England's Northwest region.

Across the United Kingdom, huge changes are being experienced in the structures, funding, and methodologies of DMOs. The "M" in DMO is beginning to mean management rather than marketing, as the realization dawns that DMOs not only have a role in selling the destination product but also in defining what that product should be. Rick Antonson, president and CEO of Tourism Vancouver, speaking at the BACD annual convention in 2003, expressed it thus: "It is our responsibility as DMOs to take the destination's personality onto the world stage. We go out there and we compete with people that those at home never even see. We know what the competition is doing—so the role falls to us to help manage the destination, to help define what it's going to become, to help develop new products or enhanced products so that what we take out to sell is what the consumer needs, and we take into the marketplace what the client wants."[2]

The hope is that, in the United Kingdom, once these many changes have settled down, there will emerge a more professional, better resourced destination management and marketing industry working in a coherent way. It will be crucial to retain a client-driven, market-centered focus. Failure to do so will mean that DMOs will be cut out of the decision-making process, or "disintermediated," to use another twenty-first-century term, as clients and consumers bypass them and go straight to the supplier.

Case Study: U.K. Destination Marketing

This case study gives a profile of York Tourism Bureau (YTB), an average-sized U.K. bureau.

York is one of the United Kingdom's smaller yet most famous cities. Steeped in history, York boasts Roman, Viking, and Norman legacies of the highest quality, with the magnificent York Minster still casting its magical spell over the city and surrounding area. York is the county seat of Yorkshire, and lent its name to the Yorkist dynasty that clashed with the House of Lancaster in the medieval Wars of the Roses. Today, one member of the British Royal family still carries the title of Duke of York.

Situated in the northern part of England but centrally within Britain, approximately halfway between London and Edinburgh, York is truly one of the gems of U.K. tourism. Its historical treasures and architectural delights make it a mecca for holiday and leisure tourists. It also acts as a gateway to a number of nearby attractions, including Castle Howard, Fountains Abbey, James Herriot Country, the North York Moors National Park with its famous steam railway, and the Yorkshire Dales.

York is not just important as a leisure tourism destination. Conferences and business tourism also play an important part in the city's visitor mix with urban and rural hotels, academic institutions, and a range of unique venues all competing actively for their share of the lucrative, high-yield conference and meetings market.

York Tourism Bureau

The YTB's role as the destination marketing organization is to maximize York's success as a leisure and business tourism destination. The bureau, an average-sized entity, has almost five hundred members who pay an annual subscription used to promote York to the travel trade, overseas and domestic markets, and the conference sector. The bureau also undertakes the marketing for First Stop York, a public/private-sector partnership that fulfils more of a destination *management* role for the city, with responsibility for marketing, training, research, product development, visitor management, and residents' issues. Other groups contributing to the overall marketing and tourism development activity include York Hoteliers, which holds a bimonthly forum for hotel managers; York Hospitality Association; the City of York Council, Yorkshire Tourist Board, based in York but representing the entire county of Yorkshire; and Yorkshire Forward, the regional development agency that provides funding and strategic direction for the expansion of the regional economy across all business sectors, including tourism.

Established in 1987, the YTB now employs forty staff in three locations, two of which are tourist information centers. It is set up as a company limited by guarantee, run on a not-for-profit basis, and has an annual turnover of approximately £1.3 million. A board of directors representing the different sectors of the industry oversees YTB's strategic direction, and the business is managed by a chief executive.

The overall purpose of YTB is to maintain ten thousand tourism jobs and visitor expenditures of nearly £300 million. It also plays a fundamental role in encouraging businesses involved in tourism to enhance their level of service.

YTB has three overarching objectives: to grow membership of the bureau by providing clear business benefits and raising its profile locally and regionally; to encourage more leisure visitors to come to York by providing new products, investigating emerging markets and delivering quality services; and to raise the profile of York as a great place for conference business and encourage more business visitors to organize and attend events in York.

These objectives are underpinned by three key principles: to be the best that it can be in delivering effective marketing campaigns and running the tourist information centers; to be a good employer, with a motivated and efficient workforce; and to have a well-managed, cohesive organization composed of members, directors, and staff.

York Conference Desk is a department of YTB. In this case, the term "conference desk" is used in a somewhat different way from that outlined earlier. The conference desk is *not* a part of the local authority, although the City of York Council contributes funding directly to its operation. The dedicated conference desk was formed in 1997 in recognition of the value of conference and business tourism to York, particularly in terms of how that sector complements the already strong and well-established leisure tourism product. The conference desk now employs two full-time staff members and also has a half-time post dealing with delegate/attendee accommodation bookings. Exhibit 2 shows the budgeted income and expenditure for York Conference Desk in 2004–05.

The conference desk's main marketing tools are its annual conference guide, in hard-copy format complemented by a Web site; the Conference York

Exhibit 2   York Conference Desk 2004–05 Budget

A. INCOME	£
1. Public Sector	
City of York Council contribution to marketing	18,000
City of York Council contribution to overheads	10,000
2. Private Sector	
Membership fees/dues	20,000
Advertising	24,500
Commission on business placed	56,000
Total Income	**128,500**
B. EXPENDITURE	
Salary/overhead	70,000
Marketing	40,000
Contribution to YTB	18,500
Total Expenditure	**128,500**

Source: York Conference Desk.

e-newsletter; a showcase; and a Web-based collaborative marketing initiative (www.conferencesinengland.com) in conjunction with the heritage destinations of Bath, Chester and Stratford-upon-Avon.

Endnotes

1. Richard B. Gartrell, *Destination Marketing for Convention and Visitors Bureaus*, 2nd ed. (Dubuque, Iowa: Kendall Hunt Publishing, 1995).

2. Rick Antonson, speech given at BACD Annual Convention, Liverpool, England, July 2003.

Chapter 15 Outline

Competencies

1. Outline the historical development of
    the Mexican tourism industry, and
    describe the role of the Mexican
    government on tourism's evolution.
    (pp. 259–263)

2. Describe the role and influence of
    Mexico's *Fondo Nacional de Fomento al
    Turismo* (FONATUR) on the country's
    tourism industry. (pp. 262–263)

3. Describe the structure, purpose, and
    funding of Mexican CVBs, and
    describe the services provided by these
    organizations. (pp. 263–267)

4. Identify the major challenges and
    opportunities faced by Mexican CVBs.
    (pp. 269–272)

5. Describe similarities and differences
    between Mexican CVBs and American
    and European tourism models. (p. 272)

15

Destination Management in Mexico

By *Elda Laura Cerda*

Elda Laura Cerda has fourteen years of experience in the tourism sector and is responsible for the Executive Director's Office of the Monterrey (Mexico) Convention and Visitors Bureau. She previously was assistant manager for the Mexican Ministry of Tourism's Northern Border Program, as well as host services coordinator for the Ancira InterContinental Hotel and convention and groups coordinator for the Camino Real Hotel. A recognized speaker in Mexico and South America, she holds a bachelor's degree in tourism and hospitality from Mexico's Universidad Regiomontana de Monterrey and a master's degree from Spain's Unversidad de Las Palmas de Gran Canaria.

DESPITE SIGNIFICANT CHANGES in destination marketing and management in Mexico, a large part of national tourism development still resides with the Ministry of Tourism, and therefore with the Mexican federal government. The mission of this agency is to plan, foster, supply, and support tourism services operations, as well as become a liaison for action among the various government levels.

This chapter examines the following topics: (1) historical development of CVBs in Mexico; (2) the institutional organization of tourism in Mexico; (3) the nature and role of CVBs in Mexico, including structure, funding, staffing, activities, services, and a case study of the Monterrey CVB; and (4) current conditions, opportunities, and challenges Mexican CVBs face.

Historical Development of Mexican CVBs

In the beginning of the 1960s, the Mexican government viewed tourism as a marketing vehicle for the country. Mexico hosted the 1968 Olympic Games, and there was some tourism infrastructure in the country to host such as event. On October 12, 1968, the nineteenth modern Olympiad was inaugurated, and with it, Mexico showed the world its capacity to organize huge events and display its tourism attractions.

Later, the 1970 Football (soccer) World Championship, organized by International Federation of Football Associations (FIFA), was held in the country. At that time, Mexico was the first country to organize and hold the world's two most popular sports events in only two years.

The first Mexican convention and visitors bureaus (CVBs) were created at the end of the 1960s and beginning of the 1970s to respond to the needs of visitors attending major events and to improve tourism infrastructure for events to come. The first known CVB in Mexico was in Guadalajara City in 1969, and the second bureau was created in México City in 1971. Through the mid-1970s, CVBs appeared in Acapulco, Puerto Vallarta, and Cancun. However, this initial trend did not become consistent throughout the country due to lack of resources.

By the end of the 1980s, a breakthrough occurred in management of Mexican tourism destinations when they began to receive tourism promotion funds from the government. After the devastating impact on the tourism industry caused by Hurricane Gilbert in Cancun in 1988, and facing a dramatic reduction of international visitors to Mazatlan, Mexican officials created a collaboration mechanism for tourism promotion called mixed funds. This mechanism was based on the creation of a fund with equal contributions from the Ministry of Tourism, state governments, and tourism service providers for destinations.

This is the way in which Mexico's collaboration effort finally started, as well as its initial attempts in managing tourism destinations, even if the core activity was focused on promotion campaigns. Financial resources were placed in a trust that had a technical committee composed of agents from the contributing parties, whose task was to direct and approve execution of promotion budgets.

Slowly, such funds were expanded throughout Mexico; more than thirty mixed funds were created. However, because contributions were voluntary, there was always the potential problem of defaulting on the financial contribution pledge. In addition, managing the funds proved to be extremely bureaucratic, diminishing their ability to enhance Mexican tourism. Consequently, termination of mixed funds began by 1997. Liquidation started, but this process has not been fully completed.

Nevertheless, it was evident that the mechanism had many advantages, mainly by involving the tourism sector stakeholders in decision making and by allowing for the possibility of having resources to conduct promotion campaigns for Mexico's tourism destinations in increasingly competitive markets.

Considering that marketing and promotion were the primary focus of most destination stakeholders, the first challenge to resolve was the availability of financial resources for these purposes. It became clear that the direction tourism administration would take involved strengthening local capabilities.

Following the initiative of the Minister of Tourism, the 1996 Value-Added Tax Law enabled state governments to charge a 5 percent tax on hotel accommodations. It was suggested that such resources be managed through a trust that would ensure that those resources were used for tourism promotion and also that the private sector participate in making decisions, as applicable.

In the future, the challenge for municipal authorities is to involve more stakeholders in destination development. Also, the private sector should more have participation, so that the process of professional management of tourism destination becomes consolidated. CVBs were officially created and launched with enactment of the room tax.

The Institutional Organization of Tourism in Mexico ———

Inclusion of tourism as a specific competence within Mexico's federal public administration started at the end of the 1920s and slowly grew in significance until reaching the level of a secretariat, which is equivalent to a ministry, in 1974. Why did the government confer such status to an agency the performance of which seemed to reside within the private business arena? There were two reasons.

On the one hand, acknowledging tourism's cross-functional role and the large number of external issues deriving from such activities, it seemed difficult for a private-sector economic agent to coordinate every requirement of tourism at any given time and cover tourism services beyond lodging and meals.

On the other hand, facing great challenges to develop economic opportunities for its population, the government recognized the highly positive impact that maintaining a sound tourism industry provides, therefore needing a government entity to push it forward.

Just as it has happened around the world, the level of government involvement and the orientation of tourism policy have evolved in Mexico. One can say that the federal government's role was primarily to regulate a migratory issue. As time went by, this regulatory role was supplemented as an effort to rule operations of tourism services.

In the early 1960s, an important contribution of the government occurred: communicating the image of Mexico abroad through creation of *Consejo Nacional* (National Board) of Tourism.

But the 1970s saw further developmental government activity—it became the owner and operator of hotels and airlines, and also assumed the task of creating cities for tourism. Case in point was Cancun, where the board carried out the master program to acquire land parcels, urbanize them, build hotels, execute promotion, and finance tourism-related companies at subsidized rates. In general terms, the government made sure that this new tourism destination—a strategic investment—appeared on the map.

The 1980s and 1990s showed that progress would not be reversed in terms of tourism. The beginning of a deregulation process and decentralization of competencies started the process toward the individual states, particularly in terms of regulation and supervision of tourism service provision.

Beyond the powers established by law, namely the Federal Public Administration Organic Law and Federal Law of Tourism, it can be stated that in the case of Mexico the current role of state government cannot be framed in just one category of tourism-related performance. On the contrary, it has acquired multiple directives, which for purposes here shall be divided into primary, secondary, and support activities. Main activities, meaning those that justify involvement of the government in the operation of the tourism system, include: (1) strategic leadership of the tourism sector, (2) promotion, and (3) encouraging competitiveness of the tourism sector.

Strategic leadership can be explained in terms of the activities that should take place to position tourism as a priority activity, not only within the government but also in society a whole. Some of the most significant activities undertaken are: (1)

designing tourism policy and reaching consensus; (2) harmonizing the overall effort; (3) setting short-, mid- and long-term goals (strategic vision); (4) fostering and directing change; (5) and becoming a source of knowledge.

In its promotion role, it goes far beyond the execution of promotional campaigns by:

- Promoting government and private investment in infrastructure and development.

- Providing access to financing for sector stakeholders.

- Directing and executing a portion of the tourism promotion effort, by harmonizing cooperative efforts (both government and private), for tourism promotion.

- Fostering linkages among tourism destinations.

Then, there is the need to build other core competencies to make Mexico globally competitive by means of such activities as:

- Definition and application of world-class quality standards for tourism destinations and services.

- Promoting this sector's modernization and professionalism.

- Strengthening the culture of tourism.

- Designing, driving, and orienting the application of and compliance to tourism regulations (promoting regulatory improvement).

- Certifying tourism service providers.

Even if not fundamental, two secondary roles do generate an important added value. They are the developer and intermediary. The developer's role comprises activities such as:

- Directly executing overall tourism projects.

- Facilitating strategic alliances as a joint investor.

- Harmonizing collective investment effort for product development.

- Assisting in sustainable tourism development.

The intermediary's role comprises such tasks as:

- Being the link between different government agencies and stakeholders of tourism.

- Harmonizing and searching for an optimum use of the resources assigned to tourism in the different agencies of the public sector.

Finally, there are certain lower-profile roles that can be considered as supplementary, such as advisor and tourism services provider.

Execution of all the roles described above is performed by *Sector Turismo*, which is basically made up of the *Ministry of Tourism (Sectur)* (Ministry of Tourism) as the head of the sector, acting as a representative and having political accountability. *Sectur* is assisted by the Mexican Tourism Board in designing and carrying out tourism promotion strategies nationwide and abroad. It has a government board, in which state and municipal governments and the private sector participate. In addition, there is another branch, the *Fondo Nacional de Fomento al Turismo* (FONATUR) (National Tourism Fund), an institution in charge of planning and developing large tourism projects on Overall Planned Centers (CIPS) represented by Cancun, Los Cabos, Ixtapa, Huatulco, and Loreto.

Responsibilities of Ministry of Tourism, State, and Local Authorities

The tourism system's daily tasks and operations also involve local authorities. Large tourism destinations started to be promoted in the second half of the twentieth century, and in the 1990s promotion became a product of federal government initiative, whereby local (state and municipal) authorities' involvement was generally limited to providing utilities for operating tourism companies within their geographical areas, with practically no capabilities or involvement in the integrated management of tourism destinations. Even in the case of areas entirely planned and developed by FONATUR, infrastructure maintenance of tourism zones is still provided by the Mexican federal government.

Entrepreneurial participation depends more on the individual economic and political weight of the sector stakeholders or the opinions and demands of entrepreneur associations.

Publication of the Mexican Federal Law of Tourism, effective in 1992, acknowledged the importance of local authorities, and it decentralized powers and passed them on to state governments. Consequently, federal tourism delegations in the states disappeared. In practice, the emphasis given to tourism in the states depended on their own goals and objectives. In some cases, the state tourism authority reached the level of a ministry or directorship. Political and budgetary weight granted to the tourism state office usually went together with the hierarchical level conferred to such entity, and in real terms, the impetus to develop destinations now depends largely on each state. Today, municipal authority involvement in these activities is very limited, even if in many places there are municipal tourism agencies that take care of utilities management just as they would provide to any other industry.

The Nature and Role of CVBs in Mexico

Approximately forty CVBs have been created in Mexico in the last ten years. However, despite that growth, some of them do not have a clear focus on their mission; that is, whether their efforts should be directed to promoting a destination in general, or whether they should focus on leisure tourism, or perhaps on business tourism. It seems that creating and starting up a CVB is like replicating commercial strategies, rather than a deep and professional analysis of the "whys" and the "what fors" of their existence, by considering key destination features: attractions, service infrastructure, hotels, transportation, restaurants, and venues. The two goals that are indeed clear for CVBs are the generation of room nights and economic development of the destination.

The term "CVB" is not yet standard in Mexico. Frequently found are similar names like *Promotora de Turismo y Convenciones, Oficina de Turismo,* and *Buró de Visitantes y Convenciones.* Some other examples include: *Promotora de Turismo y Convenciones Laguna, Promotora de Turismo de Saltillo, Oficina de Convenciones y Exhibiciones de Merida,* and *Buró de Visitantes y Convenciones de Veracruz.*

Due to the accelerated growth of this type of office, in 2002 the *Asociación Nacional de Oficinas de Convenciones y Organismos Similares,* A.C. (ANDOC) (National Association of Convention Bureaus and Similar Entities) was created. It comprises the most important CVBs in Mexico, and its mission is to promote the creation and development of CVBs, trust funds, and tourism organizations in Mexico through education and training. It also promotes joint projects and the exchange of ideas and between tourism in government and in the private sector.

In 2003, the federal Ministry of Tourism's Business Tourism Directorship proposed a project to develop step-by-step guidance for new tourism destinations interested in creating this kind of organization in their cities. The proposal involved developing for the first time a national profile of the CVBs' model of operation: structure, mission, financing, staffing, budget, training needs, and services and facilities.

ANDOC took over this proposal at the end of the same year and requested *Consultores en Turismo* (CAT) to conduct a study of the CVBs' profile in Mexico. CAT surveyed forty CVBs in the country with twenty-five multiple-choice questions and one open-ended question. This survey was applied through the Internet for six weeks, and twenty-six CVBs responded. This sample was deemed acceptable, because of the number of entities that replied and their geographical location.

Structure

The CVBs, for the most part, are not-for-profit entities created by the public and private tourism sectors, whether their service area is at a local, regional, or state level. They are managed by a board of members and specifically represent one destination, which is generally a city or town.

The governing entities to which CVBs report are primarily mixed integration. Joint participation of the private and government sectors is the rule, with only 4 percent of CVBs reporting solely to a state government agency.

Purpose

There are three main objectives for CVBs in Mexico: (1) attract events, (2) promote the destination in general, and (3) attract and promote events and tourism by highlighting destination promotion. According to the *Perfil Nacional de CVBs/Consultores en Turismo (CAT)* 2003 (CAT's National Profile), 46 percent of CVBs perform general promotion of the destination, 23 percent attract events, and 31 percent attract and promote both events and general tourism.

Exhibit 1   Training Areas of Interest

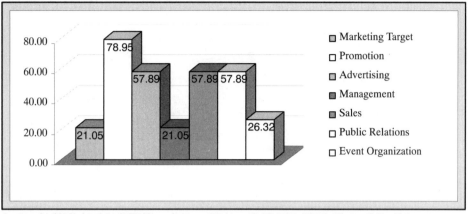

Source: *Perfil Nacional de CVBs/Consultores en Turismo (CAT)* 2003 (CAT's National Profile).

Personnel

The CVB with the highest headcount is twenty-one, and the one with the least personnel has two. The average is about seven. The main area of interest in training for CVBs is promotion, as displayed in Exhibit 1.

Funding

According to the survey, 55 percent of the CVBs interviewed are exclusively financed by room taxes, while 36 percent are financed by room taxes and other sources. Other sources of income are contributions from the state and municipal governments, as well as from members from the tourism community. Nine percent of the CVBs do not get any tax contributions, so the local authorities finance them.

The profile also shows that 59 percent of the CVBs have a budget of less than $5 million pesos, while 18 percent have a budget greater than $25 million pesos. (These include CVBs in Cancun, Riviera Maya, Mexico City, Guadalajara, and Monterrey). Some bureaus have fewer resources than others; therefore, they are more proactive in finding financing schemes. The greatest percentage of the budget (49 percent) goes toward promotion, with another 27 percent going specifically toward advertising (see Exhibit 2).

Seventy-nine percent of the CVBs receive contributions in-kind; 21 percent do not request this contribution to the tourism service providers of the destination. Contributions in-kind that the CVBs receive include land transportation, hotel accommodations, airline tickets, and meals. Twenty-seven percent of the CVBs consider these contributions as part of their income; 73 percent do not consider them as such.

This first descriptive profile on CVBs in Mexico has set an important foundation. Eduardo Yarto, Director of Business Tourism of the Ministry of Tourism, stated at the Sixth Business Tourism Meeting and CVBs in Torreón, Coahuila:

Exhibit 2   Expenditure Budget Allocation 2004

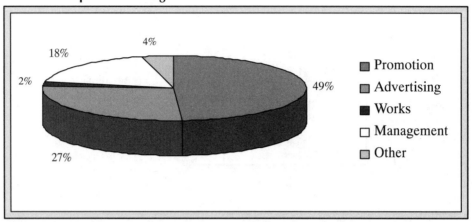

Source: *Perfil Nacional de CVBs/Consultores en Turismo (CAT)* 2003 (CAT's National Profile).

We will work together with the *Asociación Nacional de Oficinas de Convenciones y Organismos Similares* (ANDOC) to define the strategic guidelines to carry out a second study and drill down to have more elements of action that support us in defining the areas of opportunity of CVBs in Mexico in order to consolidate their professionalism and permanence.

CVB Services and Facilities

Convention and visitors bureaus in Mexico supply support and consulting services completely free, as a third-party provider to conference organizers, meeting planners, and leisure visitors. They aim to offer a "one-stop-shop" for their destination. It is important to point out that CVB services in Mexico may vary depending on the internal operation systems, such as destination goals and economic, human, and technological resources. However, in general terms one can state the following:

(1) CVBs provide information and support in selecting venues, accommodations, and suppliers for the event, and in designing a program of activities and cultural and leisure programs for delegates and escorts. Bureaus supply maps and tourism brochures of the city to participants, provide links with the city organizations and institutions for municipal and protocol services, and coordinate site inspection visits.

(2) CVBs offer logistics and economic support for congress bidders. This function entails the following: designing and producing a candidate's information, providing graphic and audiovisual materials, collaborating on the presentation sessions of the candidates, cooperating in promoting congresses once they have been awarded, and coordinating with local authorities and inspection visits by decision makers.

Monterrey CVB Case Study

The Monterrey case study is presented for three reasons, namely because of its experience with: (1) creating and starting up the bureau focusing on promoting the destination to generate leisure and business visitors; (2) evolving from a transition model to a bureau that sells the destination and hosts events, including groups, congresses, conventions, trade shows, and exhibits in the last two years; and (3) having been considered during five straight years as the leading bureau by national congress and convention organizers in the business tourism sector.

About Monterrey

Monterrey is the capital city of the state of Nuevo Leon, located in northeast Mexico and sharing the international border with Texas. Its population is 3.9 million people (4 percent of the entire country's population). It is the third largest city in Mexico with respect to population, and it contributes 9 percent of the gross domestic product (GDP). Considered an industrial and business center of Mexico, Monterrey excels in such sectors as beverages, packaging, cement, glass, steel, automobile parts, and financial services. Its education average is 8.9 percent as compared to the national average of 7.6 percent. That is the reason it is considered the "education center" of Mexico. San Pedro Garza Garcia (metropolitan area) has the highest per capita income of any municipality in Latin America. In 2003, *America Economics*, a Dow Jones publication, rated Monterrey as the best city in which to do business in Mexico and the fourth best in Latin America.

Monterrey has two airports. *Aeropuerto Internacional de Monterrey* (International Airport) averages 256 flights per day—199 domestic flights and 57 international flights—operated by approximately twelve airlines. *Aeropuerto Internacional del Norte* records 95 private flights per day.

There are currently 10,500 rooms in 106 hotels, most of which meet the quality standards for groups, congresses, and conventions. The city has a pool of venues, among them *Parque Fundidora*, a historical area made up of greenfields that hosts the *Centro Internacional de Negocios (CINTERMEX)* (International Center for Business), an ISO-9002 facility with 5,500 square meters for conventions and 18,380 square meters for trade shows; and *Arena Monterrey*, which is unique in the country, hosting up to 17,500 people. There are also stadiums, auditoriums, clubs, theaters, and other functional and versatile facilities to hold various events of organizational complexity and control.

Monterrey is characterized by the contrast of its landscapes. It is surrounded by mountains, and its natural scenery has fostered development of ecological and alternative tourism. In addition, the tourism services infrastructure developed in the last ten years comprises elements such as museums, theme parks, and malls that have supplemented the image of a business destination with a range of possibilities for leisure and fun.

Monterrey CVB

The bureau was created in 1994 as a nonprofit organization of the government of the state of Nuevo Leon, the *Asociación Mexicana de Hoteles y Moteles* (Mexican

Exhibit 3   Examples of Monterrey Events

Name	Highlights
OAS—Extraordinary Summit of the Americas (2004)	Meeting of presidents and prime ministers and other heads of state of 34 countries.
17th Karate World Championship (2004)	The most important martial arts event worldwide, with 95 participating countries.
UNO—International Conference on Financing for Development (2002)	For first time in Latin America, with the participation of 180 delegates from all over the world.
First Continental Congress on Church and Information Technology (2002)	The Vatican expressly requested it to be held in Monterrey.
Cart Series (since 2001)	For the fourth time in Monterrey.
Inaugural Match Game of the Major League Baseball Season (1999)	For the first time outside of the United States.

Source: CVB Monterrey Sales Department.

Association of Hotels and Motels), and the Monterrey Chamber of Commerce. Its source of funding comes from a 2 percent room tax. From its creation until 2002, the CVB focused on promoting Monterrey and Nuevo Leon as a leisure and business destination.

The promotion and image investment strategy provided visibility and major results in the business segment. The Monterrey CVB underwent a dramatic transition regarding its features, globalization, technology, new ways of doing business, and market demands. It reorganized itself and adopted a strategic model directed to the sale of the destination to host events. Exhibit 3 displays the tourism positioning not only of Monterrey but of Mexico as a whole in the past few years.

Vision. The vision of Monterrey's CVB is to host events from all over Mexico in the city of Monterrey, acknowledged by the organization's capacity, quality, multiple services, and economic feasibility.

Mission. Its mission is to be a stable and reliable organization, focused on attracting large events, conventions, congresses, trade shows, and exhibits to Monterrey through a joint promotion with the state of Nuevo Leon. This will increase visitation and generate a higher income that fosters job creation.

Objectives for 2004. The Monterrey CVB's several objectives for 2004 were:

- Closing the sale of 124,000 room nights.

- To continue providing follow-up to the portfolio of six world events in process, estimated to generate more than 85,000 room nights.

- Prospecting at least three world events, concluding the first stage of the sales cycle to compete on behalf of Mexico as a country.

- Adding commercial partners to the promotion and advertising campaigns (parks, museums, etc.).

- Measuring and evaluating customer satisfaction on CVB support and assistance.

- Consolidating Monterrey's positioning to host events in the national market with groups that generate more than 1,000 room nights per day.

Staffing. The Monterrey CVB's work is carried out through the executive directorship and four strategic departments: sales, consulting and customer service, marketing, and administration. A staff of eighteen professionals is dedicated to closing business.

Resources. The budget of Monterrey's CVB for 2004 is $2.5 million (U.S.) derived from room taxes. Sixty-eight percent of the budget goes to attracting events, while 15 percent is designated for tourism infrastructure development and 17 percent goes to the bureau's operating costs.

Current Conditions, Opportunities, and Challenges of Mexican CVBs

CVBs in Mexico have been going through a transition stage since the mid-1990s. This stage has been marked by strategic actions in all of the states, which have taken specific actions so that customers and suppliers of the tourism chain understand the value of tourism and the need to have institutions like CVBs.

Among strategic actions are the value-added tax zero rate on international congresses, conventions, exhibitions, and fairs. These events have been exempted from the country's 15 percent sales tax since January 2004.

This tax-free initiative, proposed by Mexico's tourism industry and passed in December 2002 by Congress, covers venue rental, lodging, airport/seaport/border transfers, and trips between hotels and meeting places. Also covered are related event services such as set-up, registration, masters of ceremonies, translators, hosts, audiovisual equipment, decoration, security, and cleaning. All related services contracted up to two nights before and two nights after an event are eligible for the tax waiver. Mexico is the second country to offer it; the first was Chile.

The tax waiver is just one of many measures taken by the Mexican government to attract and encourage international events, making Mexico more competitive worldwide. According to data from the Ministry of Tourism, there are approximately 7,750 conventions and meetings per year in Mexico, with Cancun being the favorite location. "Strategic Study Congresses and Conventions Feasibility," a study made by the agency, states that during 2001 Mexico held congresses and conventions with a total attendance of 1,524,500 people, out of which 79 percent were Mexicans and the remaining 21 percent were foreigners. Income received on this item was $1,467.3 million (U.S.), 25 percent of Mexico's total tourist expenditures in that year.

Inventory for business tourism of this type comprises 310 hotels and thirty-eight congress and convention centers located mainly in thirty-four cities and classified in four groups: beach resorts, large inland cities, historic cities, and border cities.

The Ministry of Tourism is actively promoting this new law as a package through concrete actions, such as:

- Encouraging infrastructure development for congresses, conventions, trade shows, and exhibits in most Mexican destinations.

- Joining CVBs in a common work project, through national meetings on business tourism and CVBs, to exchange information and technology as a "process to professionalism."

- Promoting business tourism campaigns through the Mexican Tourism Board. Example: In 2003, $7 million (U.S.) was invested in promotion of this segment.

- Simplifying gift and equipment import formalities for the business tourism segment.

- Building the conventions kit, specialized guide in congresses and conventions, specialized guide at trade show venues, specialized guide in incentive trips and glossary of terms, and measurement conversion tables.

Another strategic action involved creation of the *Oficina de Congresos y Convenciones (OCC)* (Mexican Convention Bureau) within the Mexican Tourism Board. The Mexico Convention Bureau was approved by the CPTM governing board on June 26, 2003, with the support of the Minister of Tourism and CPTM's director. This office derived from the perceived need to have an area specializing in promoting Mexico as the best alternative in the market segment composed of congresses, conventions, incentive trips and exhibits worldwide. It places special emphasis on consideration of supply and demand.

Concerning the former, it acknowledges interest from Mexico's tourism business sector in showcasing the country to the world. The OCC has the role of a facilitator in these instances, so that all of the stakeholders meet their positioning goals. Regarding demand in the international arena, Mexico's assets and amenities had to be assessed via a worldwide perspective and the competitive advantage that the zero-rate approval portrayed for groups, congresses, conventions, trade shows, and exhibits.

The OCC became a third-party unbiased entity linked to all of the CVBs nationwide. It facilitates and coordinates activities throughout Mexico. On the international side, its role is to facilitate communication between convention organizers and destinations, while domestically its task is to promote events held outside Mexico.

These two actions have strengthened the tourism industry and therefore the CVBs themselves. There are other variables that have prevented these entities from consolidating, so that the state and local officers and authorities understand their importance. For instance:

- Legal limitations, because every state has its own laws, and this is reflected in the CVBs' legal aspect. There is no standardization on CVBs' legal definitions.

- Duplication of roles between state and municipal government agencies. This causes distrust, especially when these organizations have a high private share because the government entities feel their territory is being invaded.

- Tourism service providers' lack of understanding of the scope of action of a CVB.

- Lack of resources to hire sufficient and well-trained personnel.

Based on the above, there are six main areas of challenges and opportunities that Mexico's CVBs face. The first entails permanence and continuity, that is, creating a culture within the private and public sectors that supports CVB permanence and consolidation. The municipal authority role should evolve to be much more involved with destination tourism. It should create opportunities for participation of the private sector, in addition to other public-sector entities involved in the development of the destination.

The second is financial guaranty. It is important that state governments guarantee the CVBs the resources coming from the room tax, because every state provides for it differently. Financial guaranty also means that tourists are supplied with adequate information once they reach the destination. This information is generated out of the room tax. Examples include information on hotels, restaurants, car rentals, land and air transportation, shows and entertaining, cultural activities, and museums. It is also critical to generate additional resources by implementing membership programs, as well as promotion and advertising cooperation programs, whereby all tourism stakeholders (museums, theme parks, airlines, PCOs, DMCs, etc.) participate. All of these view the CVBs as having the obligation to promote for free.

The third challenge involves generating metrics to demonstrate the contribution of CVBs to tourism destinations. Generally, a great many of the CVBs in Mexico are measured through the generation of room nights per location. This is somewhat contradictory, because according to the legal definition of CVBs, they should not perform the work as "housing bureaus." On the other hand, CVBs contribution in room nights is hard to measure because selling offers are always for the future and because Mexico's organized hotel industry does not have a standardized metrics system. Therefore, it is necessary to create and implement supplementary metrics, both inside and outside the CVBs.

Still another challenge refocuses on new strategies to market tourism destinations. This means several things: (1) going from the general promotion concept to an effective marketing of tourism destinations; (2) defining and/or redefining the destination purpose; (3) finding niches of special interest; and (4) developing packages of products that may define a unique sales promise (USP).

Still another is professional development. An important challenge is to achieve proper development of these CVB offices under certain professional and certification parameters. This will provide confidence both to the authorities and the tourism destination, and above all it will provide an acceptable image to the meeting planner market. At the same time, it is necessary to develop an internal service infrastructure in Mexico's CVBs, namely regarding information technology, promotion, and sale of tourism destinations.

Finally there is the matter of credibility. Once the obstacles above have been overcome, the CVBs should also have credibility in three totally different action fields: (1) with their local associates or service providers, who should see the CVB as a leader in the promotion of their destination; (2) with entities or individuals demanding the services, so that they become aware that the purpose of this office is to support them and be their main liaison with the tourism destinations supply; and (3) before federal, state, and municipal tourism officers, demonstrating the business contribution for the destination generated through the CVBs.

Learning from Other CVBs

The Monterrey CVB and other Mexican CVBs have learned much from competitive experiences with Europe, South America, and the United States when submitting applications for international conferences and events. In addition, these CVBs have continued to improve with respect to constant benchmarking against other tourism destinations such as Houston, Dallas, and San Antonio, Texas, in the United States; Rio de Janeiro in Brazil; and Madrid and Barcelona in Spain. These experiences, along with professional training received in the DMAI's Chicago conference (2002), have enabled Mexican CVBs to confirm that some of the roles the CVBs perform are very similar. However, there is a very specific difference: "the main purpose" for which these organizations were created. This is based on the essence of their destination, service infrastructure, customer needs, and the dynamics of their tourism sector.

Everything points to the continued growth of Mexican CVBs, mainly because they have been the medium through which the private sector has been involved in defining the future of their destinations facing more competitive tourism markets.

One alternative that Mexican CVBs can follow is the American model, an example that involves less bureaucracy regarding destination's administration and less marketing decision-making by state government.

Another option may be the European model and its focus on the promotion of events in different modalities: groups, congresses, conventions, trade shows, exhibits, and incentive trips. The latter is already happening in some instances, such as the Merida Convention and Exhibits Bureau, Monterrey's CVB, and the Mexico Convention Bureau, among others.

Although there is no going back in this movement of the past few years, continued progress does require national leadership from the Ministry of Tourism through its executive branches, the Mexico Tourism Board, and the Mexico Convention Bureau. This would ensure proper lobbying in coordination with the federal entities to guarantee that the CVBs may overcome the above-mentioned challenges within ten years, and that they are consolidated through clear guidelines focused on their own mission.

During this time, some CVBs will surely disappear, some others will refocus, and some others will be created. The most important things are that all of them comply with the purpose for which they were created and that they can guarantee the competitiveness and sustainability of their tourism destinations.

Glossary

By *Jan van Harssel*

Jan van Harssel, Ed.D., *a native of the Netherlands, is a professor in the College of Hospitality and Tourism Management at Niagara University. His teaching and research interests entail community tourism planning and development, guest services management, event and attractions management, and heritage tourism. A consultant, speaker, and author, he has written several textbooks, and he serves on the board of directors of the Niagara Falls (New York) Convention and Visitors Bureau.*

accountability research—Measures the performance of various CVB operations and functions, and forms the basis for CVB performance reporting.

accounting—A system that provides quantitative information about finances and serves as the basis for business decisions.

activity—A physical action taken by the CVB that ultimately supports its mission, such as attending a trade show, conducting a familiarization tour, or writing and distributing a press release.

AIDA cycle—Induces travel buying decisions through marketing efforts related to awareness, interest, desire and action.

alliance—A cooperative effort by two or more organizations that seek common goals.

attendee—Someone who attends a conference. Not necessarily a participant; may be a spouse or partner.

audit—A formal examination and verification of financial accounts.

bid—A proposal submitted by the CVB and/or hotel to a planner that includes defined dates and room blocks.

board evaluation—Because CVBs are self-governing, the members themselves must ensure that their goals are fulfilled. Self-evaluation forms are anonymously completed by the board of directors.

board of directors—Federal and state regulations require CVBs to have an uncompensated board of directors with governance and fiduciary responsibilities detailed in a set of bylaws. A CVB board of directors has philosophical, legal, and financial responsibility for the operations of the bureau.

brand—A collection of perceptions in the mind of the visitor that is the psychological, emotional, and motivational link between the customer and the product.

branding—The sum of the words, images, and associations that form the customer's perception of a destination.

budget—An itemized allotment of funds for a given period or project.

bylaws—Formal articles that detail the CVB's responsibilities and the strict guidelines to which the organization must adhere. Bylaws establish standing committees, can create temporary task forces, formalize the powers of the board, and specify the qualifications for board membership, term of office, and the nomination process.

canceled business—An event that was booked for the destination (a confirmed or contracted booking for a citywide or convention center event) that subsequently did not take place, either because the event itself was canceled or it left the destination before taking place.

cascading objectives—Sets of performance objectives, each the directive of a higher level objective.

Certified Meeting Professional (CMP)—Educational achievement awarded by Meeting Professionals International.

code of conduct—A set of ethical standards and values that become the guiding principles for professional behavior of board members. It is reflected in attendance at meetings, willingness to participate, openness and honesty, and in how members represent the bureau to external audiences.

communication—An important cornerstone of destination management. It includes media relations, crisis communication, member communication, and customer communication.

community visioning—The process of defining a community's vision or mission and developing a product plan for tourism. Also called scenario planning.

concierge—The person or staff in a hotel or visitors center who attends to guests' needs.

confirmed booking—A future event contracted in writing by the event organization for an event facility such as a convention center or hotel.

consolidated tourism marketing approach—Partners of the CVB join efforts for the common goal of increasing and marketing tourism. Partners include transportation agencies, accommodations, food service, retail, attractions, recreation, and heritage-based organizations.

consultant—One who gives professional advice or service.

Continuous and Never-ending Improvement (CANI)—The process of benchmarking and always looking to improve procedures, employee morale, revenue generation, etc.

convention and visitors bureaus—Nonprofit organizations that represent a city or geographic area in the solicitation and servicing of all types of travelers to the city or area; CVBs receive most of their operating funds from public sources and private donations.

conversion study—Determines the percentage of individuals responding positively to the specific CVB marketing effort.

cooperative advertising—A group-buying concept for businesses to advertise in the media together in a spot pre-purchased by the CVB.

corporate community—Local businesses with whom CVBs can form strategic marketing alliances.

creative brief—A one-page form that helps guide development of all graphic materials and ensures that everyone involved is informed about and agrees on the direction that development will take.

Customer Relationship Management (CRM)—Activity that provides dynamic Web site content based on the visitor's preferences, geography, and profile information. It should facilitate the expected dialogue between the visitor and the Web site.

customer service—The process of satisfying the customer relative to a product or service, in whatever way the customer defines his/her needs, then having that service delivered with efficiency, understanding, and compassion. Customer service is the ability to consistently meet external and internal customer needs, wants, and expectations involving procedural and personal encounters.

CVB product marketing dilemma—Described as having no real control over most products they promote. Sometimes referred to as accountability without authority.

destination audit—An assessment of a destination and its management organization. A comprehensive audit should include an evaluation and analysis of product mix and marketing strategies.

destination brand image study—A study that is typically used to help the CVB and its industry partners gain insight on how the destination is perceived by visitors.

destination branding—A marketing strategy that is based on the main perceptions and/or image that a customer or traveler associates with the destination in making it different, special, or unique.

destination management organization (DMO)—Organizations that lead a community's hospitality and tourism industry and are often a driving force behind local economic development plans. These gr oups are occasionally called destination marketing organizations, but have moved to a more holistic approach that now includes research, human resources, and technology.

destination management partnership—A partnership of public and private sector organizations.

Destination Marketing Association International (DMAI)—An international organization founded in 1914 that acts as a resource and advocate for the CVB industry. It provides educational resources and networking opportunities for its members.

destination research—Yields a multitude of data with components such as visitor profiles, image studies, and economic impact studies.

destination Web site—A Web site oriented in the sense of a destination marketing goal.

disclosure of information—Due to its tax-exempt status, a CVB is required to make certain records available for public inspection.

disintermediation—Removing the middleman. This term is a popular buzzword describing many Internet-based businesses that use the Web to sell products directly to customers rather than going through traditional retail channels.

drop letter—A letter sent to members who do not wish to renew their membership. It should stress disappointment, the option of renewal, and willingness to discuss any dissatisfaction with the CVB.

dues—Fees an organization or business must pay to be a member of a CVB.

e-commerce—Buying and selling products and services online.

e-lead—A sales inquiry based on Internet marketing.

familiarization tours (fam tours)—A promotional tour offered by CVBs to showcase their products and to maximize sales efforts by subsidizing the costs of airfare and providing opportunities for the customers to experience the destinations first hand.

feedback—A formal process of responding to each performance report in writing and often in a face-to-face meeting as well.

forecasting—An attempt to estimate the most likely level of visitor volume and demand based on known information, including economic, market, and social conditions and circumstances.

Form 990—U.S. federal information return that must be available for public inspection.

Form 990-T—A U.S. tax return that is not required to be available for public inspection.

front line staff—The first people the visitors make contact with when entering a facility or welcome center.

functional areas—In a CVB, they include convention sales, travel trade sales, leisure travel sales (tourism), and communication.

functional dimension of board governance—The way in which structural components are applied, how well they are applied, and whether they remain optimal in light of changing conditions.

housing bureau—Division of a CVB responsible for assisting organizers in handling hotel reservations for conference delegates.

incentive travel—Travel offered as a prize or bonus to encourage employee productivity.

industry partners—A name used for CVB members; the destination team.

infrastructure—A common city system of roads, paths, parking lots, mass transportation, water, waste disposal, electricity, signage, and telecommunications.

in kind—Services or products provided as part or full payment; used in sponsorships.

internal financial statements—Statements that can be prepared in any format that meets a bureau's needs. They include the balance sheet and income/expense statements.

invoice renewal—Sent annually as a reminder for members to renew their membership.

IRS filing requirements—U.S. CVBs organized under IRC 501(c)(6) and affiliated 501(c)(3) foundations must annually report the financial results of their operations.

job description—A tool to clarify roles and responsibilities. It includes a statement of purpose, requirements for the position, and a list of responsibilities.

leads—Potential clients for meetings, motor coach tours, and sports events.

leisure visitors—Individuals, couples, and families who have free time from work or duties.

lodging tax—A sales tax on room prices levied by cities and collected by hotels from their guests; the major source of funding for many CVBs.

lost opportunity—A potential event in the lead or tentative stage that was subsequently lost by the destination.

management—The distinct processes of planning, organizing, directing, and controlling people and other resources to achieve organizational objectives efficiently and effectively.

management letter—A letter issued to a CVB board by a CPA firm outlining deficiencies and suggesting improved operating procedures.

market annexing—Advertising across political or economic boundary lines to enhance the potential tourist perspective of an attraction area.

market segmentation—Dividing consumer markets based on demographic data such as age, education, income, gender, ethnicity, nationality, and occupation.

marketing—The management function of determining customer needs and then producing planned efforts to satisfy those needs. Marketing activities typically include research, advertising, publicity, direct mail, trade show attendance, sales calls, and Internet initiatives.

marketing mix—Those things that an organization can do to influence the demand for its products or services. It consists of four variables which are often called the four Ps of marketing: product, price, place, and promotion.

marketing plan—A bureau's business development process and resulting annual plan. A plan of action with goals, objectives, strategies and action plans.

marketing position statement—Message that describes the destination and separates it from other competitors in the eyes of the potential customer.

marketplace complications—All the impediments or roadblocks to success, including perceived complications.

Meetings Information Network (MINT)—A DMAI system for evaluating sales opportunities and marketing new meetings business.

member (of CVB)—Potentially any business that feels it may be attractive to individual leisure travelers or convention attendees.

membership benefits—Perks or bonuses members have access to as a result of holding their membership.

motivational research—A limited and focused approach for determining what community attributes, and descriptions of them, can best be employed to produce new visitor interest.

multiplier—Illustrates the degree to which the visitor dollar moves along the chain of buying and selling among the tourism industry's businesses and employees until it "leaks" out of the economy.

navigation bar—A key element of getting around a Web site. It must be user-friendly and provide clear direction to principal content of the Web site. It should include buttons or text links that can be clicked to go directly to all pages of the site.

news release—The standard tool to communicate with journalists on topics such as what's new, special events, marketing programs, and destination attributes.

nondistribution of earnings—CVBs are prohibited from distributing earnings to board members and other influential individuals. If earnings are distributed, the IRS (in the U.S.) may revoke the CVB's tax-exempt status and all related advantages.

not-for-profit organizations—Tax-exempt organizations governed by special laws that affect operations in several areas, including nondistribution of profits, tax classification, disclosure of information, tax filing requirements, and working relationships with accountants.

objectives—Statements of outcomes and of how success will be measured using direct, quantitative measurements, such as room night bookings or attendance.

ongoing coaching—Management's duty to provide an employee with guidance, direction, facilitation, morale, and technical support, and any other provisions such as tools or resources necessary to get the job done.

orientation—Planned activity for new employees and/or new board members. It includes an overview of the bureau organization, bylaws, planning activities, expectations, code of conduct, and events/activities.

pace reports—Data reported in time frames that allow comparison from month to month, quarter to quarter, or year to year, enabling management to determine if the pace of reported visitor activity such as inquiries, Web registrations, visitor guide requests, and hotel reservations is ahead of or behind projected totals.

package—A variety of travel arrangements put together and sold at one all-inclusive price.

performance coaching—Emphasizes the manager's coaching role, geared toward improving performance.

performance evaluation—The follow-up to performance reporting, an ongoing process that gauges the performance of each person and unit within an organization.

performance indicator—A number that illustrates the performance of the travel and tourism industry or one of its industry sectors (hotel occupancy, airport arrivals, attractions attendance, restaurant employment) and is sometimes a byproduct of destination's resource analysis.

performance management—Managing people in a manner that moves the organization from vision and mission statements to execution by goal planning and goal setting. A systematic cycle of events that, if performed correctly, can produce powerful results.

performance measure—A specific number quantifying the outcome of a CVB activity such as room nights sold, leads generated, or conventions booked. For evaluative purposes, these measures are often used within the context of other performance measures, such as descriptive narratives.

performance reporting—A formal process that includes reporting the progress, problems, and plans related to each CVB's performance objectives. Should be done on a periodic and formal basis.

personal and professional development—An approach to developing the competencies, skills, talent, knowledge and related attributes of employees to enable them to grow and develop. Should be completed through ongoing coaching. These developments are owed to both the employee and the stakeholders as it serves to benefit them as well as the CVB itself.

planning and documentation—Details the deliverables and expectations of a project from both the CVB and the outside provider, constructs the documentation for each detailed phase of the project, and obtains agreements on the scope of work.

postconvention tour—An extension designed to supplement a trip to a conference or convention.

preproject phase—All the relevant documentation and materials necessary to understand goals and objectives.

press kit—A packet of information about a destination's overview, including information about accommodations, attractions, history, culture, and activities.

product life cycle—A concept that suggests four main stages of a product or service: introduction, growth, maturity, and decline or rebirth.

productivity metric—Illustrates the relationship between a CVB's performance and its resources.

Professional in Destination Management (PDM)—A certificate program administrated by DMAI. It helps professional staff obtain the necessary knowledge and skills to become more effective destination leaders and CVB managers.

prospecting—Networking; meeting with prospective clients in their environment.

reception desk—The area to which delegates and others report upon arrival at a meeting.

request for proposal (RFP)—An order to communicate to the destination all the information about a meeting scheduled to be there.

return on investment—The specific, quantifiable financial returns from marketing programs for the destination.

right work environment—A workplace in which everyone has the tools and resources in order to do his or her job and that the existing structure promotes effective and efficient communications, problem-solving, and decision making.

search engine—A Web page that permits people to look for information and Web sites that they need.

segmenting—Divides customers into groups according to demographic, psychographic, or geographic variables.

site inspection—Personal, careful investigation of a property, facility, or area. Often conducted by the meeting planner in anticipation of a site selection for future meeting consideration.

SPLOTS—Strategic plans languishing on the shelf; not being used.

sponsor—Person or organization providing financial or in-kind support at an event in the expectation of promotion and publicity.

stakeholders—Various public and nonprofit entities with which a bureau works. They are the entities benefiting most from the values and successes of the destination's CVB and local tourism industry.

standing committees—Subcommittees that act on behalf of the whole board of directors to carry out ongoing functions more efficiently than the board as a whole could. Examples include the executive committee, the strategic marketing committee, and the resource development committee.

strategic planning—The act of producing a multi-year directional marketing approach, usually a three- to five-year plan.

SWOT analysis—Stakeholder analysis of a community's strengths, weaknesses, opportunities, and threats.

team building—Different CVB departments working together to reach a common goal.

tentative—The status assigned to a group or event after the bid has been submitted to the meeting planner and the destination is waiting for a decision.

third-party technologies—Hardware, software, or applications not directly owned by the CVB, but by a third party that agrees to allow others to license their technology to perform specific functions such as displaying events, calendars, maps, and hotel reservations, or conducting Web site searches.

tourism barometer—Monitors tourism-related activities for a destination on a monthly, quarterly, semiannual, or annual basis.

tourism team—CVB members joined together to exemplify the principle of interdependency and linking the CVBs with almost every facet of the tourism community, thereby helping CVBs pursue the mission of marketing their community as a destination, and often helping in promoting a region or country.

visitors guide—A publication printed by a CVB that highlights its area's attractions, accommodations, restaurants, and organizations for visitors.

visitors information centers—Sites of information conveniently available to the traveler; may provide a revenue source through sales of souvenirs, merchandise, or event tickets. A CVB can have one or more centers in its community.